Write Your Will

Sunrise   Midday   Sunset

In a Weekend

Sunset   Evening   Sunrise

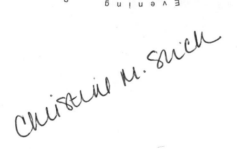

Christine M. Stich

Send Us Your Comments

To comment on this book or any other PRIMA TECH title, visit our reader response page on the Web at **www.prima-tech.com/comments**.

How to Order

For information on quantity discounts, contact the publisher: Prima Publishing, P.O. Box 1260BK, Rocklin, CA 95677-1260; (916) 787-7000. On your letterhead, include information concerning the intended use of the books and the number of books you wish to purchase. For individual orders, turn to the back of this book for more information.

Write Your Will

CHRISTINE M. SOVICH

A DIVISION OF PRIMA PUBLISHING

A Division of Prima Publishing

Prima Publishing and colophon are registered trademarks of Prima Communications, Inc. PRIMA TECH and In a Weekend are trademarks of Prima Communications, Inc., Rocklin, California 95677.

Publisher: Stacy L. Hiquet
Marketing Manager: Judi Taylor
Managing Editor: Sandy Doell
Acquisitions Editor: Emi Nakamura
Project Editor: Melba Hopper
Legal Reviewer: Cheryl Planck
Technical Reviewer: Keith Davenport
Interior Layout: Marian Hartsough
Cover Design: Prima Design Team
Indexer: Johanna VanHoose

Microsoft, Windows, and Notepad are trademarks or registered trademarks of Microsoft Corporation. WillWriter is a trademark of Business Logic Corporation.

Important: Prima Publishing cannot provide software support. Please contact the appropriate software manufacturer's technical support line or Web site for assistance.

Prima Publishing and the author have attempted throughout this book to distinguish proprietary trademarks from descriptive terms by following the capitalization style used by the manufacturer.

ISBN: 0-7615-2378-2
Library of Congress Catalog Card Number: 99-65609
Printed in the United States of America
00 01 02 03 04 BB 10 9 8 7 6 5 4 3 2 1

To my sister and best friend, Cari,
for believing that I could write this book;
to my husband, Ted,
for supporting me throughout its writing;
and to Madeline,
who was with me every step of the way.

And to my nephew, Jack,
whose recent birth required me to update my own will,
which started this whole process.

ACKNOWLEDGMENTS

I extend my deep gratitude to the folks at Prima Publishing for all of their support and assistance, especially acquisitions editor, Emi Nakamura, for remembering my previous work and asking me to author this book; Prima Tech publisher, Stacy Hiquet, for giving me the opportunity to write this book; and project editor, Melba Hopper, for helping throughout the process.

I offer my sincere thanks to Cheryl Planck for her review of the legal material in this book and to Business Logic Corporation staff and to Keith Davenport for their reviews of the technical material. I also thank Business Logic Corporation for providing the WillWriter software that is on this book's CD-ROM.

Thanks also to David Plotkin, CD-ROM developer; Marian Hartsough, interior layout coordinator; and Johanna VanHoose, indexer.

Finally, I am indebted to Professor Walter Krieger, the definitive expert on this book's subject, who taught me about wills, trusts, and fiduciary administration.

ABOUT THE AUTHOR

CHRISTINE M. SOVICH is a practicing attorney in Indianapolis, Indiana, specializing in sports, entertainment, and intellectual property law. Christine also does extensive work in the area of estate planning for her wide-ranging clients. She has worked with the estates of such legendary entertainers as James Dean, Humphrey Bogart, Greta Garbo, and Marlene Dietrich, as well as athletes such as Babe Ruth and Lou Gehrig. Christine currently works as a consultant on the estates of well-known celebrities such as George Burns, James Cagney, Vincent Price, Clark Gable, Frank Sinatra, and for living legend, Bob Hope.

Christine's undergraduate degree is from Franklin College, in Franklin, Indiana. She received her Juris Doctorate from Indiana University School of Law.

Prior to launching out on her own (and becoming an author for Prima Publishing!), Christine was vice president and general counsel for CMG Worldwide, a marketing and licensing agency for deceased and living celebrity estates, where she was instrumental in securing the Marilyn Monroe Estate as a CMG client.

A frequent lecturer in the areas of Right of Publicity law and Estate Planning, Christine sits on the executive committee of the Indianapolis Bar Association's Sports and Entertainment law section. She is also a member of the American Bar Association (ABA), serving on its Entertainment and Sports Industries Forum Committee, and is a member of the Indiana State Bar Association and its Intellectual Property and Corporate Counsel sections.

CONTENTS AT A GLANCE

CONTENTS

SATURDAY AFTERNOON
Providing for Your Beneficiaries 59

SATURDAY EVENING
Writing Your Will

INTRODUCTION

Congratulations! By deciding to write your will, you've made an important decision. A will enables *you* to decide how and to whom your property will be distributed when you die. So, by having a will, you can protect and provide for your loved ones after your death.

Your second important decision was choosing *Write Your Will In a Weekend*. Why? Because many people think that drafting a will is complicated and difficult—certainly too difficult to do themselves—so they die without a will. However, in this book, you can find the information you need *and* Business Logic's WillWriter, a software program specifically designed to walk you through the process of writing your will. In fact, with this book in hand, you're likely to discover that writing your will is not only quick and easy, but also *fun!*

What This Book Is About

This book is aimed at helping you create a legally binding will, all in a weekend, without the hassle and cost of an attorney. Along with the general legal information you need, you will find step-by-step instructions to prepare a valid, legally binding will no matter what state you live in, *excluding* Louisiana.

 NOTE If you live in Louisiana, don't use this book to draft your will. It most likely will not adhere to the state's complex requirements.

Along with the software program that comes with this book are reprinted sample documents used in creating your own will. (Most attorneys use these exact documents, or similar ones, to draft their clients' wills.)

No state law requires that a will be prepared by an attorney. As long as you meet a few general requirements (for example, you are at least 18 years old and of sound mind), you can draft your own will. Additional requirements for drafting a will are discussed during the Friday Evening Session.

What This Book Isn't About

This book is *not* a substitute for comprehensive planning of your *estate*, which is the legal term that describes your assets left at your death. A will is only one part of an estate plan. Your estate plan—depending on your age and the value of your assets—might include (among other documents):

○ A *prenuptial agreement*, which is a binding agreement between a soon-to-be husband and wife that stipulates how certain marital property or property acquired during the marriage will be owned upon their divorce or upon the death of a spouse

✿ A *life insurance policy* (or perhaps several policies)

✿ A *trust*, which is a written agreement that allows your assets to be held, controlled, and managed for your selected beneficiaries in accordance with certain directions and instructions set forth in the trust document

✿ A *durable power of attorney*, which gives your selected representative the right to make certain decisions for you regarding legal matters if you become incapacitated

✿ A *health care power of attorney*, which instructs your representative to make certain choices for you regarding your health care if you become unable to make them for yourself

✿ A *living will* (also called *Directive to Physicians*), which states your wishes about certain medical treatments and predetermines whether they will be performed in case you need them and are unable to make those decisions for yourself

For more information and software to assist you in creating a living will, please refer to the Business Logic advertisement at the back of this book.

Or you can visit **www.mir1.legaldocs.com/htmdocs/livin_st.htm** to order a free copy of the living will form for your particular state. You can also visit the Savewealth site at **www.savewealth.com/planning/estate/ livingtrusts** to learn more about living wills and how to include one in your estate plan.

CAUTION

◆ ◆

If your estate is worth more than $675,000, you need to consult a qualified financial planner or estate tax attorney who can advise you on the various federal and state tax laws that might affect the distribution of your estate.

◆ ◆

Although this might not apply to you, I need to mention one more point. You can't disinherit a spouse! So, if you're married and plan on leaving the old ball and chain out of your will, this book is not for you. You need to consult an attorney who can help you formulate an estate plan with this goal in mind.

Why You Should Have a Will

You might be thinking, "I don't need a will, I don't have anything to leave anyone."

But I bet that you have a lot more than you realize. You probably own a car, or at least a television or VCR. Perhaps you've inherited a piece of jewelry from a relative. And you most likely have a bank account, regardless of how much money is actually in it.

Five hundred dollars might not seem like a lot of money, but you might have specific ideas on who should receive that money if you die. Perhaps you want to leave it to your sister for her upcoming wedding or to a niece to help with college.

The point is that without a will, you have no control over who inherits your property at your death (and, in most cases, it would not be your sister or your niece).

With that said, my advice is that everyone needs a will, whether they're 18 or 88. If you don't currently have a will or if your will needs to be updated because of recent changes in your life (such as a marriage, divorce, or birth of a child), now is the time to protect yourself and your loved ones by stating your wishes about how you want your belongings to be distributed after you're gone.

What You Need to Begin Drafting Your Will

Surprisingly, you don't need much to draft your will. The following list includes a few items that you will need this weekend.

- ✪ **An inventory of your assets**. You will create this inventory in the Saturday Morning session.
- ✪ **A computer**. The Saturday Evening session lists the minimum computer requirements for using the WillWriter software that's on the CD-ROM at the back of this book.
- ✪ **Paper**. For printing your will.
- ✪ **A pen**. For signing your will.
- ✪ **Witnesses**. Requirements for your witnesses are covered in the Friday Evening session.

And, perhaps most important, you need a sense of humor.

How This Book Is Organized

To help you write your will in just one weekend, I've divided the necessary steps into the following seven sessions: Friday Evening, Saturday Morning, Saturday Afternoon, Saturday Evening, Sunday Morning, Sunday Afternoon, and Sunday Evening.

Each session should take only a few hours to complete, so you should have plenty of time to reflect on the important decisions you'll be making over the course of the weekend (including the names of those who will receive your belongings, the name of the guardian for your minor children, and the name of the personal representative of your estate).

You will find general information about wills at the beginning of this book and several useful appendixes at the end. I recommend that you refer to all this information in order to draft a valid will according to *your* state's particular requirements.

Here is a brief overview of what you can expect to find and accomplish over the course of the weekend.

- **Friday Evening.** "Getting Started" explains what a will is and what a will can do for you. This session also explains why dying without a will is not advisable. In this session, you begin drafting your will by identifying and selecting those qualified individuals who will act on behalf of your estate. Specifically, you will select a personal representative, the required number of witnesses, and—if necessary—a guardian for your minor children.

- **Saturday Morning.** "Finding Out What You Own and How You Own It" takes you through the process of gathering all necessary documents to inventory your estate, including what you own and what you owe. You'll locate documents such as life insurance policies, deeds to your home or other property, and bank statements. Finally, you'll learn what property should and *should not* be included in determining your estate's net worth and whether your estate is subject to taxes.

- **Saturday Afternoon**. "Leaving Gifts to Your Beneficiaries" helps you identify and decide who gets what. After you complete your inventory and calculate your estate's net worth, you will decide to whom you want to leave your personal and real property—as well as specifically what you want them to inherit. In this session, you will learn the various ways property can be left at your death and even how to leave a gift with strings attached!

- **Saturday Evening**. "Writing Your Will" walks you through the process of drafting your will using the WillWriter software provided on the CD-ROM at the back of this book. You get step-by-step instructions on how to install the WillWriter software and use it to make a valid and legally binding will (except for those in the state of Louisiana) that provides for your family and friends. It's as simple as answering a few questions and filling in a few blanks.

- **Sunday Morning**. "Editing Your Will" gives you an opportunity to review the selections that you made in the Saturday Evening session, make final changes, and print an original copy to be signed by you and your witnesses. You will also learn how to save your will document as a text file so that you can add additional provisions to your will, such as providing for a pet.

- **Sunday Afternoon**. "Signing on the Dotted Line" covers how you gather your selected witnesses in one place and instruct them on their responsibilities. This session also covers the details of signing the will in the presence of your witnesses, including both your signature and theirs.

- **Sunday Evening**. "Safeguarding Your Will (And More)" explains the precautions that you need to take in order to safeguard your newly created document. During this last session, you will find tips on when to create a new will and how to modify your existing one by drafting an amendment to your will. You will also learn about some common and uncommon problems and pitfalls and how to avoid them.

- **Appendix A**. "State-By-State Probate Matrix" provides each state's requirements for witnesses and executors of a valid will.

- **Appendix B**. "Intestate Succession" provides additional information concerning who is entitled to receive your property when you die without a will. In this appendix, you learn how states typically handle intestate succession. I even included several examples that illustrate who will inherit your belongings if you die without a will.

- **Appendix C**. "Estate Inventory Worksheet" enables you to easily record your assets — what you own and how you own it — in order to calculate your estate's net worth. You can also use the worksheet to help determine who will receive your property.

- **Appendix D**. "Probate Forms" provides a general overview of the types of documents that might be required when your estate is filed in probate court after your death. The forms in this appendix are from the Probate Division of the Marion County Superior Court in Indiana.

⚙ **Appendix E**. "Example Wills" illustrates what your will might look like after you create it with WillWriter during the Saturday Evening session. This appendix includes wills for an unmarried and a married individual, with and without children. You'll even find an actual celebrity will reprinted in this appendix just for fun.

⚙ **Appendix F**. "Tax Forms" provides copies of the actual forms that your estate might be required to file upon your death, such as a United States Estate (and Generation-Skipping Transfer) Tax Return and a United States Gift (and Generation-Skipping Transfer) Tax Return. I obtained the forms in this appendix from the Department of the Treasury–Internal Revenue Service (IRS).

⚙ **Appendix G**. "What's on the CD-ROM?" describes the WillWriter program and the other files that are on the CD-ROM at the back of this book. This appendix tells you how to download WillWriter and the files from the CD and how to install them on your computer's hard drive.

⚙ **Glossary**. Lists in alphabetical order the italicized legal terms that appear throughout this book.

Special Features of This Book

Write Your Will In a Weekend includes the following features that alert you to particular kinds of information:

⚙ **Cautions** generally provide caveats that alert you to potential problems or areas in which you need to proceed with caution. They also alert you to situations in which you might need to consult an attorney or check with your state's probate laws before proceeding.

⚙ **Find It Online** icons highlight information that is accessible online.

- **Notes** provide additional helpful or interesting information, including explanations of certain legal terms and concepts. You can also refer to the Glossary for definitions of terms that might be new to you.

- **On the CD** icons spotlight the software and files that are included on the CD-ROM at the back of this book.

- **Sidebars** provide information that supplements or illustrates a current topic. For example, a few sidebars include questions that people frequently ask and concise answers to those questions.

Getting Started

Instead of going out to a movie tonight, why not stay home and curl up with a good book? You can read this book *and* create a valid, legally binding will in just one weekend (bit different from reading *War and Peace,* isn't it?).

The information in this book provides an overview and plan for writing a personal will in all states, except Louisiana.

 NOTE You can find each state's general requirements for creating a valid will in Appendix A, "State-By-State Probate Matrix." However, because of variances and changes among state laws, I recommend that you check your particular state's laws if you have questions.

You can find your state's requirements at the library of your county's courthouse or at a local law library. Many state bar association offices also keep this kind of information on hand. And, if you have access to the Internet, you can even research state law on the Web. (Almost all states have their own Web sites on which you can look up the applicable statute.) You can also log onto the Cornell University School of Law Web site  at **www.law.cornell.edu/states/listing.html** for information on all the states' probate laws.

But, first, take a moment to read the Introduction to this book, if you haven't already. The Introduction not only outlines what you need to draft your will, but also provides helpful information regarding additional documents that you may want to include in your estate plan.

Your will can even state your preferences for funeral arrangements. (I'll talk more about preparing for your funeral in the Saturday Evening Session.)

Why do I bring up estate planning in this book? Because a will is only one part of a complete estate plan. However, a will is arguably the most important part, and for many people, the only document that they need.

ON THE

CD

In case you're not sure about your estate planning needs, check out Appendix C, "Estate Inventory Worksheet." You can also find a printable copy of this worksheet on the CD at the back of this book. This worksheet might bring to mind other documents to include in your estate plan.

In this session, you'll learn the following:

- ✿ What a will is and what a will can do for you
- ✿ Why everyone should have a will—whether you're 18 or 88
- ✿ The various state requirements for drafting a valid will so that you can determine whether you meet the necessary criteria

But, that's not all. You will also begin selecting your *fiduciaries* (that is, an executor for your estate, a personal guardian to care for minor children, and witnesses to make your will valid).

NOTE

● ●

You might notice that Friday Evening's session is a little long. Don't worry. I promise that the other sessions will be much shorter. (I've even made up for it in the Sunday Afternoon session.)

● ●

Where There's a Will, There's a Way

A *will* is a legally binding document that allows certain property left at your death to be effectively transferred to your selected successors.

In everyday terms, your will declares who (your *beneficiaries*) inherits your property upon your death and who will act as your *personal representative* (your *executor*) to carry out your final wishes. A will can also nominate one or more *guardians* to provide for your minor children after your death.

NOTE The term *personal representative* can refer to both an *executor* and an *administrator*. An executor acts as the personal representative of an estate in which a person dies *with* a will. An administrator is the personal representative appointed by a court to oversee an estate in which a person dies *without* a will.

You Have to Have Will Power!

People often wonder whether they actually need a will.

In making this decision, you may first want to consider what happens when a person dies (referred to as *decedent*) without a will. In that situation, he or she is said to have died *intestate*. (See Appendix B for more on intestate law.)

NOTE The term *testate* describes the state of dying with a will. Thus, the term *intestate* is used for the reverse situation. The drafter or creator of the will is most commonly referred to as the *testator*. This term is often used interchangeably for both a male will drafter (testator) and a female will drafter *(testatrix)*, and I will use the term testator for both men and women in this book.

No Will: No Control over the Distribution of Property

Without a will, you have little or no control over how your property and possessions are distributed *(disposed)* upon your death. Instead, a court decides how and to whom (called *heirs*) those assets are distributed based on the intestate laws in your *state of domicile* (the state in which you live). The distribution of your property under intestate laws is commonly referred to as *intestate succession*.

NOTE Heirs are the intestate recipients of property that a person did not effectively dispose of prior to his or her death. Legally, one cannot become an heir until the death of the *predecessor benefactor* (the person from whom the heir would be entitled to receive property).

Only property that is generally disposed of through a will (often called *probate property*) is subject to the laws of intestate succession. *Nonprobate property*—life insurance policies, individual retirement accounts (IRAs), pension plans, 401(k) plans, gifts made during your life, trusts, and property considered to be owned as joint tenants—is said to pass outside of probate and is inherited by the beneficiaries that you have previously named on the face of the document itself. For example, your insurance policy lists a beneficiary. This named beneficiary will be entitled to the insurance proceeds at your death.

INTESTATE SUCCESSION

Intestate succession specifies who is entitled to receive your property when you die without a will. Intestate succession is the state's version of your will; it is as though your will were drafted for you by the state in which you live.

In general, if you are married with children, property that you own at your death passes to your spouse and children. If you have neither a spouse nor children when you die, your probate estate passes to other close heirs (for example, your parents, siblings, nieces, nephews, grandparents, aunts, uncles, and cousins). If no such heirs are living at your death, your estate passes to the state. This situation is referred to as *escheating.*

Because states may vary slightly in regard to intestate succession, people who are not writing a will should check with their states' rules regarding how their property will be distributed at their death. But, you've decided to write your will, so you don't need to be concerned about most intestate succession laws.

However, I advise having a basic understanding of your state's method of intestate succession. So, I've included more detailed information on intestate succession in Appendix B.

No Will: State Appoints Guardians and Personal Representatives

If you die without a will, a state court determines who will care for your minor children. The court will appoint personal guardians and also a personal representative (commonly referred to as an administrator) to distribute your assets upon your death, without considering your wishes.

NOTE If you die without a will, the probate court will appoint an administrator for your estate, typically giving preference to the following persons, in the following order:

- Your surviving spouse, or your spouse's designated choice
- Next of kin (generally, the order is determined according to your state's intestate succession laws)
- Any other qualified person, including creditors of your estate if none of the aforementioned individuals have filed for appointment within 30 days after your death

More Reasons Why You Need a Will

This section includes some of the more common reasons why most people choose to write a will—all of which ultimately ensure that a particular loved one is provided for after a person's death. Take a look at the following situations.

Providing for Stepchildren

If your spouse has children from a prior union, these children, though not your biological offspring, are a part of your family. However, if you don't have a will, only your biological offspring or children whom you legally adopted during your lifetime can inherit from you upon your death. So, in order to leave something to your stepchildren, you must provide for them in a will.

NOTE Consider, for example, Shannon and Derek. Shannon and Derek are married and have one child (Billy) from the union. Shannon also has a son (Bobby) from a prior marriage. Derek dies without a will. His probate estate will be distributed as follows: one-half to Shannon as his spouse, and one-half to Billy (his biological child). Bobby, who was not legally adopted by Derek, is not entitled to a share of Derek's estate.

Providing for Grandchildren

You may want to leave something special to your grandchildren. Grandchildren aren't afforded rights to inherit under state intestate succession laws if their parent (your child) is still living at your death.

CAUTION

This scenario probably won't apply to you, but who knows? Be careful with large gifts or bequests in your will to grandchildren. Leaving something to your grandchildren directly and "skipping" your children is considered *generation skipping,* and the bequest might be subject to a generation-skipping transfer tax, which currently is 55 percent.

However, each person is afforded a $1,010,000 exemption from a generation-skipping transfer tax, and you and your spouse can combine your exemptions and effectively transfer up to $2,020,000 in your wills to your grandchildren. (This amount increases according to inflation from time to time.) Thus, you'd have to leave a pretty large gift before the generation-skipping transfer tax would take effect. Note, however, that this gift might still be subject to an estate or gift tax. For more information on the form required for generation-skipping gifts, see IRS Forms 706A and 709 in Appendix F.

If you want to leave a large gift to your grandchildren, check with an attorney who specializes in estate planning, or check with an accountant, before attempting to transfer the gift outright or leaving it in your will.

Don't Forget Friends, Charities, and Distant Relatives

No state makes a provision for friends, charities, and distant relatives in its intestate succession laws. So, if you want to provide for friends, charities, your alma mater, church, or distant relatives at your death, you will need to specifically do so in your will.

NOTE

If you plan on making a provision for your alma mater, check with your school. Many schools have departments dedicated solely to assisting alumnae who are interested in providing a gift of their estate.

Drafting Your Will: Are You Qualified?

As previously mentioned, no existing state laws mandate that an attorney draft or prepare your will. However, certain requirements must be met in order to create a legal, binding will. To be sure that you are creating a valid will, you must follow your particular state's rules regarding decedent's estates.

In this section, you will learn about the general requirements that you must meet in order to create a valid will in your state.

Look to Your State of Domicile

In order to create a valid will, you must adhere to the laws of your state of *domicile*. Your *domiciliary state* is the state in which you live. Each person has only one domicile. Your domicile is your legal and permanent residence. (Hint: It's generally the state in which you vote, are licensed to drive in, or, if you don't vote or drive, in which you file your income taxes. Now, I know that you file taxes. If you don't, check with the IRS. I'm sure that they'll know how to find you!)

So, if you are fortunate enough to have more than one house (say, a quaint little log cabin in the Hamptons or a luxurious beachfront pad in Malibu), be sure to use the rules of the state in which you spend most of your time (where your primary residence is located).

CAUTION

◆◆

If you're still unsure about what classifies as your state of domicile—and some people might be—it's best to consult an attorney before proceeding.

◆◆

If you move to another state after drafting your will, you will want to review the laws in your new state of domicile to ensure that your will is valid. Most likely, your will is valid under the laws of your new domiciliary state because a will is typically valid in any state, as long as it adhered to the laws of the state in which you lived when it was drafted.

NOTE   Your estate might be subject to the probate administration of more than one state. For example, say that you own that Malibu vacation home mentioned earlier. Even if your permanent state of residence is Ohio, your estate will be subject to probate administration in California—albeit to a limited extent—to effectively transfer title of that luxurious oceanfront retreat.

General Requirements for a Valid Will

Before you can draft a valid, legally binding will, you must meet certain requirements of your state. A valid will requires four basic elements:

- ✪ You must be at least 18 years of age.
- ✪ You must be of sound mind.
- ✪ Your will must be in writing.
- ✪ Your will must be witnessed.

Now, take a closer look at each requirement.

Meeting the Minimum Age Requirements

In all states, except one, you must be at least 18 years old to draft a valid will (Wyoming requires you to be 19 years old). Most states also make an exception for those who are younger than 18, but only if they meet certain additional requirements: married, member of the active armed forces, or legally emancipated (which means that although technically a minor, a court has declared the individual to be an adult).

CAUTION   If you are under 18, check with an attorney or your state's probate court before drafting your will. You want to be sure that you adhere to your particular state's requirements.

Being of Sound Mind

You've probably heard this phrase before, perhaps on a TV show or during a movie—usually when the rich, old uncle's will is read at the attorney's office. The will always seems to start the same way: "I, John Doe, being of sound mind. . . ."

NOTE   While often used in books and movies, there is no requirement that these actual words appear on the face of your will. Most wills do not contain this language, and the will you create tomorrow need not include this exact wording.

But what does "being of sound mind" really mean, anyway? Competency requirements vary for each state. Some say that you must exhibit a "sound mind"; some say that you must be of "sound mind and disposing memory"; others say that you must have the requisite "capacity" or "mental capacity" to draft a will. Although the statutes vary slightly in language, all these terms basically mean the same thing. You must be competent at the time of drafting your will by showing the following:

- You know what a will is, and you have made a conscious decision to create your will. (I've just explained what a will is, and you've purchased this book, so I think you've satisfied the latter requirement.)

- You understand who is considered the *natural objects of your bounty* (who would typically inherit from you without a will, or who would most likely be a beneficiary under your will, such as your spouse and children).

- You know the extent or worth of your estate. (You will calculate your estate's net worth during the Saturday Morning session.)

- You can determine and understand how you want your estate to be distributed.

The test for proving the testator's capacity is actually rather easy to satisfy. The fact that you are reading (and hopefully understanding) the information provided here is probably more than enough to meet your state's competency requirements. It shows that you have the necessary capacity to draft a will. That's all you need!

NOTE It's extremely difficult to prove that a testator is incompetent. The presumption is that you're mentally competent at the time of drafting. I'll talk more about contesting a will during the Sunday Evening session. I'll even give you a few tips on how to discourage anyone from contesting your will.

Putting Your Will in Writing

In order to be valid, your will must be in writing. Specifically, your will must be either typewritten or printed from word-processing software (for example, Microsoft Word). A witnessed will that is typewritten or computer-generated is considered a *formal will* and is valid in every state.

Oral or Handwritten?

Some states allow you to use oral (also called *nuncupative*) wills. And about half of the states, 22 to be exact, allow you to use handwritten, *non-witnessed* (called *holographic*) wills. However, use caution because oral and handwritten wills are more easily contested. Because you've decided to use WillWriter to write your will, you only need to take a quick look at oral and handwritten wills.

Typically, an oral will is valid only under extenuating circumstances—if you are on your deathbed or are facing imminent death (and then you obviously die from that peril). Also, the following conditions must be met:

- You, the testator, on your deathbed, must declare this to be your will before two *disinterested* witnesses, meaning someone who is not also a beneficiary in your will.

- Your oral will must be put in writing by (or under the direction of) your witnesses within 30 days of your death.

✿ After it has been put in writing, your will must be submitted to probate within six months of your death.

You are limited to the extent of property that you can leave under an oral will. These limitations make an oral will less desirable than a formal will, which is recognized in every state.

NOTE In most states that recognize a nuncupative will, your oral will can dispose only of personal property not to exceed $1,000 (or $10,000 if you are a member of the active military during a time of war). For this reason, an oral will is almost worthless.

Now, take a look at handwritten wills. A few states—for example, Indiana—recognize handwritten (holographic) wills as long as they are properly witnessed. In these states, a will need not be typed, and it can be written in any language and on any medium. For example, you can legally write your will on a chalkboard or even that napkin from last night's dinner—just make sure that you meet the other requirements discussed earlier, and make sure that you have a witness.

CAUTION Be careful! The entire holographic will must be in your handwriting. Any additional writing on the face of the will can invalidate the entire document.

Most states that recognize holographic wills (for example, Kentucky, California, and Wyoming) do not require you to have a witness. However, at probate, your signature must be authenticated either by a handwriting expert or by the testimony of a person familiar with your signature.

I strongly advise against a handwritten will. You could face too many potential problems, and your will could be invalidated or contested. Additionally, most probate courts are very strict when determining the validity of a handwritten will. Typically, this is because most handwritten wills are not witnessed; thus, they are considered to be less reliable than a formal will. Your best course is to type and print your will using word-processing software—or use a typewriter (if you still have one lying around somewhere).

CAUTION

If you plan to draft your will by hand, be sure to check with your state's probate court or an attorney in your area to confirm the specific writing requirements of your state. You can find your state's particular requirements by looking up the applicable probate code or statute in the library of your county probate court or in the library of a law school near you.

While I'm on the subject of informal wills, I might as well touch on videotaping your will. A videotaped will, while frequently used in the movies, is not yet admissible in any state. So, if you're thinking of using that camcorder that you got for Christmas, you should first check with your county's probate court or a local attorney before you start taping!

NOTE

You might be able to create a videotape of your will to supplement the actual formal will created during tomorrow's session. Check with your particular state's requirements just to be sure.

Although a video is not recognized as a valid will, many states admit videotapes as evidence of the following:

- The proper execution of a will
- The intentions of the testator
- The testator's mental state or capacity
- The authenticity of the will
- Other matters that are determined by a court to be relevant to the probate of a will

If you're interested in creating a videotape to supplement your formal will, check your state's rules of trial procedure. You can find these on your

FIND IT ON ▶
THE WEB

particular state's Web site (if your state has a Web site, that is) or by logging on to **www.law.cornell.edu/states/listing.html**.

Signing in the Presence of Witnesses

In order to create a valid, formal will, your will must also be witnessed. More specifically, you must sign and date your will in the presence of at least two witnesses (three if you live in Vermont). Then you must have your witnesses sign the will in your presence and in the presence of each other to acknowledge this exercise.

NOTE   Your will doesn't have to be *notarized* (signed in the presence of a notary public). You just need to sign it in front of witnesses, whose roles are to acknowledge your signature and then sign the will in your presence.

I discuss the requirements of your witnesses in greater detail later in this session.

Take a Break

Now that you understand wills and their functions, as well as the general requirements that you must meet in order to create a valid and legally binding formal will in your particular state, you deserve a break. After your break, you'll move on to the, perhaps, more difficult task of choosing your fiduciaries. But right now, go grab something to drink (preferably nonalcoholic) and stretch your legs. But hurry back! You still have a bit of work to do before bedtime.

Selecting Your Fiduciaries

During the final portion of this session, you will select your *fiduciaries* (those trusted individuals who will play a vital role in carrying out your final wishes).

NOTE The term fiduciary comes from Roman law, meaning a person exhibiting the characteristics of trust or confidence.

Specifically, you will select the following:

✿ A guardian for your minor children

✿ A personal representative (or executor)

✿ Witnesses to your will

Selecting a Guardian for Your Minor Children

If you don't have children, you can skip this portion and go straight to the section entitled "Choosing a Personal Representative." However, you might want to at least skim through this section in case you have children some day.

Choosing a guardian to care for your children is one of the most important, and perhaps difficult, decisions you will make. Typically, your surviving spouse (if he or she is the children's biological or adoptive parent) or the children's other biological parent will continue to provide for your minor children upon your death.

But what if the children's other biological parent (most likely your spouse) should predecease you? Or, tragically, you both meet your maker at the same time? If any of these events occur, you want to be sure that you have adequately provided for your minor children by naming a competent and trusted guardian to care for them.

NOTE In most cases, a guardian will care for a minor child only if neither parent is living.

As mentioned earlier, if you do not name a guardian for your minor children in your will, and the children's other parent predeceases you, the court will appoint a guardian for your minor children. The court will typically give preference to the children's grandparents or adult siblings, or even aunts and uncles, but this is not guaranteed.

You can specifically nominate a personal guardian for your minor children in your will. Upon your death, your nominated guardian will file a petition with the local probate court seeking judicial appointment to serve as your children's guardian under your will. Your selected guardian will most likely be appointed, unless the court determines that the selected guardian isn't in your minor children's best interests.

NOTE   Typically, children under the age of 18 are considered minors, and a guardian must be named for them. However, the *age of majority* is different in many states. Check with your state's local probate court to be sure at what age a child is considered to be an adult. If you're not sure about your particular state's requirement, nominate a guardian for any child under the age of 21.

The Role of a Guardian

A guardian is responsible for raising a child until he or she reaches the age of majority—typically 18. Your selected guardian will not only be legally responsible for providing food, housing, and clothing for your minor child, but might also be responsible for managing and investing the child's assets until he or she reaches the age of majority.

NOTE   The legally appointed guardian of a minor has all the responsibilities and authority of a parent.

The Qualifications of a Guardian

Other than being an adult, a person does not have to meet specific requirements in order to qualify as an acceptable guardian for a minor child. However, you obviously should select someone who is responsible and capable of meeting your children's financial and emotional needs. Remember, in addition to raising your children, your selected guardian might be responsible for managing any property left to your children under your will. Therefore, you will want your guardian to be both organized and trustworthy.

Most important, be sure that your selected guardian is *willing* to raise your children. Don't just assume that the person is up to the task. A person is not required to act as a guardian just because you named him or her as guardian in your will.

NOTE

Although there are no specific age requirements for a guardian—other than being an adult—you should take age into consideration.

Grandma and Grandpa might love Junior immensely, but they might not have the energy to run after a three-year-old child all day. Likewise, your 21-year-old sister, while a mature college graduate, might not be ready for motherhood. Your best option is to choose a guardian who will raise your children in a manner and lifestyle that are similar to your own.

While you're at it, if your children are old enough, why not ask their preferences as well? After all, if your children are still minors at your death, they will be the ones living with the guardian you nominate, and they need to be just as comfortable with your selection as you are. Obviously, your minor children's preference is only one consideration. You will also want to consider, among other things, the potential guardian's age, maturity level, financial stability, religious beliefs, and marital status.

ON THE

CD

To help you choose an appropriate caretaker for your minor children, I've provided a Guardian Checklist, as shown in Figure 1.1. You can also find a printable copy of the checklist on the CD at the back of this book.

Guardian Checklist

Candidate Name: _____ Age: _____

Address: _____ City: _____ State: _____ Zip: _____

Religious Beliefs:_____

Questions to Consider	Yes	No
Married?		
Existing Children?		
If No Children / Would They Like Children?		
Might They Accept?		
Financially Stable?		

Candidate Name: _____ Age: _____

Address: _____ City: _____ State: _____ Zip: _____

Religious Beliefs:_____

Questions to Consider	Yes	No
Married?		
Existing Children?		
If No Children / Would They Like Children?		
Might They Accept?		
Financially Stable?		

Candidate Name: _____ Age: _____

Address: _____ City: _____ State: _____ Zip: _____

Religious Beliefs:_____

Questions to Consider	Yes	No
Married?		
Existing Children?		
If No Children / Would They Like Children?		
Might They Accept?		
Financially Stable?		

Figure 1.1

Use this checklist when selecting a personal guardian to care for your minor children.

NOTE If you want, you can name a separate guardian for each of your minor children, although I advise against separating minor children if you can avoid doing so. However, should you want to name a separate guardian for your minor children, check with an attorney to help you draft the appropriate document (or include the necessary language in the will you create during the Saturday Evening session).

Most important, perhaps, be sure to nominate an alternate or successor guardian in your will in case your first choice is unable to serve for any reason.

Selecting a Guardian Who Is Not a Surviving Parent

Good luck trying to name a legal guardian who is *not* the minor child's surviving parent. Doing so usually isn't successful. Typically, the surviving parent automatically receives or retains custody of the minor child *unless* you can show that the other parent is (or will be) harmful to the child or has abandoned the child in the past.

You will find it difficult to prove that the other parent will be harmful to the child, unless you have evidence that that parent abuses the use of drugs or alcohol or is physically or mentally cruel to the child. Additionally, most courts will consider child abandonment only if the offending parent has failed to provide for the minor child and has not had any contact with the child for an extended period (in most states, this means more than one or two years).

Without such evidence, the court will most likely grant custody to the surviving parent.

NOTE You don't need to name the child's other parent as a guardian in your will. You should name a guardian only if you'd prefer that the other parent not serve as the child's guardian or if both of you should die at the same time.

WHEN THE OTHER PARENT ISN'T THE BEST CHOICE

Nominating someone other than the surviving biological or adoptive parent of your minor child to care for the child after your death is generally unsuccessful. However, certain circumstances might warrant you to not name the surviving parent as the child's guardian in your will. Take a look at the following fictional situation.

Question: I am a single mother raising my 3-year-old son (Steve). Steve's biological father (Doug) has not seen him in more than a year and does not financially support him. I'd like to name my mother (Steve's grandmother) as his guardian in my will. Does this guarantee that my mother will be named as his guardian?

Answer: Unfortunately, not. If Doug still has his parental rights, he will most likely be granted custody (if he seeks custody). The exceptions would be if the court were to determine that Doug's failure to provide for Steve and to have any contact with Steve this past year qualifies as abandonment, or if there is evidence to show that Doug would in any way be harmful to the child. If you prefer that someone else (rather than the child's other parent) serve as your minor child's guardian upon your death, be sure to thoroughly explain your reasoning—including the circumstances surrounding your situation and your concern for the minor child's well being.

Choosing a Personal Representative

As I previously mentioned, personal representative can refer to both executors (those individuals named in a will to carry out the testator's final wishes) and administrators (those individuals who act on your behalf when you die without a will). Because you have already made the decision to write your will, I refer to your executor throughout the book.

NOTE Some states refer to a *personal representative,* while other states use the term *administrator* or *executor* to describe this role. These terms are often used interchangeably. Legally, an *executrix* describes a female representative, whereas *executor* describes a male representative. However, *executor* is commonly used and accepted today to refer to either a male or female.

The Role of an Executor

The three primary functions of an executor are as follows:

- **Collecting assets**. Your executor will be responsible for filing claims on behalf of your estate to collect any debts owed to you on your death. Only your executor has the authority to collect debts owed to you.

  Remember, your executor will not deal with your life insurance policies, IRAs, pensions, or other property that does not pass through your will. These properties are not subject to probate and, thus, are not disposed of by your will. (This basically means that for these assets, you should have designated a beneficiary at an earlier time.)

- **Paying debts, claims, costs of administration, and taxes owed by your estate**. You can specify in your will exactly how you want your estate to handle these liabilities. I will explain your options for handling them in a later session.

- **Closing and distributing your estate to your named beneficiaries**. After your estate's debts and taxes are paid, your executor will distribute your property according to your wishes and will petition the court to close the estate.

Your executor may also be instructed to do the following:

- Obtain certified copies of your death certificate.

- Notify your creditors, beneficiaries, and others—such as the Social Security Administration and your financial institution—of your death.

- Cancel your credit cards, magazine and newspaper subscriptions, lawn care service, and so on.

- Prepare your final income tax forms.

- Manage your assets during the administration process.

For many people, choosing a personal representative is a relatively easy task. They simply choose their spouse. However, you might be different. You might be unmarried, or you just might want to select a close personal friend, an adult child, or a long-time coworker. Whatever your choice, be sure that you feel comfortable with this person and are confident of his or her ability to carry out your last—and perhaps most important—wishes.

Always ask your proposed executor if he or she is indeed up to the task. Don't let it be a surprise. The role of executor can be a rather big responsibility, one that someone may not want to undertake. Your selected executor is under no obligation to perform this role just because you named him or her in your will. Avoid any possible problems now by discussing your wishes with your selected executor.

NOTE In case your named executor is unable to carry out his or her obligations, or in the event that your executor should predecease you before you are able to change your will, you should name an alternate executor (sometimes called a *successor executor*).

Requirements of an Executor

A personal representative must act in good faith and with proper motives (within the bounds of reasonable judgment). So, who is qualified to act as an executor? Executors can be just about anyone who is an adult (typically at least 18 years old) and who is organized. And, because your executor will be handling assets of your estate and interacting with your beneficiaries during what likely will be an emotional time, you probably want to select someone who is well-liked and highly respected by your loved ones.

NOTE Because state laws vary, you should name an executor who resides in your state. For example, Montana, Nevada, New Hampshire, and Vermont require that your executor be a state resident. Florida will allow a nonresident executor, but only if the executor is also a blood relative to the testator. As you can see, the laws regarding executor residency requirements can be confusing. If you want to name a nonresident executor, be sure to check your state's specific requirements before proceeding. Each state's requirements are listed in Appendix A, "State-By-State Probate Matrix."

Disinterested Executors

Your executor does not need to be *disinterested;* that is, your executor can also be named as a beneficiary under your will. It is not uncommon for an executor to have an interest in the probate estate, and having an interest in your will (being a beneficiary) does not disqualify him or her.

NOTE Often a spouse or an adult child serves as an executor and is also named as a beneficiary in the decedent's will.

The rule is different with attorneys. The general rule is that attorneys cannot receive bequests in wills that they draft, unless they are heirs of the deceased (for example, a child, a spouse, or a parent). If you plan to use an attorney to draft your will and want to leave that attorney something in your will, inform him or her of this fact so that the attorney can refer you to another one to actually draft the will.

Unqualified Executors

Some individuals do not qualify to serve as executors. For example, anyone under 18 years of age cannot serve as an executor. Also, anyone who has been convicted of a felony is deemed unsuitable. And, depending on the state, a corporation might not be permitted to act as an executor of an estate. Check your state's specific requirements for an executor before making your final selection.

NOTE   The court gives great deference to a testator's choice of a personal representative, unless that individual is unqualified.

Paying an Executor

Legally, your executor is entitled to a reasonable fee for performing this role. However, the fee is typically paid out of your estate. Compensation can be arranged a variety of ways, depending on your state of residence. For example, you can fix a reasonable amount in the will itself or, as it is in California, the executor might be entitled to a certain percentage of your estate's net worth. Of course, executors can waive their fees, and they often do so if they are also named as beneficiaries under a will.

NOTE   Your executor might be required to post a *surety bond* in carrying out his or her duties. A surety, or *performance bond*, is a type of insurance policy that protects your beneficiaries from your executor's dishonesty or incompetence. However, you can specifically waive the bond requirement in your will.

Selecting Witnesses

As previously mentioned, your will must be witnessed by at least two people. These individuals will watch you sign and date your will in their presence, and then they will sign your will to acknowledge their witnessing of your will.

How Many Witnesses Do You Need?

In all states (except Vermont), your will must be witnessed by a minimum of two people. Be careful! Vermont requires three witnesses and Pennsylvania's statute is unclear. Pennsylvania's statute could be interpreted to require two witnesses, only if the testator does not execute the will.

NOTE Appendix A lists each state's general requirements for drafting a will, including their required number of witnesses. Again, it is always best to verify your particular state's requirements by consulting an attorney in your state or contacting your local probate court.

To be on the safe side, I strongly recommend that you use three witnesses. Why? The court (during probate) might reject one of your witnesses for a variety of reasons, including being a beneficiary in your will, not being mentally competent, or not witnessing your signature.

Why not have five or six witnesses, to be doubly sure? Because when the time comes to probate your will, your executor might need to locate all your witnesses. If you have five or six, the executor might be required to find them all, which certainly could prove time-consuming, if not downright impossible. If you limit the number of witnesses to three, you're likely to effectively protect your interests.

NOTE Your witnesses probably won't appear in court unless your will is contested. Typically, your witnesses need only sign an affidavit that acknowledges the fact that they witnessed your will and that—to the best of their knowledge—they believed that you were at least 18 years old, of sound mind, and that you drafted your will of your own volition. But, because a few states still require witnesses to testify in court, you may want to choose witnesses who are from the immediate area.

Requirements of Witnesses

When selecting your witnesses, you need to consider the following:

- ✿ A witness should be disinterested.
- ✿ A witness must be competent.
- ✿ A witness should be an adult (at least 18 years old).

Disinterested Witnesses

In order to avoid potential problems during the probate of your will, you should choose trusted, disinterested individuals to serve as witnesses to your will. In fact, Wisconsin requires that you choose disinterested witnesses.

However, all other states specifically allow you to have interested witnesses—that is, witnesses who are also beneficiaries under your will.

This means that you might be free to name one or more of your witnesses as a beneficiary under your will. Notice that I said "might." All states have rules regarding interested witnesses and their ability to receive a bequest from a will to which they attest.

CAUTION

In most states, your will is void if it cannot be proven without the testimony of the interested witness or without proof of his or her signature as a witness to your will. However, it's typically voided only as it applies to the interested witness; the witness loses whatever property was designated for him or her.

If you plan to select a beneficiary under your will to act as a witness, check with an attorney or consult your state's law. (You can find your particular state's requirement regarding interested witnesses in Appendix A.) States are all over the board about how an interested witness affects your will. A few examples of how a number of states deal with interested witnesses follow.

In Wisconsin, an interested witness invalidates your will in its entirety. In Michigan and Rhode Island, however, only the bequest to the interested witness is void. In a few states (Arkansas, Massachusetts, Missouri, Nevada, New Hampshire, North Carolina, and Vermont), the interest passed to the witness is invalidated only if the will is not witnessed by at least two other interested persons (or by three disinterested witnesses in Vermont).

Still yet, the District of Columbia and some states (Illinois, Indiana, Iowa, Kentucky, and Texas) take away the interest left to witnesses, but only in excess of the witnesses' entitled intestate share, if any. (For example, in one of these states, if your son is a witness to your will and you've left him your entire estate, he will be entitled only to his intestate share—one-half of your estate—if your spouse is still living at your death.)

A witness is not considered interested *unless* the will gives that witness some personal or beneficial interest. The mere fact that a person is named in the will as an executor, guardian, or other fiduciary does not make him an interested party. Therefore, your executor or guardian for your minor children can also serve as one of the witnesses to your will as long as he or she is not a beneficiary under your will.

Competent Witnesses

In addition to being disinterested, your witnesses must be competent at the time of *attestation* (when you sign your will in their presence and declare that the document you are signing is your will). It is enough that they understand the nature of the act. Any subsequent incompetence on the part of the witness will not prevent the eventual probate of a will.

Age Requirements

In the majority of states, there is no minimum age requirement for a witness. Your witness is required only to be competent. In other words, your witnesses must have sufficient capacity to understand the nature of the act that they are witnessing. However, a few states have interpreted "legally competent" to mean a legally competent adult.

Therefore, your best choice is to choose an adult (someone at least 18 years old) as a witness. If you choose a minor, your will might be contested.

What's Next?

You've done a great job! You identified those individuals whom you want to act on your behalf after you're gone, and you're now ready for the next step.

If you are still not quite sure about someone you've selected, take the rest of this evening to consider whether he or she is the best person to act on your behalf. You haven't started drafting yet, so you can always change your mind. You need to be comfortable with the decisions that you make tonight because the individuals that you select will play an extremely important role.

Tomorrow, you will begin to inventory your estate, and I will explain what you should and shouldn't include in determining your net worth. Now relax and get some rest, because tomorrow is a big day!

Finding Out What You Own and How You Own It

- ✿ Taking an Inventory of Your Estate
- ✿ Determining How You Own Property
- ✿ Don't Forget Your Uncle Sam

ood morning! I hope you slept well knowing that, by the end of tomorrow, you'll have a valid will that provides for your loved ones. This morning, you take an inventory of what you own so that you can determine to whom you want to leave your possessions.

In this session, you will also learn:

✪ What type of property can be left in your will

✪ What property to include when determining your estate's net worth

✪ How to determine whether your estate will be subject to federal estate taxes

You have a lot of work to do. So, grab a cup of coffee and get started.

Taking an Inventory of Your Estate

If your estate is relatively small or if you plan to leave your entire estate to one person (say, your spouse), you might not need to complete this exercise. However, if you plan to leave your property to several individuals or if your estate is large or complex, you might find it beneficial to take an inventory of exactly what you own and how you came about owning it.

You might also want to take an inventory to determine how and if your estate will be subject to federal estate taxes. That's right! Even in death, you can't escape taxes! But, enough about taxes for now. I'll talk more about Uncle Sam's portion later in this session.

After breakfast, you'll make a list of all the items you own—outright and partially. This list should include all *personality* owned by you, as well as real estate. Personality refers to your personal, *movable property,* which includes your household goods and other personal effects.

ON THE

CD

Perhaps you've already made an inventory of your household goods and possessions—in case of a fire or theft or for your insurance company. If so, you can use that list to help you with this exercise. If you haven't, you'll need to make one now. Later in this session, I refer to an Estate Inventory Worksheet (found in Appendix C) that will aid you in your calculation. The Estate Inventory Worksheet is also included on the CD-ROM that comes with this book.

Calculating Your Estate's Worth

On your estate worksheet, you need to account not only for your household items and possessions (for example, jewelry, home furnishings, clothing, art, antiques, and so on), but also for your house, automobiles, mutual funds, stocks, bonds, retirement accounts, bank accounts, life insurance policies, and so on.

Items to consider in determining your estate include the following:

- ✪ Real estate (including your home, vacation home, and other property)
- ✪ Bank accounts, certificates of deposit, cash, dividends, money market accounts, and trust income
- ✪ Stocks, bonds, mutual funds, and other securities
- ✪ Automobiles and other vehicles (for example, recreational vehicles, boats, planes, and motorcycles)

- Business interests (sole proprietorships, partnerships, and corporations)
- Personal effects (including household furnishings, jewelry, furs, clothing, art, sporting equipment, electronic equipment, tools, equipment, collectibles, coins, stamps, and antiques)
- Life insurance policies
- Retirement accounts—IRAs, 401(k)—pension plans, profit sharing, and other death benefits and annuities
- Copyrights, trademarks, patents, publicity rights, and royalties
- Miscellaneous assets, including inheritances, gifts, and promissory notes (for example, money you loaned to someone)

To determine your estate's net worth, subtract your liabilities (what you owe) from your assets (what you own). After you calculate your net worth, you will be able to determine whether your estate will be subject to estate taxes. (I'll talk more about taxes after you complete your inventory worksheet.)

Classifying Your Property: Is It Real, Personal, Tangible, or Intangible?

Before you can begin calculating your estate's net worth, you need to determine what you own. Your property can be broken into two basic categories: real property and personal property.

Real Property

Real property, sometimes referred to as *realty,* describes your real estate— for example, your home and other land that you own or in which you have an interest. *Land* includes all things that are attached to the land or that are said to *run with the land* (for example, trees and buildings).

Personal Property

As I mentioned earlier, personal property refers to your movable possessions, and it can be classified as two main types: tangible and intangible.

Tangible personal property includes those items that you can see, feel, and
touch, including jewelry (your platinum and diamond ring), clothing
(your faux leopard skin boots), art (your authentic Monet watercolor), as
well as automobiles, collectibles, antiques, household goods, animals, and
sports equipment—just to name a few.

Intangible personal property refers to other property you own or have an
interest in but that you cannot actually touch. Examples of intangible personal property include trademarks, intellectual property rights, copyrights,
royalties, stocks, mutual funds, CDs, bonds, and bank accounts.

Now that you have an understanding of how your property is classified,
take a look at what property will be disposed of by your will (also referred
to as your *probate property*).

Identifying Probate Property

Only probate property can be disposed of through a will. Examples of
probate property include:

- Possessions that you own outright
- Your interest in community property (You can leave your one-half
  interest in community property to whomever you want. See the
  upcoming section "Understanding Community Property" for more
  on this subject.)
- Your interest in property that is owned by you and another individual but that is not owned *jointly with a right of survivorship* or as
  tenants by the entirety

Nonprobate property avoids the probate process entirely by being automatically transferred to a previously designated beneficiary upon your
death.

Property that is not disposed of through your will (nonprobate property) includes:

- Life insurance proceeds
- Pension plans
- IRAs (Individual Retirement Accounts)
- 401(k) accounts
- Pay-on-death bank accounts (sometimes referred to as a *Totten Trust*), which is an account held in your name for the benefit of another where the proceeds automatically revert to the named beneficiary at your death

In each of the previous examples, a beneficiary is named on the document itself. The individual or individuals named on the document will receive the proceeds at your death. For example, say that your life insurance policy names your spouse, Melba, as the beneficiary, and your pension names your daughter, Ann. Melba will be entitled to the life insurance proceeds at your death, and Ann will receive your pension benefits. Neither Melba nor Ann need to wait until your will is probated, however, because these proceeds are from nonprobate assets.

Other nonprobate property includes property that is held as follows:

- Joint Tenants with a Right of Survivorship *(JTWROS)*
- Tenants by the Entirety (This is just a creative way of describing property jointly owned by spouses. Property owned jointly with a right of survivorship stipulates that the survivor—the one still living upon the other's death—becomes the sole owner of the whole property.)
- Property controlled by contract
- Living trust assets (assets that you choose to transfer to selected beneficiaries through a trust that you create during your lifetime)

Property owned according to the preceding examples is automatically inherited by the surviving joint owners upon your death. Or, in the case of the living trust assets, proceeds are paid to your designated beneficiaries at your death.

Determining How You Own Property

You need to understand how, or even whether, you own an item before you can effectively leave it to someone under your will. When you die, your will can effectively transfer only property that is owned by you or property in which you have an interest at your death. To determine how or whether certain property in your possession is actually owned by you, you once again need to examine the laws of the state in which you live.

Understanding Community Property

Believe it or not, your spouse might already own an interest in property that you think is yours and yours alone. In certain states—Arizona, California, Idaho, Louisiana, Nevada, New Mexico, Texas, and Washington—property acquired during marriage is considered *community property,* which means that it is owned jointly between spouses. Wisconsin's laws are similar to community property laws, but property acquired during the marriage is referred to as *marital property.*

Community property states view the marriage between a husband and wife as a partnership, in which each party has equally contributed during the partnership, regardless of each person's actual financial contributions.

For example, consider the fictional marriage of Californians named Marc and Laura. Marc is unemployed and spends most of his day lounging on the sofa at home watching "Days of Our Lives." Laura, on the other hand, works 10 hours a day, six days a week, for her healthy $250,000 annual salary. Marc and Laura live in a community property state. Therefore, although Marc doesn't contribute financially to the marriage, Laura's income is considered community property, and he is entitled to one-half of the income earned annually by Laura. That's $125,000 each year! (Between you and me, Laura didn't marry very well, did she? Maybe she should consider moving to a different state.)

Community property differs from *your* separate property (those assets that belong to you and only you). For example, a home that was purchased during the marriage—whether in your name alone or in the name of both you and your spouse—is considered as owned equally between the two of you. However, the farm you inherited upon your grandfather's death is yours alone, even though your grandpa died after you got married. Also, the savings account that you've had since college is also yours

---

IS IT COMMUNITY PROPERTY, OR IS IT MINE, ALL MINE?

Question: My wife does not work outside our home. Last year, I purchased a boat with money that I alone have earned during our marriage. The boat is deeded in my name only. We live in Arizona. Is my wife automatically entitled to the boat upon my death, or can I leave it to my brother?

Answer: In a community property state, such as Arizona, your wife is considered to be one-half owner of that boat. You, of course, can leave your half to whomever you'd like, and you might designate your brother as the recipient of your one-half interest.

But this gets sticky. Do your brother and your wife each use the boat on alternate weekends? If you've left your wife the majority of your estate, she probably won't mind giving her half of the boat to your brother, but you never know. Your brother might be obliged to buy out your wife's share if she's not feeling too generous. If she is an avid boater and wants to keep the sloop for herself, your wife might have to compensate your brother for his inherited share.

alone. (Beware! If you use those savings account funds to buy a car that is deeded in the name of both you and your spouse, your spouse then becomes one-half owner of that shiny, new automobile.)

To better understand who owns what in a community property state, refer to Table 2.1.

SPECIAL RULES FOR SPOUSES

Depending on the marital property laws of your state, your spouse might already have an interest in property that you think is yours and yours alone. And you cannot disinherit a spouse (without getting creative—too creative to go into here), even though you purposely leave your spouse out of your will.

Specifically, you cannot disinherit your spouse because your spouse likely will be entitled to *take against your will,* which means that she will receive at least her *intestate share* of your probate estate. That is, she will receive what she would have been entitled to if you had died without a will. (For more information on intestate law, see Appendix B.)

TABLE 2.1 WHO OWNS WHAT IN A COMMUNITY PROPERTY STATE

Type of Property	Ownership
Items or property owned before marriage	Owned solely by the individual.
Income earned or generated during the marriage	Owned equally by spouses.
Property acquired during the marriage	Owned equally by spouses.
Gifts given during the marriage	Owned solely by the recipient.
Inheritance received during the marriage	Owned solely by the recipient.

Ownership of Property in a Common Law State

More than 40 states are common law states; only Arizona, California, Idaho, Louisiana, Nevada, New Mexico, Texas, Washington, and Wisconsin are not.

Unlike community property states, common law states have no formal rules regarding how property is owned. (For more information regarding how property is owned in a common law state, see Table 2.2). Instead, common law states protect a spouse from being disinherited by allowing the surviving spouse at least one-third to one-half interest in the property left in a decedent spouse's will, whether or not any property has been left to the surviving spouse. This *taking against the will* allowance (as it is commonly called) does not affect most married couples because the majority of them leave the bulk of their estates to their spouses in their wills.

TABLE 2.2 HOW PROPERTY IS OWNED IN A COMMON LAW STATE

Type of Property	Ownership
Property held separately in your name (for example, title, deed, mortgage, slip)	You are the sole owner.
Property purchased by income earned or generated solely by you (for example, computer, camera, and so on)	You are the sole owner.
Property in the name of your spouse that was purchased with income earned or inherited solely by you (for example, your spouse's name on title, deed, slip, and so on)	Your spouse is the sole owner.
Property you own jointly with a person other than your spouse	You alone own your share.
Property purchased during the marriage by income generated by both partners	You and your spouse share equally.

> ### CAUTION: PRENUPTIAL AGREEMENTS CAN CHANGE EVERYTHING!
>
> **Question:** Before our marriage, my wife and I entered into a prenuptial agreement that specifically outlines how our property is owned. Is this valid in a community property state?
>
> **Answer:** Yes. A prenuptial agreement is a legally binding instrument agreed to by a couple prior to marriage that stipulates how property is to be owned or transferred upon death or divorce. A valid prenuptial agreement controls the distribution of property owned by the marital estate, even if this distribution conflicts with community property law. If you've entered into a prenuptial agreement with your spouse and have any questions regarding ownership or your right to dispose of certain property under your will, you need to consult an attorney.

NOTE

Common law states provide for a type of *forced heirship,* in which the decedent's surviving spouse is entitled to a share of the decedent's estate regardless of what the will provides.

To avoid potential problems after your death, leave your spouse at least 50 percent of your estate—or consult an attorney to help you load up on nonprobate assets! If you want to leave your spouse less than 50 percent because you are concerned that he or she will incur estate taxes, consult an experienced estate tax attorney to help you minimize any potential tax liabilities.

If you move from a common law state to a community property state (or vice versa) during your marriage, you need to consult an attorney to determine how the new state laws will affect your property. Some community property states, such as California and Washington, treat property acquired in the common law state as community property, while other states continue to treat the previously acquired property as common law property. And there is no guarantee that property acquired during the marriage in a community property state will remain the property of both you and your spouse if you move to a common law state.

Completing the Estate Inventory Worksheet

A little break in our proceedings is in order—because it's time for you to fill out your Estate Inventory Worksheet. You can use this worksheet, provided in Appendix C, to help account for what you own and how you own it. You will also use the worksheet to calculate your estate's net worth.

ON THE

CD

You can find a printable copy of the Estate Inventory Worksheet on the CD at the back of this book.

Take a Break

Now that you have completed the Estate Inventory Worksheet and calculated your estate's net worth, you can easily determine whether your estate will be subject to estate taxes. In the next section, you focus on taxes and how they might affect your estate.

But first, you might want to take a break. Now is the perfect opportunity to delegate all of the weekend chores to your husband, or wife, and kids. You can tell them that you're busy providing for their futures, so you can't be bothered with dusting and vacuuming this weekend!

Don't Forget Your Uncle Sam

It has long been said that you can be sure of only two things in this world: death and taxes. You might think that the only upside to passing away is that you will finally escape a lifetime of paying the latter. However, this might not be the case.

Your estate might be liable for both state and federal taxes. That is why you need to determine whether your estate will be subject to these taxes and how you want your estate to handle them. Many people will not need to concern themselves with federal gift and estate taxes. Most likely, the value of the gifts made during their lives, as well as the value of their estates at the time of their deaths, will be less than the personal estate tax exemption afforded under federal law.

NOTE No one gets anything in your will until your executor pays your estate's debts, taxes, and other encumbrances.

First, examine federal gift and estate taxes.

Federal Taxes

All property (probate and nonprobate) owned by you at your death is subject to federal estate taxes. *Federal estate taxes* are taxes that must be paid on the value of your estate left at your death. *Federal gift taxes* are levied on certain large gifts made during your lifetime. Both federal gift taxes and federal estate taxes (called the *unified gift and estate tax*) are levied at the same rate. However, these taxes are currently levied only when the value of your taxable estate is worth more than $675,000 or when the total value of certain property gifted during your lifetime is greater than $675,000.

If your estate's net worth is less than $675,000, it will not be subject to federal estate tax. The federal government currently gives each citizen a credit (called a *unified gift/estate tax credit*) that allows you to pass tax-free up to $675,000 (or a combined total of $1.35 million for you and your spouse) in taxable property during your lifetime or at your death.

Taxpayer Relief Act of 1997

Under the Taxpayer Relief Act of 1997, during your lifetime, you will be able to give away (or leave an estate worth) as much as $1 million by 2006 without having the estate subjected to federal estate taxes. (This is commonly referred to a *personal estate tax exemption*.) Currently, the unified gift/estate tax credit is $675,000 and will increase steadily over the next six years (see Table 2.3).

Special Rules for Spouses

Special rules apply to property that is given as a gift to your spouse during your life or left to your spouse at your death. Specifically, at your death, you can leave your spouse an estate with a value greater than the current personal estate tax exemption, and the amount left to your spouse will not be subject to federal estate or gift taxes. Consider the following hypothetical scenario.

John dies in 2005 with an estate worth $2 million. He leaves $1.5 million to his wife, Dusanka. The remaining $500,000 is left to his favorite daughter, Christine. (I would have hoped for more, but. . . .) Any amount

TABLE 2.3 AMOUNT OF UNIFIED CREDIT UNDER THE TAXPAYER RELIEF ACT OF 1997	
Year of Death or Gift	**Amount of Unified Credit**
2000	$675,000
2001	$675,000
2002	$700,000
2003	$700,000
2004	$850,000
2005	$950,000
2006	$1 million

left to a surviving spouse is exempt from federal estate tax. So, the $1.5 million left to Dusanka will pass free of tax. The remaining amount left to Christine ($500,000) will also pass tax-free because it falls within the personal estate tax exemption afforded John's estate in 2005 (refer to Table 2.3).

NOTE   A *marital deduction* is an exemption approved by the Internal Revenue Service (IRS) whereby property (no matter what the value) left to a spouse at a decedent's death is not subject to federal estate tax. In other words, the amount left to your spouse at your death is not included in calculating your estate tax liability. Seem too good to be true? Well, it just might be, because when your spouse dies, watch out!

Gifts between spouses also fall under the marital deduction exemption, meaning any amount given to your spouse *during* your life is exempt from federal gift tax. But more on gift taxes in a moment. For more information on the marital deduction, see IRC Section 2056(a) of the federal tax code.

FIND IT ON ▶
THE WEB   You can find out more about the marital deduction by logging onto the IRS Web site at **www.irs.gov**.

Excluding Charitable Organizations

Gifts made to a qualified tax-exempt charitable organization during your lifetime or at your death are also exempt from federal estate/gift taxes regardless of the amount of the gift. Such gifts are considered to be charitable deductions.

However, be careful! Some organizations are classified as tax exempt, but that might not mean that your donations to them are tax deductible. The IRS must approve the organization before the donations are considered tax deductible.

To be sure that your donation or gift is tax deductible, check out the complete IRS-approved list online at **www.irs.gov/prod/bus_info/eo/eosearch.html**.

Or you can go to **www.irs.gov** and order IRS publication 78, which is the cumulative list of tax-exempt organizations.

Also, if you own a family business, check with an attorney. A large portion of your estate might be exempt from federal taxes.

Lifetime Threshold

Many estates will not be subject to federal gift/estate taxes. You are currently entitled to give away during your lifetime or leave at your death up to $675,000 without owing federal gift/estate taxes. More important, this lifetime threshold does not include yearly gifts of up to $10,000 per person.

Therefore, you are entitled to give up to $10,000 a year to as many people as you want without having the gifted amounts subject to federal gift tax *and* without depleting your unified credit.

The IRS imposes a federal gift tax if you give an individual gift totaling more than $10,000 in a single year. The magic number here is $10,000. This amount is considered an annual exclusion and is exempt from a gift tax.

The $10,000 exemption is a total amount, which means that you cannot give your nephew a $5,000 check and then three months later, buy him a car worth $10,000. In this instance, you would owe gift tax on $5,000.

If you give more than $10,000 to one person in a single year, the overage is charged against your lifetime credit. For example, if you give your friend Curt $16,000 this year, you have exceeded the maximum by $6,000. Thus, your $675,000 lifetime unified credit is reduced by $6,000 and now totals $669,000. (Note that the $675,000 credit mentioned here applies only if you die in 2000. The credit increases yearly until it reaches $1 million in 2006.)

If you give a gift with a value greater than $10,000, you will need to file a federal gift tax return—IRS form 709 or 709(a)—when you file your annual income taxes.

NOTE Gift taxes are the responsibility of the giver and, therefore, must be paid by the giver—not the receiver. However, the recipient of the gift might need to pay the gift tax if the giver's estate fails to pay it. For example, if you give your niece $50,000 this year as a wedding gift, the $40,000 overage will be deducted from your lifetime unified credit. If at your death, your estate owes taxes that it cannot pay, your niece might be required to pay the gift tax on that $40,000 windfall.

As I mentioned, gifts to your spouse of any amount (assuming that your spouse is a United States citizen) are exempt from federal gift taxes. Also, you don't need to pay federal gift taxes for gifts totaling more than $10,000 per year to an individual if those gifts are a direct payment of that person's tuition or as payment toward medical expenses.

NOTE If your spouse is not a United States citizen, your gifts are limited to $100,000 per year. Anything beyond that is subject to federal gift tax. Even though these gifts are not taxable, you still need to file a federal gift tax return for each one.

Gifts that are exempt from federal gift tax include:

- Gifts totaling $10,000 or less to a single person in a single year.
- Gifts of any amount to a spouse, as long as your spouse is a United States citizen. If your spouse is not a United States citizen, your gifts cannot exceed $100,000 per year.
- Gifts of any amount as a direct payment of a person's tuition or medical expenses.
- Gifts of any amount to an IRS-approved, tax-exempt charity.

In case you're feeling rather generous, Table 2.4 provides a few examples of gifts and their resulting tax consequences. For all of these gifts, assume that your spouse has not consented to split the gifts made by you, so these gifts are from you alone.

TABLE 2.4 HYPOTHETICAL GIFTS AND THEIR TAX LIABILITY

Gift	Your Estate's Tax Liability
$10,000 to your nephew to use to buy a new car	No tax liability. The gift falls within your annual exemption.
A $20,000 car for your niece	Your estate will be liable for tax on the $10,000 overage amount.
An $80,000 speedboat to your spouse as a birthday present	No tax liability. Gifts of any amount to a spouse are exempt from federal tax.
$25,000 to Princeton to pay for your son's tuition	No tax liability. Gifts that are paid on behalf of an individual as payment for tuition or medical care are exempt from federal tax.

Again, if your estate worth is more than $675,000 (or worth more than $1 million by 2006), you need to consult an estate or financial planner to assist you with tax liabilities. You can do some things to diminish your tax liability and shelter your estate from a certain amount of taxes, such as the following:

○ **Create a QTIP trust**. A *Qualified Terminable Interest Property (QTIP) trust* postpones estate taxes by allowing you to pass any amount to your spouse tax-free. (Again, all amounts transferred between spouses—as long as you both are United States citizens—are exempt from federal taxes under the marital deduction.)

However, unlike leaving your entire estate to your spouse outright, a QTIP trust allows *you* to determine who will ultimately inherit your property upon the death of your surviving spouse. Under a QTIP trust, your spouse inherits only a life interest in the property transferred by you, with no right to change the beneficiaries you have selected to inherit the remainder of the trust property at her death.

While creating a QTIP trust allows you to avoid federal estate taxes at the time of your death, once your spouse dies, the value of the property remaining in the trust *is* included in your spouse's estate for tax purposes.

Note that a *Qualified Domestic Trust (QDOT)* is similar to a QTIP trust, except that it applies to transfers of property to a noncitizen spouse. Unlike a citizen spouse, who can receive any amount of money from a spouse upon the death of a spouse, noncitizen spouses can receive only an amount up to the decedent spouse's personal exemption (currently $675,000) without having the transfer subject to tax. A QDOT works to postpone tax until the death of the surviving noncitizen spouse.

- **Create an AB trust**. An *AB trust* works to reduce a couple's estate tax liability and, depending on the overall value of the couple's estate, can be used to effectively avoid estate taxes altogether. Unlike a QTIP trust, an AB trust *is* taxed upon the death of the first spouse. However, as long as the value of property passed under an AB trust is $675,000 or less (the current unified credit allowed by the IRS), no estate tax will be due.

  Because the surviving spouse inherits only the right to use the trust property or the income generated from the trust during his or her life, the property is not considered a part of the surviving spouse's estate at his or her death and passes to the final beneficiary tax-free.

  Note that the surviving spouse under an AB trust (for example, the one who inherits a life estate in the trust property at the death of the first spouse) has no right to consume or dispose of the trust principal during his or her lifetime.

  If you and your spouse are interested in taking advantage of an AB or QTIP trust, consult an attorney. A qualified attorney can help you determine which one is right for you and can also ensure that your trust meets all IRS regulations.

- **Give it away!** One of the best ways to avoid federal taxes upon your death is to give your money or property away before you go! As you learned earlier in this session, every individual is entitled to give up to $10,000 per person per year tax-free! Better yet, spouses can combine their annual exclusions and give a single recipient up to $20,000 per year without the gift(s) being subject to federal gift tax.

HOW TO CREATE AN **AB** TRUST
TO MINIMIZE ESTATE TAXES

As previously mentioned, an AB trust can be used by couples to minimize estate taxes or, in many cases, to avoid estate taxes completely. Take a look at the following hypothetical example, of how one couple could have benefited by an AB trust.

Scott and MeeWon are married. Their joint marital estate is worth $1.8 million, with each owning $900,000. During their lifetimes, Scott and MeeWon did not give large gifts (for example, gifts totaling more than $10,000 per person, per year). Scott dies in 2005, leaving his entire estate to MeeWon.

Because any amount left to a spouse at death is considered exempt from tax under the IRS marital deduction, Scott's estate will owe no tax upon his death. However, at MeeWon's death two years later, her estate is worth $1.8 million (her own $900,000 and the $900,000 she inherited from Scott).

She leaves the entire amount to her daughter, Nakita. At her death in 2007, MeeWon can effectively transfer up to $1 million dollars tax-free. However, this leaves $800,000 in her estate that will be subject to tax—straight to Uncle Sam!

Now, take a look at what would happen if Scott and MeeWon were to create an AB trust.

Instead of transferring their estates outright to the surviving spouse at death, Scott and MeeWon create an AB trust in which the surviving spouse is named a life beneficiary of the decedent spouse's estate. Their daughter, Nakita, is named the ultimate beneficiary of the trust property and will inherit it upon the death of the life beneficiary.

Scott dies in 2005. The property left in the AB trust to MeeWon is subject to estate tax. However, because the amount of property transferred was less than the $950,000 unified credit in 2005, no tax is owed by Scott's estate. MeeWon has "inherited" a life interest in the trust property, with the ability to use the income for the remainder of her life. At her death, the remainder of the trust property will then pass to Nakita. Her own estate, which she has also left to Nakita, does not include her life interest in the AB trust and is, therefore, worth only $900,000. Her entire estate, like Scott's, will also pass tax-free because it is less than the allowable unified credit in 2007.

If you have a large estate, you will undoubtedly benefit from consulting a qualified financial planner or an attorney specializing in estate planning. I highly recommend doing so. Federal gift and estate taxes start at 37 percent and can be as high as 55 percent, depending on the value of the gift or estate left at death. With rates that high, a qualified financial planner or estate tax attorney is certainly worth considering.

For more information or to speak with an estate tax specialist, visit the Preservation Group's Web site at **www.savewealth.com/planning/estate/taxes.html**.

FIND IT ON ▶
THE WEB

NOTE Estate taxes are due to the IRS within nine months following the testator's death.

Your State Might Want a Piece of the Pie

State-imposed taxes can be broken down into two main types: *inheritance taxes* and *estate taxes*. These state taxes are generally referred to as *death taxes.* Every state imposes some type of state death tax. However, tax rates vary according to the state in which you live.

State Inheritance Tax

The following 17 states impose an *inheritance tax*: Connecticut, Delaware, Indiana, Iowa, Kansas, Kentucky, Louisiana, Maryland, Michigan, Montana, Nebraska, New Hampshire, New Jersey, North Carolina, Pennsylvania, South Dakota, Tennessee.

NOTE Connecticut's inheritance tax will be phased out by 2005.

Inheritance taxes are levied according to what each beneficiary received from your estate—not on the overall value of the estate left at your death. Your estate, however, is responsible for paying this tax. Typically, the value of the beneficiary's inheritance is reduced by the amount of tax owed on the gift. However, if you live in a state that imposes inheritance taxes, you can make a provision in your will that informs your executor how you want your estate to handle these taxes.

The rate at which your bequest will be taxed depends upon your relationship with the recipient. For example, in most states that impose an inheritance tax, gifts left to spouses are usually taxed at the lowest rate. Gifts to children and parents are taxed at a lower rate than those left to more remote relatives or other nonrelative beneficiaries.

NOTE Most, if not all, states provide the same exemptions as the federal government. Therefore, gifts to a spouse or charity might not be subject to state death taxes. Check your state's tax laws to be sure.

Check the laws of your particular state to determine when inheritance taxes will be due following your death. If the tax isn't paid on time, your executor could be personally liable for the tax!

Estate Taxes

The overwhelming majority of states (all but Connecticut, Delaware, and New York) and the District of Columbia impose an estate tax levied on the overall value of the decedent's estate left at his or her death. This estate tax is similar to the federal estate tax imposed on larger estates, except that the rates at which these state taxes are levied are typically much lower than the current federal estate tax rates. However, the bad news is that state death taxes generally start for estates with a much lower net value than the federal estate tax, which currently is levied for estates worth more than $675,000.

Your estate will most likely be taxed on the following:

- All real estate located within the state
- All other personal property owned by you, regardless of where it is located

There is good news, however. Only four of these states (Mississippi, North Carolina, Ohio, and Oklahoma) require this tax to be paid in addition to your estate's federal tax liability. The remaining states that impose an estate tax merely deduct the owed state tax from your estate's calculated federal tax liability. This is called a *pick-up tax.*

CAUTION   Even though no additional tax is due, your executor will still be required to file the appropriate state death tax return for your estate.

The following states (and the District of Columbia) qualify as pick-up tax states:

Alabama	Missouri
Alaska	Montana
Arizona	Nebraska
Arkansas	New Hampshire
California	Nevada
Colorado	New Jersey
District of Columbia	New México
Florida	North Dakota
Georgia	Oregon
Hawaii	Pennsylvania
Idaho	Rhode Island
Illinois	South Carolina
Indiana	South Dakota
Iowa	Tennessee
Kansas	Texas
Kentucky	Utah
Louisiana	Vermont
Maine	Virginia
Maryland	Washington
Massachusetts	West Virginia
Michigan	Wisconsin
Minnesota	Wyoming

In a pick-up tax state, your estate will not be required to pay additional taxes beyond its owed federal tax liability. Consider John as an example. He lived in Arizona, a pick-up-tax state, when he died last year (1999) and left an estate worth $750,000. Because $650,000 of his estate was not subject to federal estate tax, John owed federal tax on only the $100,000 overage (which was taxed at 37 percent). John's estate also owed approximately $750 in state death taxes. However, his estate's total tax liability was only $37,000 and not $37,750. He paid $36,250 to the federal government and $750 to the state of Arizona.

NOTE

Connecticut, Louisiana, North Carolina, South Carolina, and Tennessee also impose a state *gift tax*. State gift tax rates are typically equal to the respective state's death tax rate. If you live in one of these states and are concerned about large gifts (gifts totaling more than $10,000 to an individual in a single year) that you have made recently, check with an accountant or a tax preparer in your state.

Your will can explicitly state how you want your executor to handle these estate or death taxes, if owed. Generally, you can do one of the following:

⚙ Direct your executor to pay these taxes from a specific property (for example, a bank account, mutual fund, or the sale of your home). As long as the value of the described property meets or exceeds your estate's tax liability, your other property will not be affected. If the property you designate, however, does not cover the tax liability of your estate, your executor must determine which assets to use to make up the difference.

⚙ You can instruct your executor to pay any tax liability from all property held in your estate proportionately. In this case, all gifts of property to be distributed under your will are decreased by an equal amount to take care of the owed taxes.

If your will does not state how estate or inheritance taxes are to be paid, your executor will be left to determine the best way of handling these taxes.

Again, don't be fooled. Some people think that you can avoid paying taxes simply by avoiding the probate process, meaning that, if they only own nonprobate property at their death, their estates will not be subject to tax. This is not the case.

Avoiding probate merely allows your estate to avoid certain court costs, attorney fees, and probate fees associated with administering your estate. Taxes will be due on your estate's overall worth, whether or not your estate goes through probate. (Probate is discussed in greater detail during the Sunday Evening session.)

If you have specific questions regarding your estate's potential federal or state tax liability, check with an attorney in your area who specializes in estate planning and probate.

What's Next?

Now that you've finished the somewhat tedious part of gathering documents and taking inventory of your estate, you can take a break! But don't go too far. In the next session, you'll identify the natural objects of your bounty (your spouse, children, and other close relatives), as well as anyone you want to provide for in your will.

Providing
for Your
Beneficiaries

Now that you've completed an inventory of your estate, you need to decide who will inherit your possessions after your death. This exercise might take longer than you think; you might have a favorite aunt or a close friend to whom you want to leave something special, or you might want to make a provision for your alma mater, place of worship, or favorite charity.

In this session, I provide my version of a Beneficiary Worksheet for Specific Requests that you can use to do this session's exercise. In fact, I suggest that, before continuing, you take a quick look at the worksheet, shown in Figure 3.1. That way, you can refer to it as you work through this session.

In this session, you will learn how to do the following:

- ✪ Select your beneficiaries
- ✪ Leave a contingent bequest
- ✪ Provide for a life estate
- ✪ Provide for minors in your will
- ✪ Determine how to leave a gift
- ✪ Disinherit a beneficiary
- ✪ Name your residuary beneficiary

You begin this session by determining who gets what.

Beneficiary Worksheet
for Specific Bequests

_____ to
Description of Item(s) to Be Left

_____   _____
Name of Beneficiary   Relationship to Testator

_____   _____
Alternative Beneficiary   Relationship to Testator

_____ to
Description of Item(s) to Be Left

_____   _____
Name of Beneficiary   Relationship to Testator

_____   _____
Alternative Beneficiary   Relationship to Testator

_____ to
Description of Item(s) to Be Left

_____   _____
Name of Beneficiary   Relationship to Testator

_____   _____
Alternative Beneficiary   Relationship to Testator

_____ to
Description of Item(s) to Be Left

_____   _____
Name of Beneficiary   Relationship to Testator

_____   _____
Alternative Beneficiary   Relationship to Testator

_____ to
Description of Item(s) to Be Left

_____   _____
Name of Beneficiary   Relationship to Testator

_____   _____
Alternative Beneficiary   Relationship to Testator

Figure 3.1

Use this handy
worksheet to keep
track of who gets
what in your will.

Leaving Gifts to Your Beneficiaries

In the Friday Evening session, you discovered that if you die without a will, your property is distributed by intestate succession, which provides only for your close relatives. A will, on the other hand, enables you to make provisions for anyone you choose. In essence, with a will you are limited only by your imagination. (A more detailed discussion of intestate succession is in Appendix B.)

You might want to consider including the following people in your will:

- ✿ Your spouse or mate
- ✿ Your children
- ✿ Your parents, siblings, and other relatives
- ✿ Your close friends
- ✿ A university and charities
- ✿ Even the nice attorney who wrote this book in order to help you create your will quickly and effortlessly . . . why, the possibilities are endless!

However, before you start doling out the goods, mull over the questions in the following sections.

Leaving Something with Strings Attached

Most people want to provide for their loved ones; however, they want to retain some control over how that gift will be used at their death. A common question asked by many testators is, "Can I leave something with strings attached?"

Leaving a gift to a beneficiary under your will with strings attached is considered a *conditional gift* (also called a *contingent* or *conditional bequest*). Every bequest left under a will is technically a conditional gift. Although the bequest might not state as such, the gift is contingent on the beneficiary surviving the testator.

Often the bequest, on its face, will state this condition. For example, you might write, "I leave my crystal polar bear collectible to Sonia Sovich, should she survive me" or ". . . provided that she is living at my death."

Many times the bequest is silent, simply stating, "I leave my crystal polar bear collectible to Sonia Sovich." However, as you have learned, unless Sonia is alive at your death, this gift will either lapse and become part of your residuary or, depending on your relationship to Sonia and the state in which you live, this gift might pass to Sonia's descendent.

But, what if you want to impose upon a beneficiary other conditions or incentives? For example, say that you want your grandson to attend your alma mater, or you want your daughter to divorce your son-in-law? Are these conditional bequests permissible?

It depends on the intent behind the gift and whether the condition is enforceable.

Unenforceable Will Provisions

Gifts that are contingent upon certain acts—such as an unlawful act, a divorce, marriage, or change of religion or sexual orientation—are against public policy and are unenforceable. Most courts will not enforce bequests that are against public policy for obvious reasons. By allowing these types of bequests, the courts are, in essence, taking away a beneficiary's fundamental right to choose a spouse, practice a certain religion, and so on.

Here are a few examples of unenforceable will provisions:

> *I leave $100,000 to my sister, Zelda, if she divorces that no good husband of hers, Sigmund Zigfield.*
>
> *I leave $20,000 to my friend, Joyce Radziwill, if she kills my husband.*

> *I leave my daughter, Madeline, $250,000 if she converts to Buddhism.*
>
> *I leave $10,000 to my friend, Mindy Macey, provided that she uses it to purchase cocaine.*

Permissible Contingent Bequests

As previously mentioned, most other conditions—such as stopping smoking, going to college, and being gainfully employed—are valid contingent bequests. These types of lesser-controlled matters are viewed as incentives, and are perfectly legal.

Here are examples of permissible contingent gifts:

> *I leave my Fleetwood Mac CD collection to John Sovich, provided he stops smoking.*
>
> *I leave $25,000 to my niece, Olivia Montgomery Davis, if she should graduate from college.*
>
> *I leave my sapphire necklace to my friend, Angela Alberts, provided that Angela leave it in her will to her daughter, Ashtynne.*
>
> *I leave my art collection to my grandson, Caden Theodore, if he should attend Princeton.*

Some so-called *conditional gifts,* while permissible, are difficult to enforce. For example, who determines whether John has indeed stopped smoking? What if he stops smoking, but only for a month and then resumes the nasty habit again? Is he required to return the CD collection? Can he keep a portion of the collection for the time he didn't smoke? As you can see, this bequest might be impossible for your executor to enforce. For this reason, often it is preferable to leave a gift with no strings attached.

However, circumstances exist in which leaving a conditional gift or bequest might be warranted or even necessary. For example, "I leave my daughter $100,000 if she should be divorced or widowed upon my death," might not be viewed as an incentive for your daughter to divorce (or even kill) her husband, but a way to guarantee financial security for your daughter if she becomes divorced or widowed.

◆ ◆

Because of the potential for problems, you need to consult an attorney when you're considering leaving a conditional gift. An attorney can help you create a valid incentive trust to ensure that you have some say in how your money and possessions are spent or used after your death.

◆ ◆

Leaving a Life Estate

You might prefer to leave one person a limited interest in your property, with a second person receiving the remainder of the property (or the entire property) upon the death of the first person. If so, you can legally structure a bequest to be enjoyed by more than one person over a long period of time.

Leaving a gift of limited duration is commonly referred to as a *life estate.* A life estate is a gift in which you leave the use of certain property (for example, a vacation home) or the income derived from certain property (income from a trust account) to a person for his or her lifetime only. A separate beneficiary (sometimes called a *remainderman*) is named to inherit the property upon the death of the owner of the life estate.

Here is the most common example of a life estate:

> *I leave an interest in our vacation home to my loving wife, Vinnie, for her lifetime, and then to our sons, Clarence, John, Whitney, and Harlan, as tenants in common.*

NOTE Typically, a life interest—that is, an interest in a life estate—does not give the beneficiary of the life estate the right to sell or otherwise dispose of the property, only the right to use the property (or the income from the property) for his or her lifetime. After the life estate beneficiary's death, the remaining property passes to the second beneficiary (also called the remainderman).

Leaving Property to a Minor

If you are planning to leave gifts under your will to minor children, note that special rules will apply. You will need to check your particular state's requirements to determine how much you can leave without the child needing an adult to manage the gift. Typically, minors cannot own property worth more than $5,000 without being required to have an adult manage the property. (Generally, a minor child reaches the *age of majority* at age 18, but the exact age depends on the state in which the child resides.)

If you want to leave a minor child a significant gift, you can do so by doing one of the following:

- Creating a trust for the minor child
- Naming a custodian to manage the minor child's property

NOTE Before creating a trust for a minor child, consult an attorney to be sure that your trust meets all the requirements needed to make it valid and enforceable.

If you choose to name a custodian for the minor child, you can do so under your state's Uniform Transfer to Minors Act (UTMA).

Uniform Transfer to Minors Act (UTMA)

All states, except Michigan, South Carolina, and Vermont, have adopted the Uniform Transfer to Minors Act. If you live in a state that has not yet adopted the UTMA, you will need to check with a local attorney to help you effectively transfer property to your minor child before your death, either by creating a trust or using your state's Uniform Gifts to Minors Act (UGMA). Every state has adopted the UGMA.

Under the UTMA, naming a custodian is a relatively easy task. Simply designate an adult in your will to manage the minor child's property and leave the property to the custodian directly. You can also designate the child's guardian or your executor as the custodian for the minor child's property. The custodian is instructed to manage the property and to use its generated income, if any, for the welfare and benefit of the child.

When the minor child reaches your state's majority—typically age 18 but perhaps as old as 21, depending on your state of residence—the custodianship ends, and the child takes control of the remaining property. See Table 3.1 to find specific state UTMA custodian age guidelines.

TABLE 3.1 UTMA CUSTODIANSHIP AGE GUIDELINES	
State	**Age**
Alabama	21
Alaska*	18-25
Arizona	21
Arkansas*	18-21
California*	18-25
Colorado	21
Connecticut	21
Delaware	21

TABLE 3.1 UTMA CUSTODIANSHIP AGE GUIDELINES *(CONTINUED)*	
State	**Age**
District of Columbia	18
Florida	21
Georgia	21
Hawaii	21
Idaho	21
Illinois	21
Indiana	21
Iowa	21
Kansas	21
Kentucky	18
Maine*	18-21
Maryland	21
Massachusetts	21
Minnesota	21
Mississippi	21
Missouri	21
Montana	21
Nebraska	21

TABLE 3.1 UTMA CUSTODIANSHIP AGE GUIDELINES *(CONTINUED)*

State	Age
Nevada*	18-25
New Hampshire	21
New Jersey*	18-21
New Mexico	21
New York	21
North Carolina*	18-21
North Dakota	21
Ohio	21
Oklahoma	18
Oregon	21
Pennsylvania	21
Rhode Island	18
South Dakota	18
Tennessee	21
Texas	21
Utah	21
Virginia*	18-21
Washington	21

TABLE 3.1 UTMA CUSTODIANSHIP AGE GUIDELINES (CONTINUED)	
State	Age
West Virginia	21
Wisconsin	21
Wyoming	21

*These states allow the testator to select the age (within the above ranges) at which the custodianship ends and the beneficiary will be entitled to own the property/money outright.

DESIGNATING A CUSTODIAN TO MANAGE GIFTS TO A MINOR

Because children cannot typically own outright property valued at more than a few thousand dollars, making a bequest for a child in a will requires additional safeguards. The following question is commonly asked in cases regarding gifts to minors.

Question: I'd like to make a $25,000 provision in my will for my goddaughter, Payton Justice Williams, who is three years old. Is there anything special I must do to make sure that Payton receives the money when she is older? I trust her mom, Tracy, to handle the money until PJ is old enough.

Answer: If Payton is still a minor when she becomes entitled to the bequest, you will need to name a custodian in your will (under your state's Uniform Transfer to Minors Act) to manage Payton's gift. You can name her mother, Tracy, if you'd like and leave the gift to Tracy as a custodian for Payton. Tracy will need to set up a bank account in her name as custodian for Payton and will be responsible for managing the money and using it for Payton's welfare and maintenance. Depending on where you live, the custodianship will most likely end at Payton's eighteenth or twenty-first birthday, and she will then own the remaining money outright.

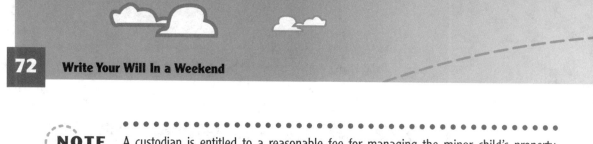

NOTE   A custodian is entitled to a reasonable fee for managing the minor child's property. However, the custodian might waive any such compensation and often does.

Take a Break

Whew! It's time for a break! Take a few moments to check the mail or grab a quick snack (cheese and crackers sound good). When you return, you'll find out how to leave gifts of your personal property to your selected beneficiaries.

Gifts Come in Three Flavors: Specific, General, and Demonstrative

In general, you can leave three types of gifts in your will: specific bequests, general bequests, and demonstrative bequests,

Now take a quick look at each one.

Leaving a Specific Bequest

A *specific bequest* refers to leaving a particular item (personal property) in your will. A *specific devise* refers to leaving a gift of real property in your will. For the sake of simplicity, I refer to both as specific bequests.

Specific bequests include, for example, your BMW, the wedding ring from your first marriage, your baseball cards, your jet ski, your faux fur, and your autographed Phish CDs.

These bequests are tangible personal property. They might be a tangible asset or a specific amount of money payable from a particular source.

Specific bequests are the safest bequests to make because they are the last gifts used to pay creditors, costs of administration, and other expenses if your estate becomes unable to meet these obligations.

However, specific bequests might cause other problems. For example, you might be wondering, "What if Harry dies before me? Then who gets the baseball card collection that I left him in my will?" Or you might be wondering, "What if I don't own the baseball card collection at my death? Then what happens?" These are good questions. Take a look at the first scenario.

When "Eli" Predeceases You

Typically, if your will does not name another beneficiary for a specific gift (such as the baseball card collection in the preceding example) and the named beneficiary for that specific gift dies before you die, the baseball card collection passes into your estate's *residuary* and becomes the property of your *residuary beneficiary.* (I'll talk more about your estate residuary in a moment, and you'll select a residuary beneficiary during this evening's session.)

NOTE The general rule is that if a gift of property (also called a *bequest* or *devise*) is void, revoked, or lapses, it becomes part of the estate's residue and passes to the residuary beneficiary.

Most states, however, have an *antilapse statute* (also referred to as a *no lapse statute*) that gives the gift to another one of your close descendants rather than your residuary beneficiary. For example, say that you leave your prized baseball card collection to your son, Harry. Harry dies before you, leaving his child, Larry (your grandchild). In states with antilapse statutes, the baseball card collection will automatically go to Larry, rather than to your residuary.

NOTE Antilapse statutes apply only to gifts left to your descendants. For example, if you leave $10,000 to your neighbor and she dies before you—and you don't change your will—that $10,000 will *not* go to your neighbor's heirs. Instead, it will pass into your residuary and become the property of your residuary beneficiary.

Be careful. In a few states, antilapse statutes apply only to a decedent's *lineal descendents* (children and grandchildren) and not to the decedent's collaterals (brothers and sisters). In this instance, say that you leave the baseball card collection to your brother, Cemal, who dies before you die. He leaves a daughter, Lola (your niece). Lola will not inherit the baseball card collection. Instead, it will come back to your estate, passing into the residuary.

If you are concerned that your particular state's antilapse statute provides only for your lineal descendents, simply name your niece (Lola) in your will as the alternate beneficiary of the baseball card collection, in the event your brother (Cemal) predeceases you.

ALWAYS NAME AN ALTERNATE BENEFICIARY

John's will provides as follows: *Because my only son, Ted, has neglected me in my declining years and has led a life of sin, I hereby leave him nothing at all. Everything I own I give to my friends, Phil and Nan Rowles, to share equally.*

Both Phil and Nan predecease John, and the provision for them fails under the lapse doctrine. (Because Phil and Nan are merely John's friends, and not his relatives, the provision for Phil and Nan will not pass to their descendants.)

John's only sister, Mary Helen Stoycos, claims John's estate under intestate succession laws as his closest next of kin after Ted.

Question: Who will inherit John's estate?

Answer: Ted, his good-for-nothing son. John had not effectively transferred his property to another beneficiary, and he had not named a residuary beneficiary in his will. Thus, the laws of intestate succession apply. And even though John purposely tried to disinherit Ted in his will, John's estate will pass to Ted under his state's laws of intestate succession. (For a more detailed discussion on intestate succession, see the Friday Evening session and Appendix B.)

CAUTION

◆◆◆◆◆◆◆◆◆◆◆◆◆◆◆◆◆◆◆◆◆◆◆◆◆◆◆◆◆◆◆◆◆◆◆
In case your first beneficiary dies before you (*predeceases* you), you might want to name an alternate or successor beneficiary for each specific gift.
◆◆◆◆◆◆◆◆◆◆◆◆◆◆◆◆◆◆◆◆◆◆◆◆◆◆◆◆◆◆◆◆◆◆◆

Now that you understand what typically happens if a named beneficiary predeceases you (as illustrated by the earlier baseball card collection example), it's time to find out what happens if either you do not own the baseball card collection at your death or the baseball cards are lost or destroyed.

Ademption by Extinction

In most states, when an item is not part of your estate at your death, it is said to be *adeemed by extinction*. This term means that the beneficiary named for that particular gift will not receive anything from your will because the item that you left him or her no longer exists. Ademption by extinction applies only to specific bequests left under a will. A specific bequest can be considered adeemed in one of two basic ways:

✪ The testator does not own the item at death.

✪ The item is lost or destroyed.

Take a look at the following example situations. (The names have been changed to protect the innocent.)

First scenario: Carrie Gutman drafts a will, leaving her diamond ring to her daughter, Katie. Several years later, at Carrie's death, the diamond ring is not found among her possessions. Her executor files the loss with her insurance company, which reimburses her estate the value of the ring.

Question: Is Katie entitled to the value of the ring?

Answer: No. The court found the gift of the diamond ring to be adeemed by extinction. Because the article (diamond ring) specifically bequeathed by Carrie under her will was lost during her lifetime, the bequest failed and Katie took nothing.

Second scenario: Bob Jones leaves his Porsche to his girlfriend, Hannah. Three months after drafting his will, however, Bob dies tragically in a car accident, wrecking the Porsche. His insurance company pays his estate the value of the car.

Question: Is Hannah entitled to the value of the crunched car?

Answer: Yes. The court found that Hannah was entitled to the insurance proceeds from the car accident because the ademption occurred at the very moment of the testator's (Bob's) death.

The preceding examples are based on actual case law, but they are not indicative of every state's interpretation of ademption by extinction. Some states, although not the majority, look to the testator's intent in leaving the gift to determine if the gift will lapse. (This is considered the *intent theory* and is not widely recognized.)

IT'S A MATTER OF INTENT

In several states, however, a change in the *form* of an item is *not* necessarily considered to be adeemed. Instead, the testator's intent determines the outcome. Consider this example, in which my will might state the following:

I leave all my interest in my law partnership, Sovich & Minch, to my good friend, Curt Cavin.

After executing my will, I incorporate my law partnership (and call it, Legally Speaking, Inc.). This is considered a change in the form of the bequest—from a share of a partnership to a share of a corporation.

However, because the gift still technically exists at my death (except in a different form), some states will hold that the gift will not fail. Instead, Curt will be entitled to all of the stock I own in the new corporation.

Typically, however, states follow the *identity theory,* which states that if the item is not there at the testator's death, it is said to be adeemed by extinction. This is the modern rule.

The majority of states still follow the identity theory. Thus, the specific bequest must be in the exact form as stated in the will or the gift will fail.

Understanding the Doctrine of Satisfaction

Under the doctrine of satisfaction, a general or residuary gift might be satisfied in whole or in part by the testator's *inter vivos* gift to the beneficiary *after* the execution of the will.

An *inter vivos* gift is a legal term meaning a gift made during the testator's lifetime, for example:

> *I leave Chase Alberts $40,000.*

Two years after the will's execution, I generously give Chase $20,000. (As you learned in the Saturday Morning session, unless my husband joins me in this gift, my estate will be liable for gift tax on $10,000. But that is not the issue here.)

Question: Will the $20,000 gift to Chase during my life be considered partial satisfaction for the $40,000 bequest left to him in my will?

Answer: It depends. States vary in regard to gifts made during the testator's life. Many states require additional evidence that the testator intended the gift as an advancement against the recipient's share under the testator's will. Other states automatically consider *any* substantial gift (made by the testator during his or her lifetime) as an advancement against a bequest in a will. And other states consider only a substantial gift from a parent to a child to be an advancement.

> ## I CAN'T GET NO SATISFACTION!
>
> One Indiana court ruled that there was no satisfaction of a bequest when an older man left a younger married woman $50,000 in his will. However, his son argued that the bequest was partially adeemed by satisfaction because his father had given the young woman *many* gifts over the years.

NOTE
The doctrine of satisfaction does not apply to specific bequests. A specific bequest (for example, a diamond ring) given to the beneficiary during the testator's lifetime is considered to be adeemed by extinction—no longer a part of the testator's estate at his or her death, although it is sometimes incorrectly referred to as *ademption by satisfaction*.

If you made a rather large gift to one of your beneficiaries before drafting your will and you want that gift to be considered an advancement against what the beneficiary would have received under your will, be sure to state your reasons in your will in order to avoid any confusion or misunderstanding regarding your decisions. Take a look at the following hypothetical situation.

Dusanka Sovich has two daughters, Cari and Chris. She wants to leave $50,000 to Cari, but only $30,000 to Chris because she gave Chris $20,000 to finish law school in 1995. Dusanka should specifically state (in her will) her reason for the reduced gift to one daughter so as to avoid a possible will contest by Chris later on. (I'll talk more about will contests in the Sunday Evening session.)

Leaving a General Bequest

A general bequest is a gift that is payable out of your general estate; it does not require distribution of, or payment from, a particular asset or source. Commonly, a general bequest is a gift of money (called a *pecuniary legacy*). For example, a gift of "$10,000 to my nephew, Jack" would not be considered a specific bequest *unless* I state a source for the gift ("$10,000 from my ABC bank account to my nephew, Jack").

 NOTE Specific and general bequests can be tricky. Suppose that I leave Chris O'Donnell (yes, the actor) 100 shares of Walt Disney World (WDW) stock upon my death. Soon after my death, the stock splits 6 to 1. If during probate, the court finds that this was a specific bequest, Mr. O'Donnell gets 600 shares of WDW stock. If the court classifies my gift in my will as a general bequest, Chris gets only 100 shares. (Note to Chris O'Donnell: I'm not really leaving you 100 shares of WDW stock. However, give me a call; I might change my mind.)

Leaving a Demonstrative Gift

A *demonstrative bequest* is a gift (typically, an amount of money) that is payable primarily from a particular source. If that source fails or is inadequate, the gift becomes payable from the general assets of the estate.

Consider the previous example of a general bequest, in which $10,000 from my ABC bank account was given to my nephew, Jack. For this to become a demonstrative bequest, I would say "$10,000 from my ABC bank account to my nephew, Jack. However, if the funds in my ABC bank account should be insufficient to meet this gift, then out of my other property." This is a creative way of splitting specific and general bequests, and it provides a better guarantee that Jack will get the $10,000 that I obviously want him to have.

Distinguishing among Bequests

Now, you're ready to test yourself. See whether you can tell which of the following examples are specific, general, or demonstrative bequests. (You can find the answers immediately following the last question.)

> **Example #1:** *I leave all of my dining room furniture to Martha Stewart.*
>
> **Example #2:** *I leave Morticia Addams any money Gomez owes me at my death.*
>
> **Example #3:** *I leave Chris O'Donnell $10,000 worth of my Disney stock.*
>
> **Example #4:** *I leave $10,000 to Dave Benner.*
>
> **Example #5:** *I leave $10,000 out of my saving account at National City Bank to Jon Short.*
>
> **Example #6:** *I leave Anna Radziwill all my personal property.*
>
> **Example #7:** *I leave Stacy Fellure 100 shares of Microsoft stock.*
>
> **Example #8:** *I leave Doug Solmos $5,000 to be paid from a debt owed me by Tom Grinslade, but if that debt is insufficient, Doug gets the money out of my other property.*

Answers:

1. specific; 2. specific; 3. specific; 4. general; 5. specific (because of the source);
6. specific; 7. general (could be viewed as directive to my executor to purchase 100 shares);
8. demonstrative (combining specific and general)

I Don't Want Him to Have Anything!

Okay, so you want to disinherit someone. Say that you really dislike your sister because she stole your date to the senior prom. Or, perhaps your brother wrecked your car. (Although these seem like minor squabbles that would not warrant disinheritance, it's your property and your decision.)

Except for your spouse, you can disinherit anyone who would normally inherit property from you after your death (unless you live in Louisiana, which might not allow you to disinherit a child). You might be thinking, "That is why I am drafting a will—to avoid dying intestate and having no control over how my property is distributed. Isn't not naming some-one or not leaving someone something in my will, good enough?" The answer, unfortunately, might be "No." It all depends on your relationship to the person you want to disinherit.

CAUTION

◆ ◆

Some states, such as Florida, require that you leave your house to your spouse or your minor children. Therefore, expressly disinheriting your child in your will might not stop your child from receiving the house. Again, check with an attorney if you want junior off the dole permanently.

◆ ◆

By not naming a brother or sister in your will, you can ensure that he or she will not inherit any of your probate property after your death. How-ever, this is not the case with your spouse and children.

As you learned in the Saturday Morning session, your spouse might be entitled to a share of your probate estate regardless of what your will pro-vides. What about your children? Can a child be disinherited?

Can I Disinherit My Child?

Disinheriting a child might not be as easy as you think. Simply leaving Junior out of your will might not be enough to ensure that he will not receive a share of your estate.

Is It Intentional?

To disinherit a child, your will must explicitly state your intent to do so. Otherwise, your child might be considered *pretermitted* (to have been unintentionally omitted) and, therefore, entitled to a share of your probate estate.

Or Was Junior Merely Pretermitted?

In many states, when a testator fails to provide for one of his children in his will (that is, a child who was born or adopted after the last will was made), that child—whether born before or after the testator's death—is entitled to receive a share of the testator's estate. Specifically, the child is entitled to receive a share of his or her parent's (the testator's) estate that is equal to the value of what the child would have received had the testator parent died without a will.

The exceptions include the following:

- When the will makes it clear that the omission was intentional
- When the will was created, the testator had one or more known children, but left most of the estate to his or her surviving spouse

Once again, to clarify, a pretermitted child is considered to be *unintentionally* left out of a will and is entitled to a share of his or her deceased parent's probate estate.

CAUTION Many states use the theory of pretermitted issue to prevent subsequently born or adopted children from being unintentionally omitted. Be careful! In some states, *any* child left out of a will is considered pretermitted—even if that child was alive at the time the will was drafted.

◆ ◆

If you want to disinherit a child, your will must specifically state this desire. You can generally accomplish this by including a phrase in your will similar to the following:

> *I have specifically made no provision in my will for my son/daughter _____, and direct that he/she take nothing under my will.*

You might also want to explain your reasons for disinheriting your child in your will so that there is no confusion. Perhaps you made substantial provisions for your child during his or her lifetime, or perhaps the child is self-sufficient and needs no further help.

Dealing with Leftovers: Property without a Specific Beneficiary

Now that you understand how gifts of your property can be left at death, take a look at what happens to probate property that is not effectively distributed in your will.

Your *residuary estate* is what is left after all your bequests of personal and real property are distributed and all taxes, debts, and other encumbrances are paid. The remaining property, if any, is said to pass into the residuary and will be left to the individual of your choosing, called your *residuary*

A QUICK LOOK AT THE THEORY OF PRETERMISSION

No mention of a child within a will raises a presumption that the child was unintentionally omitted *unless* one or more of the following rules apply:

Rule #1: An intentional omission is evident from the face of the will.

Rule #2: Other known children of the testator were also omitted from his will, and the decedent's surviving spouse was left all or substantially all of the decedent's estate.

Take a look at this example, in which Tim's will states the following:

I leave everything to my wife, Alison. I intentionally leave $0 to any other person who might be considered my heirs.

After execution of the will, a daughter, Olivia, is born to Tim and Alison. (Tim also has two daughters, Lindsey and Mallory, from a prior union). Tim dies.

Question: Is Olivia entitled to a share of Tim's estate as a pretermitted heir?

Answer: No. Tim left his entire estate to his surviving spouse (see rule #2) and any child of his living at the time of his death was intentionally omitted as evident on the face of the will (see rule #1).

Additionally, Tim had other known children (Lindsey and Mallory) at the time his will was drafted, and he still left his entire estate to his wife (see rule #2).

---

beneficiary. You can also name a successor beneficiary to your residuary, in case your first choice predeceases you or cannot inherit the residuary for any reason.

Even if you think you have effectively disposed of all your probate property in your will, it's still a good idea to name a residuary beneficiary. If part, but not all, of your probate estate is disposed of by your will, the remaining part will be distributed under your state's intestate succession rules—*unless* you named a residuary beneficiary in your will.

Understanding the Rules of Abatement

Abatement describes the order in which your bequests will be appropriated (used) to satisfy your estate's liabilities if your estate is unable to pay claims. If you made provisions in your will for how your taxes, claims, and other encumbrances are to be handled, then the rules of abatement most likely will not apply to you. If you didn't make such provisions, your property will most likely be appropriated as follows:

- Intestate property
- Residuary property
- General bequests
- Specific bequests

Any intestate property of the decedent will first be used to pay estate debts and other encumbrances (for example, state and federal taxes, funeral expenses, legitimate claims of creditors, and probate fees). As you learned in the Friday Evening session, intestate property is property not effectively disposed of in a will.

For example, say that you fail to name a beneficiary in your will for your porcelain purple cow collectible *and* your will does not designate a residuary beneficiary. Your purple cow will be considered intestate property and will be sold first to meet any unpaid obligations of your estate. (You won't have intestate property if you have a will and have named a residuary beneficiary.)

Under a will, the residuary is typically the first to go because it is considered to be a catchall and, therefore, is used first to meet your estate's obligations. If your residuary property is insufficient, your general bequests (for example, gifts payable out of the general estate) are used next. Finally, specific bequests (diamond earrings, porcelain purple cow, and so on) are used.

You might want to keep the rules of abatement in mind when you complete your beneficiary worksheet (refer to Figure 3.1, shown at the beginning of this session).

What's Next?

Believe it or not, you've finished the most difficult, as well as the most time-consuming, sessions. Your next steps are to draft your will and have it witnessed. In the Saturday Evening session, you will draft your will by using the WillWriter software that is provided on the CD at the back of this book. Drafting your will with WillWriter is as easy as answering a few questions and then printing the created personalized will.

Writing Your Will

- ✿ Installing WillWriter
- ✿ Setting Up WillWriter
- ✿ Drafting Your Will Using WillWriter
- ✿ Creating and Viewing Your Will

Now that you've completed the Saturday Morning and Saturday Afternoon sessions, you're ready to actually draft your will by using Business Logic Corporation's WillWriter software.

NOTE Business Logic Corporation prepared a special version of its WillWriter software just for you. You will find that version on the CD-ROM at the back of this book. For information about the commercial version of WillWriter, you can contact Business Logic Corporation at **www.blcorp.com**.

Drafting your will with WillWriter is a quick and easy task. You might even have time to catch a late movie after you're done!

In this session, you will learn how to do the following:

✪ Install the WillWriter software

✪ Draft your will using WillWriter

✪ Review your newly created will

✪ Save your answers for reloading

Before continuing, however, you might want to skip to Appendix E and look at some sample wills that I created using the WillWriter software.

ON THE

CD

WillWriter is a legal will-writing software system that makes writing personal wills fast and easy. As you complete the exercises in this book, you will use the "full" version of WillWriter that is included on the CD-ROM in the back of the book.

NOTE Two versions of WillWriter are on the CD-ROM and will be installed onto your hard drive when you download WillWriter. The "full" version contains all the functionality of the program. This is the version that you should use. The demo version is much more limited, so there is no reason to use it.

This version includes features that enable you to do the following:

○ Answer simple questions that help you write your will.

○ Create your will at the press of a button.

○ Review the document before printing.

○ Print wills that look professional.

NOTE For information about additional legal forms that you might need, visit **www.blcorp. com/willwriter.htm**.

This evening, you use WillWriter to write a will that outlines how to provide for your loved ones after your death.

Before beginning, however, you need to make sure that your computer meets the following minimum system requirements:

○ 486 or faster processor

○ Microsoft Windows 95 or higher

○ 4MB of RAM

○ CD-ROM drive

Okay, it's time to fire up your computer and install WillWriter from the CD-ROM. Don't panic! Even if you have little or no computer experience, you will be able to easily install the WillWriter program.

CAUTION WillWriter permits you to use this software to prepare legal documents for friends and family members. However, remember that if you start charging for this service, you might be in a position of liability. If you are still interested in charging or preparing legal documents for others, contact a lawyer for local state regulations.

NOTE As you work through the steps in this session and the next one, the dialog boxes that appear on your screen may look slightly different from the ones in this book (depending on the version of Microsoft Windows that you use). However, the options in your computer's dialog boxes will be similar, and you should have no trouble following along.

Installing WillWriter

If you have not already installed WillWriter from the CD-ROM, you can follow these steps. With your computer up and running and the Autorun feature enabled, insert the CD-ROM in the CD-ROM drive, close the tray, and wait for the CD-ROM to load.

If you have disabled Autorun, place the CD-ROM in the CD-ROM drive and follow these steps:

1. From the Windows taskbar, click on the Start button. The Start menu appears (see Figure 4.1).

2. Click on Run. The Run dialog box appears.

3. In the Open box, type **d:\WillWriter\setup.exe** (assuming that D is your CD-ROM drive). If your CD-ROM drive is not D, just substitute the correct letter.

4. Click on OK.

5. The WillWriter Installation welcome screen appears. When you are ready, click on Next to continue.

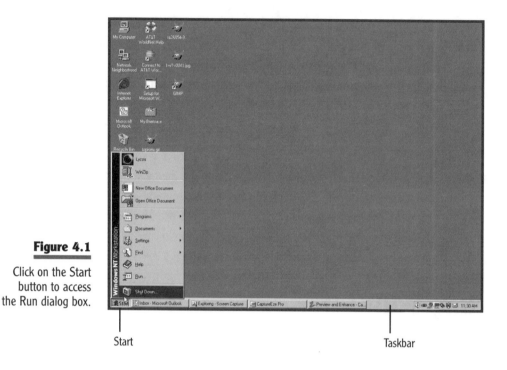

Figure 4.1

Click on the Start
button to access
the Run dialog box.

Start   Taskbar

6. The WillWriter License Agreement window appears. Read the
   agreement, and then click on Next to continue. If you do not agree
   to the license agreement, click on Cancel.

7. Enter your name and, if desired, your organization or business
   name.

From here, the Setup Wizard appears and guides you step-by-step
through the installation process.

NOTE

Note that c:\blcorp\willwrtr is set as the default pathname. That is, the WillWriter program folder (willwtr) will be stored named as willwrtr within a subfolder named blcorp.
If you want to change this pathname, you can do so at the appropriate wizard screen. If
you're not familiar with Windows, I recommend that you just accept the default settings.

After you install the software, if you have questions about creating a will, you can access WillWriter's Help menu that's included with the software. Just click on the Show Help Contents button, which is the little question mark on the Button Bar (see Figure 4.2).

By clicking on the Show Help Contents button, you can learn about the topic or problem that you are experiencing. Many common problems and questions are identified here, along with easy-to-follow solutions and answers. You can also get answers to Frequently Asked Questions at Business Logic's Web site.

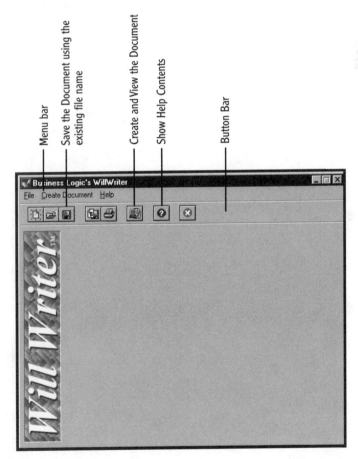

Figure 4.2

The user-friendly Button Bar enables you to quickly perform a variety of tasks in WillWriter.

Setting Up WillWriter

With WillWriter successfully installed onto your computer, you just follow these easy steps to set up WillWriter and begin creating your own customized will.

1. Go to the Windows taskbar and click on Start.

2. Choose Programs.

3. Choose WillWriter, and then select Business Logic's WillWriter.

Now you're ready to create your personal will:

1. Click on File, located at the upper-left corner of the menu bar (or press Alt+F).

2. From the File drop-down menu, choose Create a New Personal Will (or press Ctrl+N). See Figure 4.3.

   After you select Create a New Personal Will, a quick legal liability window appears (look familiar?), stating the legal conditions under which the developers of the program allow you to use the software.

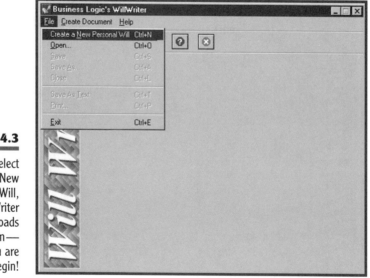

Figure 4.3

When you select Create a New Personal Will, WillWriter automatically loads its program— and you are ready to begin!

3. After you read it, simply click on I Accept the Terms, and immediately the first Last Will and Testament interview screen appears (see Figure 4.4).

NOTE

Under common law, a will could dispose only of a testator's personal property. A *testament* was a separate written document needed to dispose of all real property (real estate) owned by the testator at death. Hence the phrase that is still used today, "last will and testament." Today, however, a will is universally accepted as being able to dispose of both personal and real property.

Now that you have successfully loaded and set up WillWriter on your computer and read all the legal mumbo jumbo, you're ready for the next step—actually drafting your will.

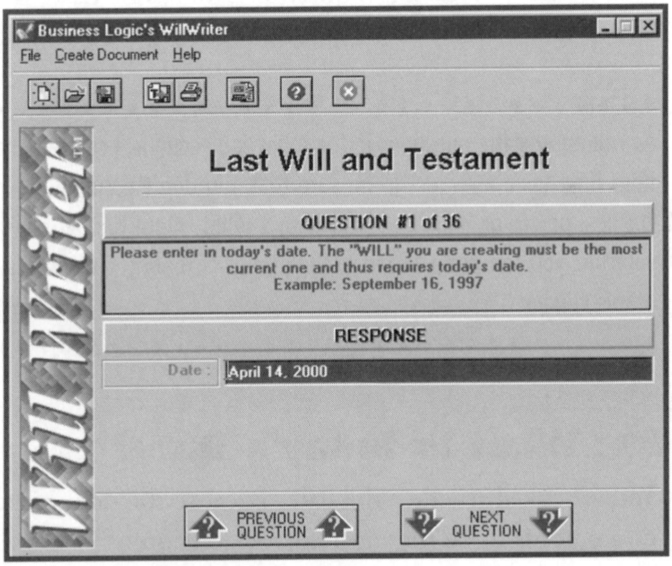

Figure 4.4

Here's the first Last Will and Testament interview screen.

Drafting Your Will Using WillWriter

You're ready to begin writing your will, which you do just by answering the questions asked by WillWriter. Most of the questions require only a short answer or a "Yes" or "No" response.

♦ ♦

CAUTION Always start typing your answers at the beginning of the field. *Do not leave a blank space!* If you leave a blank space, WillWriter assumes that you have left the field blank, and when you create the will, that area will not have your answer.

♦ ♦

After answering each question, click on the Next Question button at the bottom of the screen. The Previous Question button enables you to cycle back through the questions, in case you happen to change your mind or make a mistake (refer to Figure 4.4).

WillWriter provides 36 questions for your Last Will and Testament "interview." Your current question is always shown just below the title.

♦ ♦

CAUTION As you answer the questions in the following sections, I suggest that you save your work from time to time—just to be sure that you don't accidentally lose it (your computer crashes, power goes off . . . who knows what might happen!). For the steps on saving your file, you can jump ahead to the section "Creating and Viewing Your Will," at the end of this session."

♦ ♦

Question #1: What Is Today's Date?

You are asked to enter the date. Because the document you are about to create needs to be the most current version of your will, be sure to enter today's date. (Refer to Figure 4.4 for an illustration of what your screen should look like.)

Question #2: What Is Your Name?

Next, WillWriter asks you to type your name in the space provided.

You must use your full legal name. For me, it is Christine M. Sovich (see Figure 4.5). This name appears on my driver's license, social security card, and other important documents.

However, if your legal name is Barbara but everyone calls you Barbie—and you even have credit cards and other important documentation in the name of Barbie—be sure to include this name as well. Therefore, your answer to Question #2 might look something like this:

> Barbara C. Stolzmann, a.k.a. Barbie Stolzmann

Question #3: What Is Your Gender?

Next, you are asked to select your gender. If you are female, enter "No," and WillWriter will tailor your will accordingly (see Figure 4.6).

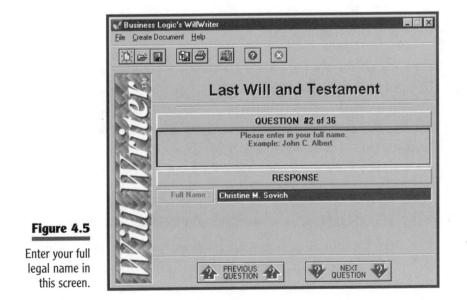

Figure 4.5

Enter your full legal name in this screen.

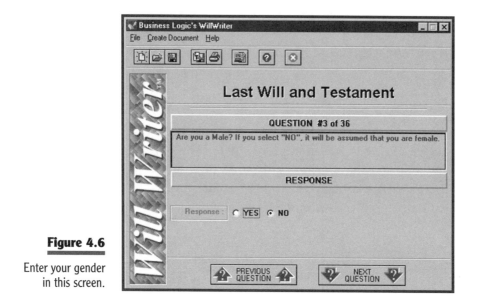

Figure 4.6

Enter your gender
in this screen.

Question #4: In What City and State Do You Reside?

Next, you are asked to enter the city and state in which you reside (see Figure 4.7). Remember to enter the city and state in which you are considered to be a legal resident.

◆◆

CAUTION   Disregard the Province portion of this question. If you live in Canada, you must consult an attorney before proceeding. WillWriter is not valid in the province of Quebec and therefore cannot be used to create a will there. Also, remember that if you live in Louisiana, you cannot use WillWriter to draft your will.

◆◆

Question #5: Handling Funeral Arrangements

The next few questions are geared toward your funeral arrangements. Before you answer them, take a moment to consider your plans.

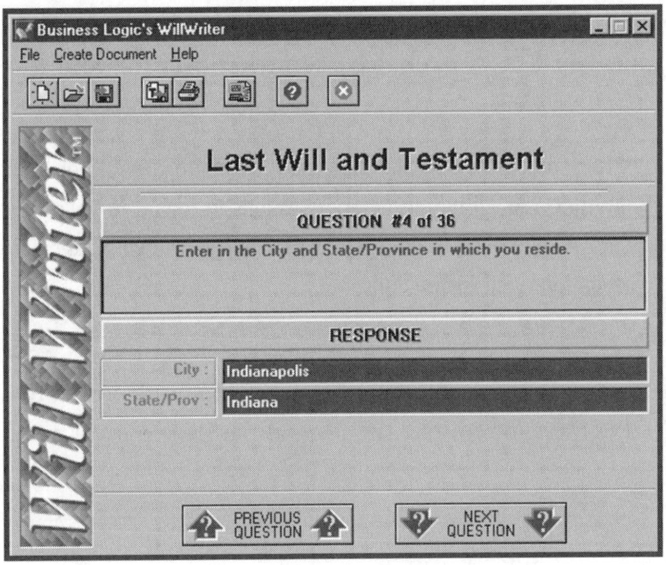

Figure 4.7

Enter your "legal" city and state here.

Throughout this book, you've learned the importance of drafting a will to protect and provide for your family and friends at death. However, you haven't learned anything about preparing for your actual funeral. You should make these decisions now (such as the type of funeral you desire and whether you prefer to be buried or cremated), though you shouldn't pay for your funeral before you die.

Prepaying funeral expenses is big business. According to a recent article in *Modern Maturity* (September/October issue), death in the United States is a $10 billion industry. Many older adults think that by prepaying for their funerals, they are sparing their loved ones additional stress and burden. Although prepaying for your funeral might seem like a good idea, there are reasons why you shouldn't.

Instead of prepaying for your funeral, invest that money in a CD, money market account, or a mutual fund. Just think of the return that you can make on that investment—money that would otherwise be realized by the funeral home or cemetery of your choice.

Your executor can then use the invested money to cover your expenses, and you'll most likely have some left over for your loved ones.

NOTE Just be sure to specifically state your ultimate desires for your funeral in your will. WillWriter asks all the necessary questions in regard to your preferred funeral arrangements. All you need to do is type your choices, and your executor will be responsible for carrying out your instructions.

If you move, your prepaid funeral expenses probably will not be refunded (unless, of course, the funeral parlor is part of a chain).

INFORMATION ON PREPAYING FOR FUNERALS

For more information regarding funerals and their prepayment, contact the following:

> American Association of Retired Persons (AARP)
> 601 East Street NW
> Washington, D.C., 20049

Or you can call AARP at 800-424-3410. You can also visit their Web site at **www.aarp.com**.

Also, you can read "Funeral Related Options and Costs: A Guide for Families," a booklet by Mercedes Bern-Klug. The booklet can be purchased for $4 by contacting the following organization:

> The Center on Aging / FIP
> University of Kansas Medical Center
> 5026 Wescoe
> Kansas City, Kansas 66160-7117

To learn more about planning for your funeral, contact the National Funeral Directors Association (NFDA)—the world's largest funeral service organization. You can visit NFDA at **www.nfda.org**.

Question #6: Cremation or Traditional Burial?

Now, you must decide whether you prefer cremation or a traditional burial. If you prefer to be cremated, you don't need to type "Yes" in the Response. By making a provision for the disposition of your ashes, WillWriter automatically incorporates the appropriate language. However, be sure that you leave explicit instructions for disposing your ashes. If, for example, you want them to be buried at sea, you might type **scattered over the Atlantic Ocean** in the Response box, as I did in Figure 4.8. You don't need to type "Please scatter my ashes over the Atlantic Ocean" because WillWriter already knows you're discussing *your* ashes.

CAUTION   If you choose to be buried at sea, you will need to check your state's laws. Scattering ashes in public areas is illegal in most states.

If you chose a traditional burial, leave this question blank and click Next Question.

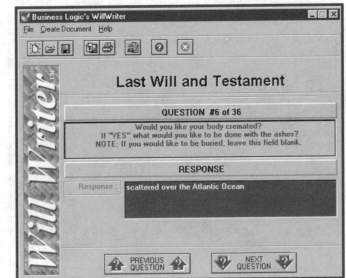

Figure 4.8

Enter your preference for burial here.

Question #7: What Are Your Funeral Arrangements?

This question deals with your wishes concerning specific funeral arrangements. You need to be as specific as possible (see Figure 4.9).

Question #8: Are You an Organ Donor?

Here, you are asked about possible organ donation. If you wish to donate your organs, be sure to specifically state which organs you are willing to donate (see Figure 4.10).

NOTE You can also fill out an organ donation declaration (or card) stating your specific wishes as an organ donor. This document should be included with your other important estate planning papers and should be readily accessible to your executor, spouse, or other interested persons.

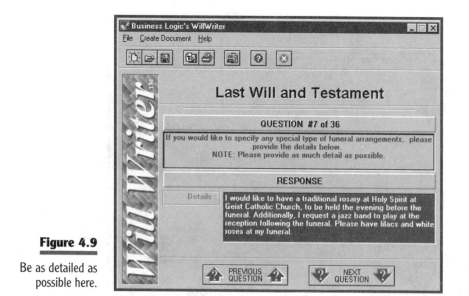

Figure 4.9

Be as detailed as possible here.

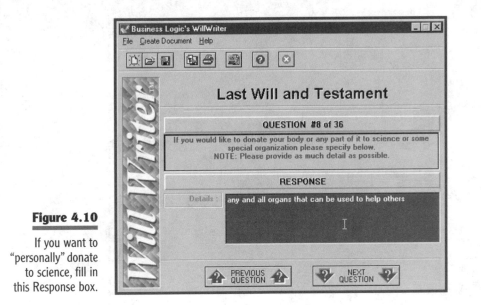

Figure 4.10

If you want to "personally" donate to science, fill in this Response box.

Take a Break

You deserve it! You have successfully installed and set up the WillWriter software. You've even started writing your will by answering the first few questions of the WillWriter interview process. Now is the perfect time to take a quick break. Go walk the dog, make some popcorn, or call your mother. When you return, you can finish answering the rest of the Will-Writer questions, thereby creating a will that is tailored to meet your specific needs.

Question #9: What Is Your Spouse's Name?

If you are married, you need to list your spouse's full legal name (for example, Linda Jane Minch, not Jane Minch or L. Minch). If you and your mate are merely living together or living as a Common Law husband and wife, leave this response blank. Question #9 applies only to those who are *legally* married (see Figure 4.11).

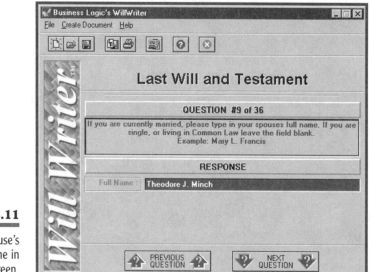

Figure 4.11

Enter your spouse's full legal name in this screen.

Question #10: Are You Leaving Your Entire Estate to Your Spouse?

This next question allows you to leave your entire estate (or the majority of your estate) to your spouse (see Figure 4.12).

NOTE If your answer to this question is "Yes," you can still leave specific gifts to other beneficiaries under you will.

If you don't want to leave your entire estate (or the bulk of your estate) to your spouse, skip this question and proceed to the next one.

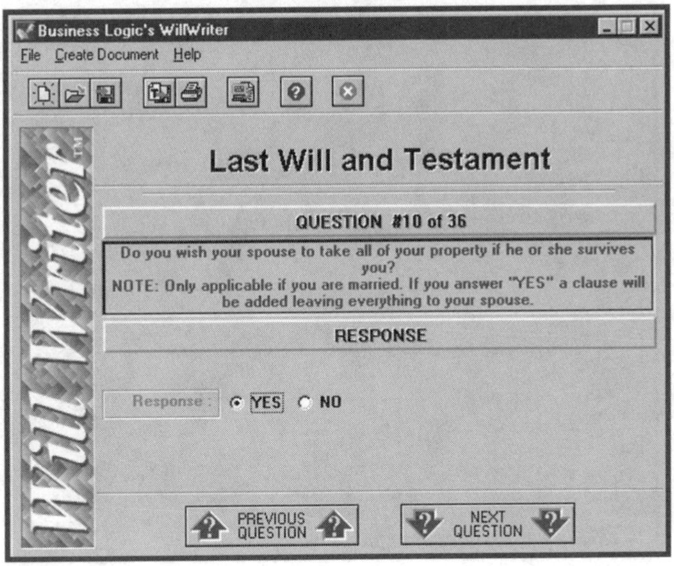

Figure 4.12

Click Yes, and you leave everything to your spouse.

Question #11: Are You Leaving Your Entire Estate to Your Children?

This question allows you to leave your estate to your children in the event that conditions such as the following ones apply:

○ Your spouse didn't survive you.

○ You aren't married.

○ You chose not to leave the majority of your estate to your spouse at death.

If you want your children to inherit your estate at your death, click "Yes" (see Figure 4.13).

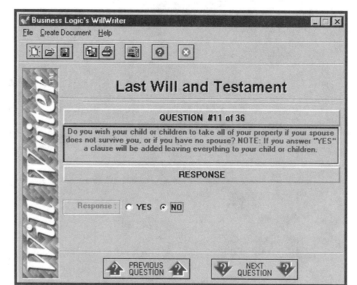

Figure 4.13

Click Yes to leave everything to your children.

Question #12: Who Is the Guardian of Your Minor Children?

Question #12 deals with nominating a guardian for your minor children. Remember that your named guardian must provide for all minor children living at your death and might also act as a custodian for gifts left in your will to your minor children.

Type your nominated guardian in the Response box.

You don't need to name your spouse or the children's other parent because, in most cases, this person automatically receives custody of the minor children. Instead, you most likely want to list an alternate guardian in case your spouse or the children's other parent is not living at the time of your death.

WillWriter states that the "other parent" will automatically be named the guardian of minor children left at your death. However, if you prefer that someone other than your spouse or the children's other parent care for the children at your death, you may state this in your answer.

Simply list your choice for a guardian here (see Figure 4.14). After you complete this exercise, I will show you how to delete the reference to the surviving parent and how to include your reasons for doing so.

NOTE Getting the court to appoint someone other than the children's other parent to serve as their guardian can be difficult. Without proof that the surviving parent shows the potential to inflict mental or physical harm upon the children, the surviving parent usually is automatically awarded custody.

Also, you should name a successor or alternate guardian; your first choice might not be living at your death or might not be able to care for your minor children. Simply make a provision for an alternate or successor beneficiary in your response, as the following example does:

> *Cari Sovich, my sister, should she be living at my death, or to Trev and Angela Alberts.*

That's all! WillWriter takes care of the rest.

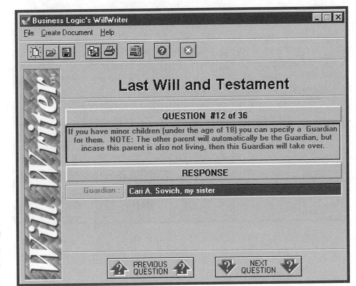

Figure 4.14

Enter your choice for guardian in the Response box.

Question #13: What Are Your Children's Names?

If you answered "Yes" to Question #11, list the names of your children here (see Figure 4.15). Remember to type each child's full legal name.

Question #14: Do You Have Specific Bequests?

WillWriter allows you to leave specific gifts (or bequests) to six individuals. Again, a specific bequest refers to a gift of personal property. Here's an example of a specific bequest:

> *I leave to Kathy Utley, my aunt, my rare book collection.*

As I mentioned, you can name family members, friends, or anyone you choose. You can also leave specific gifts to charities or other institutions (such as your alma mater or church), but don't use these next ques-

Figure 4.15

If you answered "Yes" to Question #11, enter your children's names in these boxes.

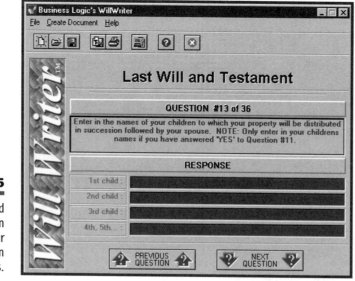

tions for those gifts. WillWriter makes specific provisions for these types of charitable gifts, and I'll get to those questions in a moment. Use these next few questions for the specific bequests that you decided to include in your will this afternoon.

Question #15: Who Is Your First Beneficiary?

List the specific beneficiary for your first bequest here (see Figure 4.16). Be sure to type his or her full legal name. You might know who "Skip" is, but your executor might not. By providing Skip's full legal name, you make it easier for your executor to locate this person and distribute the gift.

You also need to enter Skip's relationship to you in the response area provided. You don't need to type "My friend" or "Skip is my friend." Just type **Friend**.

Figure 4.16

Enter the full name of your first beneficiary.

NOTE Be sure to type the beneficiary's full name and relationship. If you simply put "my aunt" rather than "Darlene Bursac" and you have more than one aunt, your executor might be forced to divide the gift among all persons who qualify as your aunt (or the gift might lapse and pass into your residuary).

Question #16: What Is the Specific Bequest for Your First Beneficiary?

Now, list the specific bequest you want to leave this individual (see Figure 4.17). When describing the gift, be as specific as possible.

Question #17: Who Is the Second Beneficiary?

List the second recipient of your specific bequest. Don't forget to include his or her relationship to you (see Figure 4.18).

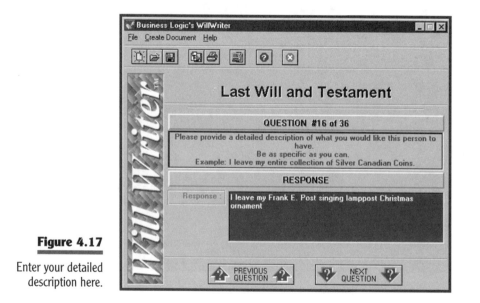

Figure 4.17

Enter your detailed description here.

Figure 4.18

Enter your second beneficiary's name here.

Business Logic's WillWriter

File   Create Document   Help

Last Will and Testament

QUESTION #17 of 36

Enter the name of the next individual you would like to leave part of your estate to:
NOTE: If you do not wish to leave anything else to anyone, just leave the fields blank, and skip to QUESTION 27.

RESPONSE

Full Name : Cari A. Sovich

Relationship : sister

PREVIOUS QUESTION   NEXT QUESTION

NOTE You can name more than one beneficiary for a specific gift that all beneficiaries will share equally. For example, "I leave my Porsche 911 to my daughters, Claudia, Emerson, and Ellery, to be shared equally."

Question #18: What Is the Specific Bequest for Your Second Beneficiary?

Describe the gift you want to leave this individual. Remember, be as specific as possible (see Figure 4.19).

Questions #19, #21, #23, and #25: Who Are Your Remaining Beneficiaries?

Again, type the full names of the individuals who will receive specific bequests of your estate after your death. List their relationships to you in

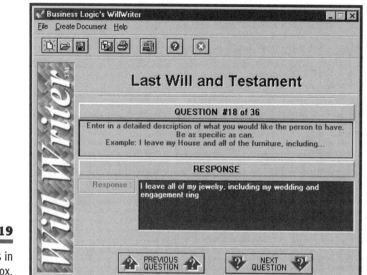

Figure 4.19

Enter the details in
this Response box.

the appropriate spaces provided. If you are leaving the gift to more than one person, simply list all of them in the space provided. For example, your answer for Question 19 might be "John and Dusanka Sovich (parents)."

Questions #20, #22, #24, and #26: What Are the Specific Bequests for Your Remaining Beneficiaries?

You need to describe the specific bequests that you're leaving for each of the preceding beneficiaries.

Now also might be a good time to qualify your gifts or leave a contingent bequest, which you learned about in the Saturday Afternoon session. Here's one example:

> *I leave my BMW to Steve, provided that he gives his personal vehicle to my niece, Lindsey.*

NOTE As explained in the Saturday Afternoon session, you need to consult an attorney when leaving a conditional gift or a gift of a life estate. Typically, these types of bequests are best handled by creating a trust to be included in your will and by naming a trustee to ensure that the condition is satisfied.

To protect your selected beneficiary, you probably need to provide a *gift-over* for each of your specific bequests. A gift-over ensures that your named beneficiary is left something even if you don't own the item at your death. An example of a gift-over to your Aunt Darlene might be as follows:

> *To my Aunt Darlene, I leave my diamond earrings. If I do not own the diamond earrings at my death, I leave my Aunt Darlene $10,000.*

Remember, some states mandate that if you don't own the earrings at your death, Darlene will get nothing. Other states provide for Darlene to receive cash that is equivalent to the value of the earrings. Thus, it's best to clarify your intentions.

Question #27: Do You Have Bequests for Charities?

The next few questions deal with gifts to charities or other institutions.

NOTE If you don't want to make a provision to a charity or other organization, you can skip the next several questions and go straight to Question #32.

WillWriter enables you to leave gifts to two charities. Just in case you want to make bequests to more than two charities, I show you how to add additional provisions at the end of this session.

Question #28: What Is the Name of the First Charity?

First, list the name of the charity for which you want to make a provision. Be sure to enter in the full name of the charity. For example, "Humane Society" is too general. Do you mean the Hamilton County Humane Society (as shown in Figure 4.20), the Humane Society of Indiana, or the American Society for the Prevention of Cruelty to Animals?

Question #29: What Is the Specific Bequest for the First Charity?

Now, type the specific bequest that you want to make. You can also name a successor or alternate charity here (in case your first choice is not a recognized charitable organization at the time of your death or in case the

Figure 4.20

A general bequest could be confusing for your executor, so be sure to enter the full name of the charity of your choice.

Business Logic's WillWriter

File   Create Document   Help

Last Will and Testament

QUESTION #28 of 36

Enter in the name of a Chartiy or Institution that you would like to leave a gift to:
NOTE: Continue with QUESTION 32 if this is not applicable.

RESPONSE

Charity : Hamilton County Humane Society

PREVIOUS QUESTION   NEXT QUESTION

IRS doesn't consider it a tax-deductible charity). To provide for a successor charity, your response to Question #29 might be as follows:

> $25,000 should this organization be an IRS recognized, tax-deductible charity at my death; otherwise, I leave the $25,000 to the United Way.

Question #30: What Is the Name of the Second Charity?

List your second choice for a charity here (see Figure 4.21).

You can also leave a gift to your alma mater, another university, or any other organization or institution (such as your place of worship).

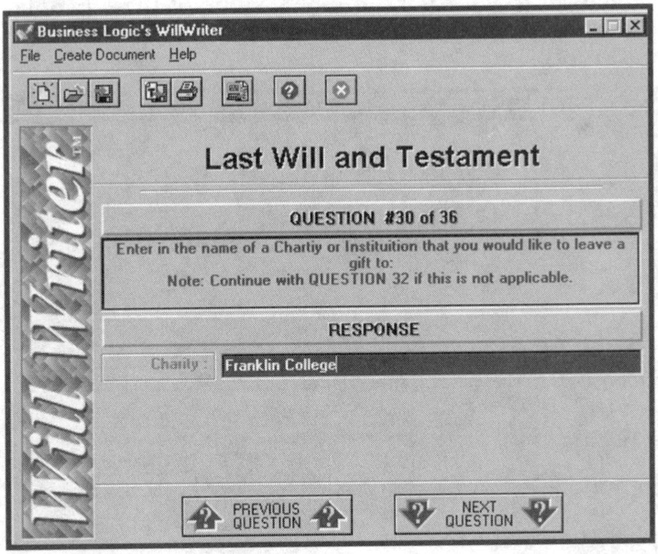

Figure 4.21

Enter the name of the second charity here.

Business Logic's WillWriter

File Create Document Help

Last Will and Testament

QUESTION #30 of 36

Enter in the name of a Charity or Instituition that you would like to leave a gift to:
Note: Continue with QUESTION 32 if this is not applicable.

RESPONSE

Charity : Franklin College

PREVIOUS QUESTION   NEXT QUESTION

Question #31: What Is the Specific Bequest for the Second Charity?

Describe the gift to be bequeathed (see Figure 4.22).

Question #32: Who Will Act as Your Executor?

Here's where you can appoint a personal representative to handle your estate at your death. As previously mentioned, you need to state your choice for a personal representative in your will; when appointing an executor (or personal representative), a court gives preference to the person named in the will.

Remember, if your will makes no provision for a personal representative, the court gives first consideration to your spouse (if your spouse survives you) or to an individual designated by your spouse. If your spouse doesn't survive you or declines the role of executor, the court will then give consideration to your next of kin. If none of these people exist at your death

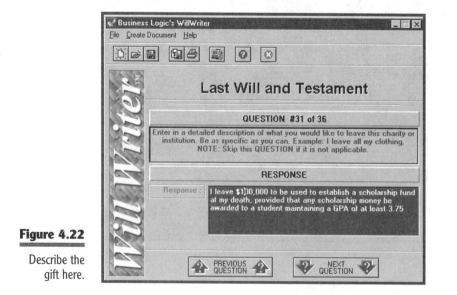

Figure 4.22

Describe the gift here.

or if they don't file with the court within 30 days following your death, any other qualified person (including one of your creditors!) can act as your estate's representative.

Again, be sure to enter the full legal name of your selected executor (see Figure 4.23).

Question #33: Is Your Executor Male or Female?

You are asked to state whether your executor is male or female (see Figure 4.24).

Question #34: Who Is Your Successor or Alternate Executor?

You can also nominate a successor or alternate executor in your will, and I highly recommend doing so. Simply type the full legal name of the successor (see Figure 4.25).

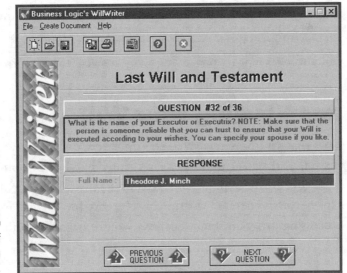

Figure 4.23

Enter the name of your executor in this Response box.

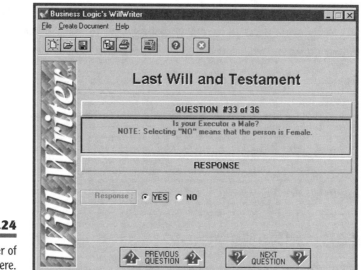

Figure 4.24

Enter the gender of your executor here.

Question #35: What Are the Names of the County and State in Which You Live?

List the county and state in which you reside. Please note that WillWriter is asking you to provide the name of the *county*—not the country.

That's it! You're done. See how easy that was? You're ready to create your will and review it before saving your answers for tomorrow's session.

Creating and Viewing Your Will

Now that you have answered the interview questions, you can save your answers and reload them at a later time. The buttons on the Button Bar help you create a new will, save and reload existing documents, and export your generated document as a text file for use in another word-processing program. First, however, you must create your will and review the document.

Figure 4.25

Enter the name of your secondary executor here.

The following appears in the figure:

Business Logic's WillWriter

File Create Document Help

Last Will and Testament

QUESTION #34 of 36

What is the name of the Secondary Executor? It is always a good idea to have a secondary executor to take the place of the first one, in case he/she is unable to or unwilling to carry out the duties. Leave the field blank, if it is not applicable.

RESPONSE

Full Name : Cari A. Sovich

PREVIOUS QUESTION   NEXT QUESTION

Simply go to the Button Bar and click on Create and View the Document (the third button from the right on the Button Bar, shown earlier in this session in Figure 4.2).

Note that you *don't* press the Write the Will button as shown on-screen.

WillWriter automatically creates your will as a printable document in a matter of seconds, incorporating the information you provided during the interview process. After it's written, the document appears in a viewer that you can use to scroll up or down the document.

NOTE

You will undoubtedly find grammatical and spelling errors during your review. You can easily fix these errors, and I will show you how to make all these changes Sunday Morning.

For now, check to make sure that the content is correct. For example, make sure that your beneficiaries are receiving the appropriate bequests and that you correctly spelled the names of your spouse, children, and executor.

If you want to go back and make changes, just close the viewer. Doing so returns you to the WillWriter interview screen, where you can scroll back through the questions (by using the Previous Question button) until you reach the answer that requires revisions.

When you complete your changes, you can instantly rewrite the document by pressing the Create and View the Document button. You can carry out this procedure as many times as necessary until you are satisfied with the overall content.

In the Sunday Morning session, I take you step-by-step through the process of saving this document as a text file and printing it. For now, follow these steps to quickly save the document in WillWriter:

1. From the WillWriter menu bar, click on File and choose Save.

   The Save As dialog box appears.

2. Click on the Save in selection box arrow, and choose drive C from the drop-down menu that appears.

3. In the list of folders, double-click on blcorp and then on willwrtr, unless you used a different name when you installed WillWriter.

4. In the File name box, type a name for your will.

5. Click on the Save button, and *voilà!* . . . your document will be saved in the willwrtr folder.

What's Next?

Tomorrow you will save your will as a text document and then print and review it, making any last-minute changes and correcting misspellings or typos. You will also gather and educate your witnesses for the signing of your will. But you've done enough for one day . . . save the printing and editing of your will for tomorrow!

Oh, and one last thing. Feel free to sleep in late tomorrow morning. The Sunday Morning session shouldn't take much time at all.

Editing Your Will

- ✿ Opening Your Document in WillWriter
- ✿ Saving Your Will as a Text File
- ✿ Printing a Draft of Your Will
- ✿ Making Final Changes to Your Will
- ✿ Printing a Final Copy of Your Will for Signature

In the Saturday Evening session, you created and saved your will. Now you will resave it as a text file and print a draft copy for review. By saving the document as a text file, you can make additional changes to the will (such as adding a third witness or making a provision for your pet). You can also edit and correct spelling and grammar errors.

In this session, you will do the following:

- Open your will in the WillWriter program.
- Review your answers to the WillWriter questions.
- Save your will as a text document and print a draft copy of your will.
- Make final changes to your will.
- Designate a residuary beneficiary.
- Name a custodian for your minor child's property.
- Add a third witness.
- Provide for a pet.
- Print a final copy of your will for signature.

You've still got a lot of work to do, so those Sunday funnies will have to wait. Let's get started!

Opening Your Document in WillWriter

To open the document that you saved in the Saturday Evening session, just follow these steps:

1. Go to the Start menu, select Programs, click on WillWriter, and then click on Business Logic's WillWriter.

   Business Logic's WillWriter screen appears (see Figure 5.1).

2. Go to the Button Bar, and click on the Open an Existing Document button (second button from the left, as shown in Figure 5.1).

   The Open File As dialog box appears. (The dialog box should look similar to the one shown in Figure 5.2.)

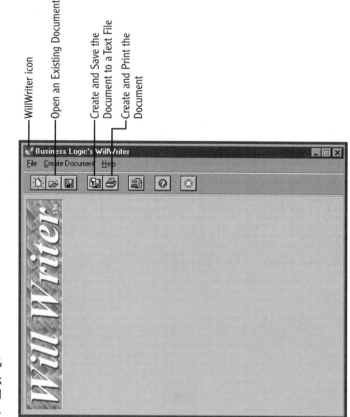

Figure 5.1

Take a look at the initial WillWriter screen.

Figure 5.2

Here you can find the will that you created and saved last night.

3. On your hard drive (C drive), locate the will you created last evening, and double-click on it to open it.

WillWriter automatically opens the previously saved document.

At this point, you probably want to take a moment to review your will (see the upcoming sidebar, "Reviewing Your Answers," for more on that topic). After you review your answers, you're ready to save your will as a text file.

Saving Your Will as a Text File

You can save your will as a text file so that it can be imported and used on any word processor. As I mentioned earlier, saving the document as a text file enables you to make additional changes to your will, such as correcting spelling and grammar errors and providing for additional beneficiaries.

CAUTION   After you export your will as a text file, you cannot open that version of your will in Will-Writer. (WillWriter recognizes only its file format, which is indicated by the file extension .wil—for example, mywill.wil—whereas text documents save in the .txt format.) Therefore, be certain that you answer *all* the questions that WillWriter presents exactly as you want to before you save your will as a text file. Of course, once you save the file as a text file, you can make additional changes or provisions by editing the will in a text editor or word processor.

To save your will as a text file, perform the following steps:

1. With the will document you created in WillWriter open, click on the Create and Save the Document to a Text File button located on the Button Bar (refer to Figure 5.1).

   The Save Text File As dialog box appears (see Figure 5.3).

2. In the File name text box, type the name of your will (Figure 5.4 shows mywill as the filename) and click on Save (or OK).

   The new text file is saved on the same drive and in the same directory in which you saved the WillWriter program.

   If you selected the default drive when installing WillWriter, the pathname is c:\blcorp\willwrtr.

   If you previously saved your file in a different folder, WillWriter points back to that folder instead.

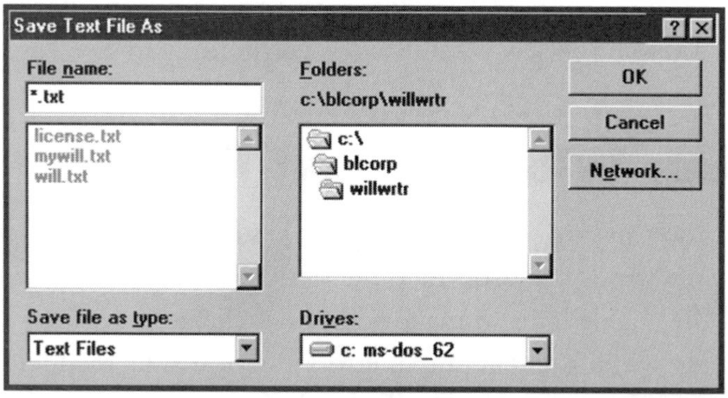

Figure 5.3

By saving your will as a text file, you can add provisions and fix errors.

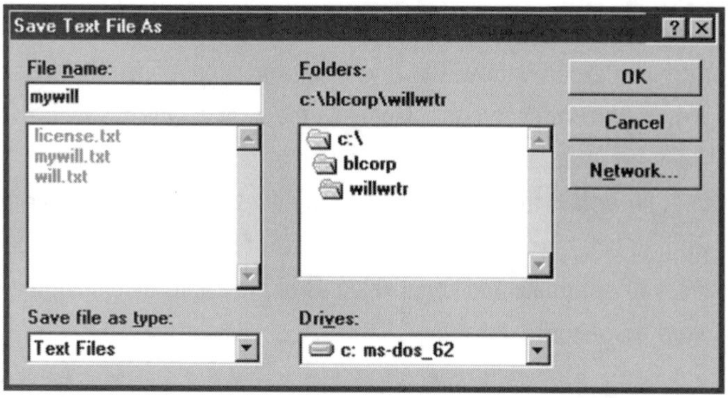

Figure 5.4

You can use the same name for the text file that you used when saving your will last night.

Printing a Draft Copy of Your Will

After you save the document, you can print a draft copy of your will and review it for errors and possible revisions to make during this session.

With the document open, you can easily print the draft by following these easy steps:

1. Click on the Create and Print the Document button located on the Button Bar (refer to Figure 5.1 to see this button).

   A Print dialog box appears.

2. Just click on OK, and your will is printed.

REVIEWING YOUR ANSWERS

It's always a good idea to review your will carefully before printing a draft copy. Remember, you can change any of the answers that you provided last night. Simply scroll through the questions—using the Previous Question and Next Question buttons at the bottom of your screen—making changes where necessary.

You might want to compare your answers to the Beneficiary Worksheet that you created in the Saturday Afternoon session. Ask yourself the following questions:

- Did you use your full legal name?
- Did you include all your desired bequests?
- Does your will make provisions for all your selected beneficiaries?
- Did you nominate an executor and, if applicable, a personal guardian for your minor children?
- Did you name an alternate executor?
- Did you state your wishes for specific funeral arrangements?

If you closed the WillWriter program after saving the document as a text file, you need to follow these steps:

1. Locate the text file on your computer's hard drive.

2. Open the document by double-clicking on it. The document will appear as a Microsoft Notepad file (as mine did in Figure 5.5) unless you have associated text files with a different program.

3. From the Notepad menu bar, click on File and choose Print from the drop-down menu. The document prints automatically.

That's all! You now have a printed draft of your will.

Making Final Changes to Your Will

Take this time to make final changes or revisions to your will. (Perhaps your spouse's snoring has changed your mind about what you're leaving him or her!) Now is also the time to verify vital contact information (such as the correct spelling of your fiduciaries' names and their addresses and

Figure 5.5

In Notepad, you can easily make additions and revisions to your will.

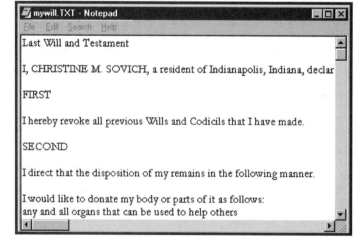

phone numbers). You must include the correct information in order to avoid lengthy delays at probate. And be sure to fix grammatical or sentence structure problems that appear in the document.

Finally, you might want to add provisions to your will that you didn't create during the WillWriter interview, such as the following:

- Name a specific residuary beneficiary for your estate.
- Select a custodian to manage property left to your minor children.
- Add an additional witness.
- Make a provision for the family pet.

If you saved your will as a text file, you can easily make changes to the document. Just open the file and type your changes.

NOTE As with all added provisions, you need to number the provisions and then renumber the remaining paragraphs in the document accordingly.

Designating a Residuary Beneficiary

Remember, a residuary gift is a gift of whatever remains in the estate after payment of all obligations and after all other bequests and devises are satisfied. To be on the safe side, name an alternate residuary beneficiary in the event your first residuary beneficiary is unable to receive the bequest for some reason.

WillWriter automatically provides for the residue of your estate to be distributed to your named heirs in the order of succession. However, you can name a completely different beneficiary of your residue estate or direct that the residue be left solely to a previously named beneficiary under your will.

To provide for a residuary beneficiary, you will want to include the following language (or similar language) in your will:

> *I leave my residuary estate, that is, the rest of my property not otherwise effectively disposed of under my will, to (name or names of your residuary beneficiary or beneficiaries), in equal shares or in the following shares: (_____); or if he/she/they should not be living at my death, I leave my residuary estate to (name of alternate/successor beneficiary or beneficiaries), in equal shares.*

Simply type the preceding language after the last specific bequest in your will. You also need to delete the language that WillWriter provided—that is, for the residue of your estate to be distributed to your named heirs in the order of succession.

Naming a Custodian to Manage Your Minor Child's Property

WillWriter automatically provides for your executor to hold and manage all property left to your minor children. In case you prefer a different individual (adult) to act as a custodian, delete the WillWriter language and replace it with the following provision in your will:

> *If at my death, any of my children shall be minors, I appoint (name of nominated custodian) to act as a custodian to manage and/or handle any property left in my will to any such minor child, according to the Uniform Transfer to Minors Act of the state of (name of your state). Should (name of nominated custodian) not be able to serve for any reason, I appoint (name of alternate/successor custodian) to act as my minor child or children's custodian. I direct that no bond be required of any custodian appointed hereunder.*

NOTE If you do not want your nominated guardian to be required to post a bond, be sure to add language to that effect in your will. You can do this simply by adding the following sentence to the end of the provision for your minor children: "I direct that no bond be required of any Guardian nominated hereunder."

Adding a Third Witness to Your Will

As you can see, WillWriter provides for only two witnesses in the document you just created. Beware! If you live in Vermont, the state requires three witnesses.

I strongly recommend adding a third witness no matter where you live, just in case the probate court deems one of your witnesses as unqualified for the task.

You most certainly want to add a third witness if one of your witnesses is also a named beneficiary in your will.

To add a third witness, you just make a provision for another witness after the provisions for the first two witnesses, leaving space for a third signature. If you saved the WillWriter document as a text file, you can easily make this change. A sample additional witness provision is shown in Figure 5.6.

Please Don't Overlook Spot and Fluffy!

Believe it or not, you can also make provisions in your will for your pets, ensuring that Riley, Abraham, or Pigger (or whatever the name of your

Witness #1

John Q. Public residing at 123 Madeline Boulevard, Merrillville, Indiana 46410

_____
Print Name

_____
Signature

Dated: _____

Witness #2

Barbara C. Stolzmann residing at 456 Sweet Water Canyon, Crown Point, Indiana 46037

_____
Print Name

_____
Signature

Dated: _____

Witness #3

Pauline Stolzmann residing at 789 Rocky Pointe Road, Indianapolis, Indiana 46355

_____
Print Name

_____
Signature

Dated: _____

Figure 5.6

Note the addition of the third witness.

furry buddy) is adequately taken care of upon your death. To make a provision for your pet, incorporate the following language into your will:

> *I leave my pet(s) (name of pet or pets), (description of pet or pets), in the care of (name of selected guardian or guardians) should my pet(s) be living at my death. Should (name of selected guardian or guardians) be unable to care for my pet(s) for any reason, I leave my pet(s) to (name of alternate/successor guardian). I also leave the sum of (name sum) to help the guardian appointed hereunder to care financially for my pet(s).*

CAUTION

You cannot name your pet as a beneficiary under your will! Animals cannot directly receive money or property under a will.

You can add your pet provision *after* you've listed all your specific bequests, but *before* the bequest to any charity or other organization.

NOTE

As you did with your executor and guardian, it might be wise to name an alternate caretaker for "Oscar" and "Charcoal." You wouldn't want them wind up at the Humane Society with no guarantee that they'll be adopted by another family as loving as yours. Before you name someone as guardian of your four-legged friends, be sure to ask whether the individuals are willing to assume the responsibility. Aunt Bertha might be excited to hear that she's inherited something under your will that has fur, but might not be too happy to find out that her gift has feet!

Printing a Final Copy of Your Will for Signature

When you finish editing your will—for the last time—and are comfortable and confident with the decisions that you've made, you're ready to print a final copy in preparation for signing your will.

You can print your will by following the procedures laid out in the section titled "Printing a Draft Copy of Your Will," earlier in this session. It's that easy!

What's Next?

Now that you've completed drafting and editing your will, all you need to do is validate it. When all your witnesses arrive, you're ready for that next step.

In the Sunday Afternoon session, you will sign your will in the presence of your witnesses and watch as they sign and acknowledge it as well.

(By the way, you might want to take this time to tidy up a bit before they arrive.)

Signing on the Dotted Line

- ✿ Gathering and Educating your Witnesses
- ✿ Executing Your Will
- ✿ Self-Proving Your Will
- ✿ Checking for Proper Execution

Now that you've drafted your will and printed an execution copy, it's time to sign your will and make it valid. As you learned in the Friday Evening session, in order to make your will legal, two things must be done: You need to sign your will in the presence of at least two witnesses (you'll need three if you live in Vermont), and your witnesses must sign your will in your presence and in the presence of one another. To verify your particular state's witness requirements, check out the State-By-State Probate Matrix in Appendix A.

In this session, you will do the following:

○ Gather your witnesses and instruct them on their role in acknowledging your will.

○ Execute your will: Sign your will in the presence of all your witnesses, and then watch each witness sign your will.

○ Learn how to self-prove your will.

○ Check for proper execution to protect against your will being contested.

You are ready to sign your will. So, round up your witnesses and get ready to sign on the dotted line.

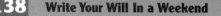

Gathering and Educating Your Witnesses

When your witnesses arrive, you need to take the time to instruct them on their duties as witnesses to your will. You need to explain their roles and tell them that, after your death, they might be called upon to verify or legitimize your will. Specifically, your witnesses might be asked to do the following:

- Testify as to your mental competency at the execution of the will.
- Verify your age at the time you drafted your will.
- Verify your signature on the will.
- Prove that you drafted your will as a free and voluntary act.

If a witness is unfamiliar with the signing ceremony, you should instruct him or her now. Typically, you do this by stating aloud that the document you are about to sign is your last will and testament.

 NOTE Remember, your witnesses do not need to read your will or be told of its contents. They need only be told that you intend for this document to be your will and that you have executed this will of your own volition.

Next, you need to acknowledge, in the presence of all of your witnesses, that you want each of them to serve as a witness to your will.

Executing Your Will

Now, it's time to actually sign your will and make it official. In most states, to properly execute a will, you must do one of the following:

- Sign and date your will in the presence of your witnesses.
- Declare in front of your gathered witnesses that the signature on the document is *your* signature. If you signed your will before your witnesses arrived, your will is still valid as long as you acknowledge

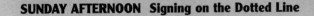

your signature on the document by declaring it to be your signature in the presence of your witnesses.

✿ If you are unable to sign, appoint someone to sign the will for you. For example, say that your wrist is in a cast from all that typing during Saturday's sessions. That's okay, as long as you appoint someone to sign the will (your name, of course) on your behalf in the presence of you and your witnesses. Be sure that your will also states that another person signed for you at your request.

Signing and Dating Your Will

In most states, you don't need to sign your will at the end of the document. Therefore, it's okay to sign right after the first occurrence of your name in the document, as Figure 6.1 illustrates.

However, some states—Pennsylvania is one—require you to sign your will at the end of the document, which is considered the *logical end* of the will. Specifically, you want to sign your will *after* all the *dispositive provisions* (the clauses in your will that direct how your property will be distributed to your named beneficiaries).

In case you are unsure about your state's requirement, sign your will at the end of the document to avoid any potential problems. All states consider the end of the will as a proper place for signing.

 NOTE You are not required to sign *every* page of your will, just the last page. But if you're concerned that your stepson or mother-in-law might replace a page of your will with a false page after you die (giving them more of your estate than you've actually planned to leave them), you can protect your will by initialing every page. You might even want to have each of your witnesses initial every page, although this, too, is not required.

After you sign your will, you need only your witnesses' signatures.

Last Will and Testament
of Christine M. Sovich

I, CHRISTINE M. SOVICH, _____Christine M. Sovich_____, a resident of McCordsville,

Indiana, declare that this is my Last Will and Testament.

Figure 6.1

In most states you can sign your will at the bottom—or at the top, as shown here.

Requirements for Witnesses' Signatures

As previously mentioned, your witnesses must sign your will in your presence *and* in the presence of each other.

Although your witnesses should sign your will in each other's presence, some states allow them to sign the will in the presence of the testator at separate times. However, I strongly recommend that you ask everyone to sign your will during the same session to avoid potential problems during probate.

In case one of your witnesses cannot make it *today,* before proceeding, you need to check your state's requirements concerning witnesses and their need to sign your will in each other's presence.

Regardless of these factors, your witnesses *must* sign your will in your presence. Most states interpret *in your presence* to mean that you must actually *see* each witness sign your will. However, a few states have applied a *conscious presence* standard, allowing you to be in the vicinity of where the witnesses sign the will, as long as you know the signing is taking place.

For example, say that someone just rang your doorbell. You can walk away from the dining room table where your witnesses are taking turns signing your will and see who is at the door. In a state that applies a conscious presence standard, you are considered to be in the vicinity of the signing, and that is acceptable. To be on the safe side, however, stay put. Tell you husband or kids to answer the door, or let the paperboy wait!

NOTE A recent Minnesota case held that a testator had met the requirement of observing his witnesses' signatures, even though the testator could not actually see the table where the witnesses were signing his will. (One of the witnesses was inadvertently blocking the testator's view. However, if the testator had moved two or three feet, he could have seen the actual signing ceremony.) The court applied a conscious presence standard, saying that the testator was in the vicinity of the witnesses' signing and knew what was going on.

Take a Break

Your will is signed and witnessed. Now it's time to take a break. I hope you prepared something yummy for your witnesses to eat. After all, you didn't name them in your will, so you at least should provide a light lunch for them to enjoy.

After lunch, you'll learn how to self-prove your will to protect it from being contested. So, be sure to tell your witnesses not to eat and run. Their services might still be needed!

Self-Proving Your Will

When you *self-prove* your will, you help validate your will if and when your witnesses don't remember signing your will. Also, self-proving provisions can be used to rebut witnesses who later claim that the signing ceremony never occurred.

A will is presumed to be self-proven if it includes an *attestation clause* (see the upcoming section "Attestation Clauses") signed by a witness (or witnesses) that indicates the following:

- ✿ The testator executed the instrument as his or her will.
- ✿ The testator signed the will, acknowledged his or her signature on the will, or had someone else sign the will in the presence of witnesses.
- ✿ The testator executed the will as a free and voluntary act.
- ✿ The testator was of sound mind (mentally competent) at the time of drafting.
- ✿ The testator was 18 years old or older (19 years old in Wyoming).
- ✿ Each witness signed the will in the testator's presence and in the presence of the other witnesses.

Attestation Clauses

You do not need an attestation clause to validate a will. However, it is recommended. An attestation clause attached to the document itself can act to self-prove the will, which means you might not have to rely on your witnesses' memories or testimonies in order to prove your will.

Until 20 to 25 years ago, a will could not be self-proved. Basically, an executor had to drag your witnesses to probate court to prove the will. If no witnesses could appear in court, an executor had to present the witnesses' affidavits under oath to prove the will. Also, if witnesses weren't still alive or couldn't be located, an executor had to retain a handwriting expert to testify as to the testator's signature on the will.

Now, under the Uniform Probate Code (UPC)—to which most states adhere—any will can be simultaneously executed, attested, and self-proven. The only requirements are the acknowledgment of the will by the testator and affidavits of the witnesses (made before a notary).

Notarizing and Self-Proving Your Will

As previously stated, you don't need to notarize your will. However, the probate process might be expedited if you and your witnesses sign and date your will in the presence of a notary public. In case you don't have a notary among you, you can accomplish the same thing by having one of your witnesses sign an *affidavit* (a sworn statement) before a notary at a later date.

The will you created during the Saturday Evening session provides for a self-proving provision (called an *affidavit of execution*) at the end of your document. You might have one of your witnesses sign this affidavit in the presence of a notary public. (See Figure 6.2 for an example of an affidavit of execution.)

THE LAST WILL AND TESTAMENT OF ADAM A. ADAMS
Affidavit of Execution

I, John Q. Public, of the City of Merrillville, in the County of Lake, in the State of Indiana,

Make oath and say:

1. On the 1st day of April, 2000, I was present and saw the paper annexed and marked as LAST WILL AND TESTAMENT of this my affidavit executed by Adam A. Adams.

2. At time of execution, I knew such person(s) who was on that date of the full age of Eighteen (18) years to the best of my knowledge.

3. The said paper writing was executed by such person in the presence of myself, Barbara C. Stolzmann, of the City of Crown Point, in the County of Lake, and Pauline Stolzmann of the City of Indianapolis, in the County of Marion. We were all present at the same time, whereupon we did, in the presence of such person, attest and subscribe the said paper writing as witnesses.

_____

John Q. Public
Witness

SWORN BEFORE ME AT THE City of Crown Point in the County of Lake

this _____ day of April, 2000.

_____ Commissioner for Oaths
_____ Notary Public

_____

Commissioner/Notary

Figure 6.2

To self-prove your will, have a witness to your will sign an affidavit such as this one before a notary public.

UNDERSTANDING THE IMPORTANCE
OF ATTESTATION CLAUSES

Although an attestation clause is not required to create a valid will, it can be useful. An attestation clause raises the presumption of a will's validity if a witness's memory fails. An attestation clause can even be used to rebut a witness who claims the signing ceremony never took place. Consider the following situation.

At Mrs. Lola Lotsamoney's death, a document is offered for probate as her will. Three witnesses' signatures are below Lola's signature on the will: Penny Pincher (Lola's longtime friend), Freddy Freeloader (Lola's only child, to whom she did not leave anything under her will), and Nina Nottoobright (the secretary of Lola's attorney, Eve N. Mooremoney). In each of the following scenarios, consider the will's ability to be accepted to probate if, first, the will *does* contain an attestation clause and, second, the will *does not* contain an attestation clause.

Scenarios:

✪ **A:** All witnesses to the will have predeceased Mrs. Lotsamoney, but their signatures are readily identified.

✪ **B:** Only Nina Nottobright is surviving at Lola's death. Nina recognizes her signature, but she can't recall signing the will, any of the circumstances surrounding the execution, or even the identity of Mrs. Lotsamoney.

✪ **C:** Freddy Freeloader is the only surviving witness at Mrs. Lotsamoney's death. Freddy identifies his signature, but says he never saw his mother sign the will and never even heard her acknowledge the document as her will. Freddy even testifies that his mother lacked the requisite mental capacity to draft the will. (Freddy is clearly hoping the court will invalidate the will and pass his mother's fortune to him intestate!)

Answers:

✿ **A:** With or without an attestation clause, the will should be admitted to probate with no problems.

✿ **B:** With an attestation clause, Nina's poor memory shouldn't cause a problem because an attestation clause raises the presumption that the will was properly executed. However, without an attestation clause, problems might arise if the other witnesses' signatures cannot be identified.

✿ **C:** An attestation clause is necessary. It would raise a question of fact for the court to consider. (Other testimony could then be introduced regarding the fact that Freddy is merely attempting to invalidate the will so he can inherit his mother's fortune by an intestate process.) Without an attestation clause, the will would not be admitted to probate (as it could not be proven to be valid). Mrs. Lotsamoney would be out of luck, and Freddy would be a wealthy man!

Checking for Proper Execution

Before you dismiss your witnesses, you want to check your will for proper execution. Did you sign and date your will in the presence of your witnesses? Did all your witnesses sign your will in your presence and in the presence of each other?

Be sure you signed your will first and then had your witnesses sign after you. Also make sure that you've signed your will at its logical end (the bottom of the document, or at least after all of the provisions to your beneficiaries).

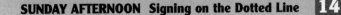

Now, you need to make copies of the fully executed agreement, and be sure to keep these copies separate from the original will.

CAUTION Don't sign multiple original copies of your will. If you decide to change your will at a later date, you will need to locate all the originals of your will and destroy each and every one. It is better just to make copies of the original and store the original in a safe, readily accessible place.

What's Next?

Your will is signed and properly witnessed. You need to attend to just a few more minor—and not so minor—details before you're done.

In the final session of this book, you will learn how to protect your will so that it is ready when you need it. You'll also find out what happens after you're gone and how the probate process works. I'll even explain will contests to you, in case you're concerned that one of your heirs might become a bit greedy and contest his or her bequest.

Safeguarding Your Will (And More)

- ✿ Revoking and Destroying Old Wills
- ✿ Determining When a New Will Is Needed
- ✿ To Draft a New Will, Or Not to Draft a New Will?
- ✿ Storing Your Will
- ✿ Understanding Probate
- ✿ Will Contests and Dealing with Uncommon Situations

Now that you have legalized your will (by having it witnessed), you need to take precautions to safeguard it so that it's ready when needed. (With any luck, that won't be for a while, but it's better to be prepared.) You must do more than just store it in a safe and easily accessible location. You must ensure that your most current will is your *only* will, that you update your will when necessary, and that you safeguard it against contests.

In this session, you will learn about the following:

- How to revoke and destroy old wills
- When you need to draft a new will, and when an amendment suffices
- Where you need to keep your will and other important papers
- The probate process and what happens after you're gone

I'll even explain some common and uncommon will contests and how to avoid them.

Revoking and Destroying Old Wills

To ensure that your newly created document will be accepted as your valid and controlling will, you must revoke and destroy all wills that you've previously created. To revoke an existing will, you must expressly state your intention to do so at the beginning of your new will.

Specifically, your new will must contain a written *revocation of prior wills* clause. (Don't worry, WillWriter automatically included a revocation clause in the document that you created last night.) A typical revocation clause reads as follows:

> *I hereby revoke all wills and/or codicils that I have previously executed.*

NOTE If you happen to know the date(s) of your previous will(s), you could have included this information in the revocation clause that you wrote last night. For example, you might have typed language similar to the following:

> *. . . that I have previously executed, specifically, my will dated _____, 19__.*

However, including the dates of your old wills is not necessary. Merely stating that you revoke all prior wills in the will is more than enough to ensure that your new will—the one you created during Saturday Evening's session—is your only valid will.

As previously mentioned, the WillWriter program automatically incorporates the necessary revocation language in your will. Therefore, you need only to physically destroy the old will as well as all copies of it. (To destroy a will, you can burn it, tear it up, or strike through each page with an ink pen.) Only one will can be offered and accepted to probate, so make sure that your most current will—the one that stipulates your most current wishes—is your *only* will in existence.

Three Common Revocations

A will can be revoked three basic ways:

- ✪ Through a physical act
- ✪ Through a subsequent instrument

✿ Through an operation of law

All states recognize one or more of the preceding ways to revoke a will. Take a quick look at each way.

Revocation by a Physical Act

If you physically destroy the will—burning, tearing, or defacing—it's considered revoked and invalid. All states recognize the revocation of a will by a physical act as long as the testator intended to revoke it. However, the actual wording of each state's statute might vary. For example, Indiana's statute says the testator must "mutilate or destroy." As long as your intention is to revoke the will and you either tear, burn, or strike through each page of the document, you have successfully revoked your old will.

Revocation by a Subsequent Instrument

You can revoke a will by drafting another will or codicil in which you expressly revoke or amend the previous will. As mentioned earlier, you can accomplish this by including a revocation of prior wills clause in your newly created will.

Revocation by an Operation of Law

Upon the subsequent divorce or annulment of the testator, all gifts made to a former spouse under the testator's will are revoked by operation of law.

Additionally, as you learned in Saturday Morning's session, in common law states, a surviving spouse has the right to take against the will his or her entitled intestate share. In this instance, the provisions of your will that concerned your surviving spouse's share are revoked.

Determining When a New Will Is Needed

At the beginning of this book, I strongly advised drafting a new will—or at least amending your existing will—when you encounter significant life changes (for example, marriage, divorce, or the birth of a child). I suggest that you revisit your will every five or 10 years. Perhaps your feelings have changed or a named beneficiary has died. Maybe you have sold or disposed of certain assets or acquired new property.

Many people wonder whether they really need to change their wills when they get divorced. My standard answer is a resounding "Yes!"

Often, I'm asked what effect a divorce has on a will. Actually, state law varies as to how, or if, a final divorce decree or annulment will affect your will. In some states, the decree has no effect at all, and therefore any bequest made in your will to your former spouse will still be honored. (This probably is not what you would like to have happen.)

However, in most states a final divorce or annulment decree will nullify any bequest left to a former spouse. Under this circumstance, if you have not named a successor beneficiary for the particular gift, the unclaimed gift usually passes into the residuary and becomes the property of your residuary beneficiary.

Still in other states, a divorce or annulment decree nullifies or voids your entire will.

CAUTION   Check with an attorney or your state's probate office to determine how a divorce or annulment will affect the validity of your will. If you're in doubt, it's best to draft a new one!

But how can you distinguish between needing an entirely new will and needing just a basic amendment to the original document?

To Draft a New Will, or Not To Draft a New Will?

That certainly is the question.

Determining whether you need to draft a new will (and destroy your current will) or just create a *codicil* (amendment) to your existing will depends on the extent of the changes you are contemplating.

First, take a look at what a codicil is.

A *codicil* is a separate legal document that amends or changes the terms of an existing will—without revoking it entirely—after it has been signed and properly witnessed. Essentially, a codicil acts as a supplement to your will.

NOTE To be valid, a codicil must be executed with the same formalities as a will. Specifically, a codicil must be in writing and witnessed, and it must refer to the will that it seeks to amend or change. Some states recognize a *holographic* (handwritten) codicil as valid, but only if the codicil is written in the testator's own handwriting. To be on the safe side, your best course is to create a typewritten codicil.

A codicil can revive a previously revoked will or validate an instrument that had been improperly executed (under what is considered the *doctrine of incorporation by reference*). It also republishes a will as of the date of the codicil.

For example, say that you draft your first will in April 2000. Ten years from now, you create a new will (in April 2010) *without* destroying the April 2000 will. Five years later, in 2015, you create a codicil that specifically refers to your first will—the April 2000 will.

In this example, your April 2000 will now acts as your controlling will, with a new "republished" date of 2015.

As previously mentioned, however, your April 2000 will must be physically present to be valid. Physically destroying a codicil does not destroy the will, but destroying the will does destroy the codicil to that will. In other words, a codicil does not stand alone without a will.

CODICILS: YOU HAVE TO HAVE INTENT

A codicil will not revive a gift that has been revoked by law, unless there is clear intent on the testator's part to still leave the (revoked) gift to the previously named beneficiary in the will. (This is a bit confusing, so here's a fictitious couple, Mike and Jeanine Smith, who illustrate the preceding point.)

When Mike drafts his will, he leaves the residuary to his then-wife, Jeanine. Several years later, Mike and Jeanine divorce, and Mike does not create a new will at that time. Mike and Jeanine reside in Indiana, a state in which a divorce revokes any bequest or provision in favor of a former spouse.

Three more years pass, and Mike supplements his old will with a codicil (because he now wants to leave a portion of his estate to his favorite attorney and not to Father Phil, the pastor of his church). Although he specifically references his old will, revoking the gift to Father Phil and making a new bequest to the attorney (she did not draft his will, by the way, so this bequest is okay), he does not change the beneficiary of his residuary.

What effect does this have? The general rule in most states is that, although this codicil republishes the will to the date of the newly created codicil, it does not revive the gift to Jeanine *unless* there was clear evidence of Mike's continuing intention to leave the residuary to Jeanine.

If Mike had wanted his former wife to inherit the residue of his estate at his death, he would have been required to expressly state that intention in the codicil he created.

CAUTION

◆ ◆
You can't use a codicil to revive a will that has been physically destroyed.
◆ ◆

If you and your spouse have a child after you draft your will and you plan to create a codicil to update or amend your will, be sure to mention the subsequently born child in your codicil.

Without a codicil, under your previous will, your child would have been considered pretermitted (accidentally left out of your will) and would have been entitled to a share of your probate estate.

However, in many states, if you draft a codicil to your will after your child is born but do not mention the child in the codicil, your failure to mention the child will be considered intentional. Therefore, in this circumstance, the child would not receive anything under the will.

Why? Because the codicil republishes the will as of the date of the codicil and the child will have been born by that date, but the child will not be mentioned in either the will or the codicil.

In case you are still confused about codicils and how they effect a will, take a look at the following sidebar.

DRAFTING YOUR CODICIL: DON'T FORGET JUNIOR

Scenario: Darren and Samantha are married with one child (Tabitha). After Tabitha's birth, Darren drafts a will. Shortly thereafter, Darren and Samantha have a second child (Adam). Darren makes a codicil to his will two years later, in which he specifically refers to his first will, but fails to mention or provide for Adam. How does this affect Adam?

Answer: In most states, Adam can no longer claim to be pretermitted and, therefore, can take nothing under Darren's will.

Storing Your Will

Now that your will is complete, you might be wondering, "Now what do I do with it?" Good question . . . with a simple answer. Keep your document in a safe place that will be easy for your interested parties—specifically your executor—to locate.

If you have a safe deposit box, check with your bank or financial institution to determine whether it will be accessible to your executor, spouse, or other interested parties upon your death. Many states require that the safe deposit box be sealed at death until an audit determines your estate's tax liability. You want your will to be accessible to your executor and other interested parties, so I suggest that you keep your will in a storage box at home with other important papers (such as birth certificates, insurance policies, and so on). If you don't mind your executor knowing your will's contents beforehand, give him or her a copy for safekeeping.

 NOTE If you keep certain investments in your safe deposit box—such as stock certificates or CDs—you can deduct the box's rental fee on your federal income tax return.

Understanding Probate

Although many people don't like to talk about the circumstances surrounding death, most people are curious about what happens to their estate upon their death. At your death, your estate will most likely go through probate. Unless and until it is admitted to probate, a will does not effectively prove title or right of property.

In general, *probate* is a proceeding to establish a will and administer certain assets of the deceased person (*decedent*). It is a state court proceeding in which the authenticity of your will is established. Your will might be proven by the following:

- A self-proving affidavit.
- The testimony of your witnesses.
- The testimony of an expert identifying the handwriting of the testator or a witness. This testimony is permissible only when the witnesses are dead, out-of-state, incapacitated, or cannot be located.

During probate, the following occurs:

- Your personal representative is officially appointed by the court.
- Your nominated guardian is appointed by the court.
- Your taxes and debts (if any) are properly paid.
- Your heirs are identified.
- Your property in your probate estate is distributed according to the specific instructions in your will.

NOTE Typically, a will must be admitted to probate within three years from the date of the testator's death. Or it must be admitted to probate before the court rules that the decedent died intestate and issues a final judgement as to how the decedent's property will be distributed to his or her heirs.

Your executor needs to be able to easily locate your will and then petition the court to admit your will to probate. (This is typically accomplished by filing an application with the probate court in the county in which you reside.)

When a will is offered for probate, the court must first find that the testator is dead and that the will was executed in all respects according to law. After confirming these conditions, the will is admitted to probate as the last will of the deceased testator *unless* objections are filed in a timely manner.

NOTE Before a will can be admitted to probate, the will must be proven by at least one of the witnesses. If all the witnesses are dead, out-of-state, or have become incapacitated since attesting the will, the will is admitted to probate upon the proof of the handwriting of one of the witnesses or of the handwriting of the testator.

On a petition for the qualification or appointment of an executor, the court will issue *letters of administration* (also called *letters testamentary*) giving your executor the power to act for your estate. Your executor will also sign an *oath of personal representation* promising to faithfully perform his or her duties. (Turn to Appendix D to see samples of a Letters Testamentary and an Oath of Personal Representative. Your particular county's probate court will have these forms.)

NOTE Depending on the state in which your will is probated, a hearing might be required to formally appoint your executor.

Normally, your executor will be required to post a *surety bond* (also known as a *performance bond*). However, you can specifically state in your will that no bond need be posted for your executor or personal guardian that you have named for your minor children. (By the way, WillWriter assumes no bond will be required and automatically incorporates language to that effect in your will.)

Once appointed, your executor will notify your named beneficiaries. At this same time, your known creditors will also be notified. The court generally posts a notice in your local and regional newspaper(s), informing creditors of your death and allowing them to file a claim against your estate for monies owed, if any. This notice is commonly referred to as a *notice of administration*. Creditors then typically have a five-month statute of limitations in which to file a claim against your estate. (You can

find samples of a Notice of Administration and a Claimant form—
which is required of all creditors filing a claim against an estate—in
Appendix D.)

NOTE Your estate is responsible for paying the cost of placing the notice in the newspaper.

Your executor will collect or account for your assets and file an inventory
of your estate with the court. Your executor also is responsible for filing
an estate tax return on your behalf with the Internal Revenue Service
(IRS).

CAUTION Check with an attorney or the laws of your state to determine whether your executor will
need to file an income tax return for your estate as well. Typically, if your estate generates more than $600 during the administration, an estate *income* tax return will be
required. Also, remember, if your estate is worth more than $675,000, your executor will
need to file an estate tax return.

As previously mentioned, your executor is required to pay your debts,
your estate taxes, and the costs of administration (including probate costs,
court fees, and so on) before assets can be distributed to your beneficiaries. If your estate does not have enough liquid assets to meet your debts,
assets must be sold to raise money to pay these liabilities. (That's why it's
best to determine how you want these encumbrances handled and to
make a provision stating your wishes in your will.)

Your executor will also file an accounting (called a *notice of final account*)
to be accepted by the probate court. Your executor then petitions the
court to close the estate, and your property is distributed to your named
beneficiaries. (A sample Notice of Final Account form is reprinted in
Appendix D.)

When Probate Is Required

If you own certain property in your name upon your death, your estate must be probated. Any property (personal effects, household furnishings, bank accounts, and so on) left by a will must go through the probate process. Additionally, your executor will need *marketable title* (title that is good and clear and free from any claim) in order to later transfer your property according to the wishes outlined in your will. Only probate can provide such title for your executor.

NOTE Most states allow smaller estates—typically $15,000 or less, but sometimes as much as $150,000—to avoid the normal probate procedures and the associated costs. And many states even eliminate probate if property is left to a spouse. Check with your state's requirements, or check with an attorney in your area, to see whether your estate qualifies.

Benefits of Probate

Probate has its benefits. As you have learned, your will enables you to nominate a personal guardian to care for minor children you might leave at your death. Also, after your will is probated, your creditors are officially put on notice of your death, and the statute of limitations in which to file a claim against your estate begins. If a creditor does not file within the five-month time limit, his or her claim against your estate will expire and be forever barred. Without probate, a creditor could theoretically make a claim against your estate and your beneficiaries for an indefinite period of time.

Avoiding Probate

Your estate is not required by law to go through probate. As you learned previously, only probate property left at your death needs to go through the probate process. Nonprobate property (for example, life insurance proceeds, 401(k) plan proceeds, and pension plan proceeds) does not have to go through probate. Instead, these assets are automatically transferred at your death to the beneficiaries you previously named on the documents themselves.

Probating an estate can be costly. When you add up all the filing fees, executor's fees, attorney's fees, and other costs (such as those for accountants and appraisers), probate can quickly reduce the value of your estate. Also, the probate process can be time consuming, typically lasting anywhere from four months to a year or more. I've personally worked on estates that have been in probate for more than five years.

When you consider the time and cost involved, it is no wonder that many people look for ways to avoid probate.

NOTE Another disadvantage to probate is a lack of privacy. Once a will is admitted to probate, it is a matter of public record. Therefore, anyone can obtain a copy of your will and see to whom you've left your belongings. Privacy regarding specific distributions and bequests is out the window!

Here are some common costs you can expect to incur:

- **Filing fees.** Court filing fees vary from state to state. Typically, the filing fee is $100.

- **Executor's fee.** As previously mentioned, your executor is legally entitled to a fee for performing his or her duties. This fee can range from nothing (if your executor waives the right to a fee) to a percentage (typically two or three percent) of your net probate estate.

- **Attorney's fees and costs.** These costs are for retaining a probate attorney to handle the estate during the probate process. Each state has its own structure for fees that a probate attorney can charge. Fees can range from a lump sum to an hourly rate, depending on the complexity of the estate. (Typically, the more complex the estate, the higher the fee charged by the attorney.)

- **Appraiser's fee.** These costs relate to obtaining a qualified individual to appraise the value of your estate, including specific items within your estate.

- **Surety bond.** Again, this fee varies. However, it's typically $100.

You created a will during the Saturday Evening session, and the property that you left in your will (probate property) must go through the probate process. However, in case you are thinking about restructuring your estate in the future to avoid probate, read on.

Probate Alternatives

You can structure your estate to pass directly to your named beneficiaries without going through probate. The following assets do not require probate:

- Life insurance policies
- Property held as joint tenants with a right of survivorship (ROS)
- Property held as tenants by the entirety
- Pay on death accounts (also called *Totten Trusts*)
- Property transferred by contract
- IRAs
- Pension plans
- 401(k) plans
- Certain types of trusts (for example, Qualified Terminable Property Interest trusts and AB trusts). For more information on QTIP and AB trusts, see the discussion in the Saturday Morning session.

If you are concerned about probate costs, see an attorney who can help you formulate an estate plan designed to reduce these costs. Also, some states allow *unsupervised probate administration,* which is typically faster and cheaper than the traditional supervised administration. Unsupervised probate administration allows your executor to perform a variety of duties without court supervision. (You can find a reprinted Letters Testamentary for Unsupervised Administration form in Appendix D.) Check with an attorney in your area to see whether unsupervised probate is available in your state and whether your estate qualifies.

Will Contests

You've probably found a good deal about contesting wills in movies or books, but it's time to weed out fact from fiction.

In most states, any interested person can contest the validity of a will. However, there is a time limit in which a will can be contested. Typically, a will contest must be filed in the court that has jurisdiction over the probate of the estate no later than five months from the date the will is admitted to probate. The interested person must file his or her written allegations setting forth an objection to the will's validity with the court, and the allegations must be verified by affidavit.

NOTE In a will contest, the contesting party is the plaintiff; your executor and beneficiaries are defendants.

Four Basic Grounds for Contesting Wills

First, will contests are rare, and successful will contests are even more rare. However, in that rare instance in which your will is contested, it will most likely be challenged on one or more of the following grounds:

- Improper execution
- Mental incapacity (or *testamentary capacity*)
- Undue influence
- Fraud or duress

If your will is successfully contested on these grounds, it is invalidated, and your probate estate will pass under the intestate succession laws of your state (see Appendix B for more on intestate law).

Improper Execution

A will contest on the grounds of improper execution is usually brought because the testator failed to have the requisite number of witnesses to his or her will (or a witness is later deemed interested and therefore unqualified). Also, perhaps all witnesses didn't sign in each other's presence (if required), or a witness did not actually witness the testator's signature.

Capacity of the Testator

Your will can be contested on grounds that you were not mentally competent at the time of its drafting (or that you were of unsound mind). If so, your executor or other beneficiaries must prove that you understood the nature of making a will, understood the extent of your estate, and that you knew who would be considered the natural objects of your bounty.

As previously mentioned, there is a presumption that you were competent at the time of drafting your will, which must be overcome before your will can be successfully invalidated.

NOTE   The burden of proof is on the person contesting the will—not on the estate being contested—to prove the testator was not competent when he or she drafted the will.

Undue Influence

If your will is challenged on the grounds of undue influence, the contesting party must prove that you did not draft the instrument of your own free will and volition. Undue influence contests usually claim that testators were coerced into making their wills or certain provisions in it.

In other words, undue influence must be something that destroys the free agency of the testator at the time the will is made, and which, in effect, substitutes the wishes of another for that of the testator. Here are some examples of relationships in which a presumption of undue influence might arise:

- Priest and parishioner
- Attorney and client
- Doctor and patient

Undue influence can be difficult to prove. This is because influence is not considered undue if it merely involves persuasion—a "please" calculated to arouse the testator's sympathy or favor, even with the intent to obtain benefits under a will.

NOTE "Pretty please, Daddy" is not considered undue influence. (Boy, am I lucky!)

Furthermore, general influence over the testator is not enough to invalidate a will. For example, a wife's influence over her husband to leave a portion of his estate to her child by a previous union most likely will not qualify as undue influence. And most states no longer recognize a presumption of undue influence between spouses because it is now common for spouses to discuss estate-planning issues.

NOTE Courts are reluctant to invalidate a will because of undue influence because some influence is proper. Additionally, a determination of what constitutes undue influence is difficult; most often there is little direct evidence to prove that the influence was undue.

A court will consider several factors when examining undue influence:

- Mental and physical capacity of the testator at the will's execution. "Was the testator susceptible to undue influence?" Consider the testator's age, personality, physical and mental health, and ability to handle business affairs.

- Relationship between the testator and the individual who supposedly exercised undue influence (the *influencer*). "What was the relationship between the testator and the influencer; that is, was the influencer in a position to exercise undue influence over the testator?"

- Influencer's involvement in the testator's making of the will or in the testator's decision to make a will. "Did this person have an opportunity to exercise such influence and to cause a wrongful purpose?"

- The extent of the influencer's profit under the testator's will. "Did the influencer inherit a much larger gift or portion of the testator's estate than a reasonable person would expect him or her to receive?"

As with a contest challenging mental capacity, the contestant bears the burden of proving that a testator was unduly influenced into drafting his will or a certain provision in it. The main factor to consider is whether the influencer, by his or her conduct, gained an unfair advantage (by receiving bequests that a reasonable person would regard as improper).

Fraud or Duress

Some fraud claims are similar to claims of undue influence. For example, to prove a testator was fraudulently induced into creating or changing a will, the person contesting the will must prove the following:

- The testator relied upon a beneficiary's false statement of promise.

- That false promise caused the testator to write or revise his or her will to benefit the beneficiary.

Consider the following hypothetical situation.

An 83 year-old, enormously wealthy man meets a young, beautiful woman who lavishes the man with attention and love. (He lavishes her with diamonds and exotic vacations, so loving him is quite easy for her.) The young woman promises to accept his marriage proposal and care for him for the rest of his life (which won't be long) if only he changes his will to provide for her and her young son. The man does, and young and beautiful doesn't (marry him that is). The man dies one month later, without making a new will. What effect does this have?

Most likely, the man's legitimate beneficiaries (his children and grandchildren) would contest the will as being invalid, claiming that old, feeble Grandpa was fraudulently induced into making his will.

It's difficult to prove that a testator was fraudulently induced into creating a will. Again, to successfully invalidate a will, the challenger must show that the testator would not have drafted the will if he or she hadn't been fraudulently induced into doing so.

Other types of fraud, however, are easier to prove. For example, it's relatively easy to prove that the testator was mistakenly tricked into signing a document that was later fraudulently admitted to probate as his or her will. In this situation, the challenger must show only that the testator had no intention of making the signed document his or her will; this can be proven through the testimony of other interested parties or through the testimony of the testator's relatives.

No-Contest Clauses

Take a moment to consider no-contest clauses, which are also referred to by attorneys as *in terrorem clauses.* Most people use no-contest clauses to discourage their beneficiaries from contesting their wills. Such a clause works to disinherit anyone who unsuccessfully contests your will and his or her provision under your will.

 NOTE *In terrorem* is a Latin term that means "in order to frighten."

Following is an example of an acceptable no-contest clause:

> *Should any beneficiary named hereunder contest my will or any of its provisions, the property, share, or interest in my estate left to that contesting beneficiary shall be revoked and shall pass into my residuary or shall be disposed of as though the contesting beneficiary had predeceased me without children.*

NOTE A successful will contest will invalidate not only the no-contest clause, but also the entire will. In this instance, your estate will pass under your state's laws of intestate succession. Therefore, a no-contest clause really works only to disinherit an unsuccessful contestant to your will.

WillWriter automatically provides for a no-contest clause in your will. However, you can delete the provision if you don't want to include a no-contest clause in your will.

CAUTION You might want to consult an attorney if you have any indication that your will might be contested by one of your beneficiaries. Your attorney can help you further safeguard your will against such contests, beyond the inclusion of a no-contest clause.

I've said it before, and I'll say it again: You can't disinherit a spouse. (At least not with information in this book, anyway.) So, a no-contest clause will likely have no effect on your spouse.

Dealing with Uncommon Situations

Here are some final words on some uncommon situations. Although these situations might never apply to you, it never hurts to learn a little about them:

O Murder of the testator

O Adulterous spouse

O Abandonment

States vary slightly in how a beneficiary inherits under these situations. All states, however, *generally* view these circumstances in the same way.

Murder of the Testator

While uncommon, the murder of a testator by a beneficiary in his or her will certainly makes a great movie of the week. But, just in case you are curious as to what would really happen in this situation, wonder no more.

If a named beneficiary is found guilty (or guilty but mentally ill) of murdering or causing the suicide of the testator, the beneficiary will be treated as though he or she predeceased the testator and will not inherit under the testator's will. Simply put, bad deeds will not be rewarded.

This typical rule also applies to life insurance policies. No proceeds will pass to a named beneficiary if that beneficiary is found to have caused the death of the policyholder. Instead, all insurance proceeds will pass to the alternate beneficiary (if you named one) or to the policyholder's (your) estate and will more than likely pass into the residuary.

 NOTE The murder of the testator by a beneficiary is actually just another type of fraud wherein the beneficiary accused of murdering the testator stands to gain from the testator's death and subsequent probate of his will.

Adultery

A more common situation exists when a testator drafts a will leaving the bulk of the estate to his (or her) spouse, only to have the spouse leave the testator for another man (or woman, as the case may be), and then the testator dies before changing his will.

The good news is that, in many states, if either a husband or wife has left his or her spouse and is committing adultery at the time of the spouse's death, the adulterous spouse will not be entitled to a part of the deceased spouse's estate.

NOTE In a recent Indiana case, a court held that a husband was not entitled to a part of his deceased wife's estate because he was living with a "female friend" while his wife—who was suffering from Alzheimer's disease—was living in a nursing home.

However, proving adultery can be an extremely difficult task for your executor and other interested parties to your will—a task that they might not be able to successfully accomplish.

Abandonment

Typically, if you abandon your spouse without *just cause,* you're not entitled to a share of your deceased spouse's estate, even though you normally would be afforded a share under intestate laws.

CAUTION Most states do not define *just cause,* and, as with adultery, it is difficult to prove.

What's Next?

Congratulations! You have finished this book (except for the appendixes, of course)! More important, you have successfully created a will that is legally valid and recognized in your particular state. You and your loved ones are now protected when that unfortunate, yet inevitable, event occurs.

Remember, you can always use WillWriter to create a new will if you change your mind in a few years, or in the event the contents of your estate change.

Now, be honest. Writing your will wasn't too difficult, was it?

I'd ask you whether you had fun, but I don't want to press my luck.

State-By-State Probate Matrix

As you learned in the Friday Evening session, in order to determine whether you meet the necessary criteria to draft a valid, formal will, you must look to your *state of domicile*—your legal and permanent residence.

In this appendix, you will find each state's applicable probate statute as well as its requirements for drafting a valid will. Specifically, you will learn the following:

- The number of witnesses required in your state to make your will valid

- Whether your witnesses can be interested (also a named beneficiary in your will)

- Whether your executor must be a resident of your state

For more information about the preceding topics, you can turn back to the Friday Evening session.

Don't forget that all states require you to be at least 18 years old (19 years old in Wyoming) and to be competent at the time of drafting of a will (which means that you need only minimal ability to perform the act).

Again, if you have questions about your particular state's requirements, you need to review your state's probate statute before proceeding. The applicable statute is listed in the following matrix to aid you in your search.

NOTE I gathered this information from the Cornell University Web site at **www.law.cornell. edu/states/listing.html** and the Indiana University Law School library. Louisiana is not included in the following matrix.

STATE - BY - STATE PROBATE MATRIX

State & Applicable Statute	# of Required Witnesses	Witnesses Interested?	Non-Resident Executor?
Alaska - Tit. 13 / Chap. 16	Min. 2 Witnesses	Yes	Yes
Arizona - Tit. 14	Min. 2 Witnesses	Yes	Yes
Alabama - Tit. 43 / Art. 7	Min. 2 Witnesses	Yes	No Direct Reference
Arkansas - Tit. 28 / Chap. 25	Min. 2 Witnesses	Yes[1]	Yes[2]
California - Prob. Code 6380-6390	Min. 2 Witnesses	Yes	Yes
Colorado - Chap. 15	Min. 2 Witnesses	Yes	Yes
Connecticut - Sect. 8029	Min. 2 Witnesses	Yes[3]	No Direct Reference
Delaware - Tit. 12 / Sect. 202 - 203	Min. 2 Witnesses	Yes	Yes
District of Columbia - Sect. 18	Min. 2 Witnesses	Yes[4]	Yes[5]
Florida - Tit. XLII	Min. 2 Witnesses	Yes	Yes[6]

[1] May be interested, but if only one interested witness, he will receive bequest equal only to that he would have taken intestate.

[2] Non-resident executor must appoint a resident to accept service on his behalf.

[3] Bequest to interested witness shall be void, unless will is legally attested to without signature of witness or unless witness is otherwise an intestate heir.

[4] Interested witness may not take in excess of what he would have been entitled to through intestate succession.

[5] Non-resident executor must prove he has been rightfully appointed as well as submit to jurisdiction within the District of Columbia.

[6] Non-resident executor is permissible as long as the executor is an adopted child or adopted parent, a blood relative, spouse, or spouse of person otherwise qualified to serve as the executor.

STATE - BY - STATE PROBATE MATRIX (CONTINUED)

State & Applicable Statute	# of Required Witnesses	Witnesses Interested?	Non-Resident Executor?
Georgia - Chap. 53	Min. 2 Witnesses	Yes[7]	Yes
Hawaii - Tit. 30A	Min. 2 Witnesses	Yes	Yes
Idaho - Tit. 15 / Chap. 2 / Part 6	Min. 2 Witnesses	Yes	Yes[8]
Illinois - 755 / 4 & 5	Min. 2 Witnesses	Yes[9]	Yes[10]
Indiana - Chap. 29 / Sect. 1	Min. 2 Witnesses	Yes[11]	Yes[12]
Iowa - Section 633	Min. 2 Witnesses	Yes[13]	Yes
Kansas - Chap. 59	Min. 2 Witnesses	Yes	No Direct Reference
Kentucky - Sect. 394	Min. 2 Witnesses	Yes[14]	Yes
Louisiana	N/A	N/A	N/A
Maine - Chapters 2 & 4	Min. 2 Witnesses	Yes	Yes[15]

[7] Witness to the will may be interested though the interested witness loses his right to the bequest if there were not two other disinterested witnesses who also attested the will.

[8] Non-resident executor must submit authenticated copies of appointment as well as post bond and agree to jurisdiction within Idaho.

[9] Bequeath must not exceed the value of intestate property interested witness would be otherwise entitled to.

[10] Non-resident executor must produce affidavit showing authority to act as executor.

[11] Interested witness may not take in excess of intestate share unless otherwise proven by such witness that bequest was not unduly influenced.

[12] Non-resident executor must post a bond and appoint resident to receive service as well as agree to jurisdiction in Indiana.

[13] Interested witness may not take in excess of intestate share.

[14] Interested witness may not take in excess of intestate share.

[15] Non-resident executors must provide proof of authority to act under the will.

STATE - BY - STATE PROBATE MATRIX (CONTINUED)

State & Applicable Statute	# of Required Witnesses	Witnesses Interested?	Non-Resident Executor?
Maryland - Art. Estates & Trusts / Sec. 4	Min. 2 Witnesses	No Direct Reference	Yes
Massachusetts - Sect. 192 & 193	Min. 2 Witnesses	Yes[16]	Yes
Michigan - Chap. 720	Min. 2 Witnesses	Yes[17]	Yes
Minnesota - Sect. 524.2 & 524.3	Min. 2 Witnesses	No Direct Reference	Yes
Mississippi - Tit. 91 / Chap 5 / Sect. 1 & 13	Min. 2 Witnesses	Yes	Yes
Missouri - Chap. 474	Min. 2 Witnesses	Yes[18]	Yes
Montana - Chap. 72	Min. 2 Witnesses	No Direct Reference	No
Nebraska - Chap. 30	Min. 2 Witnesses	Yes[19]	Yes
Nevada - Sect. 133 & 139	Min. 2 Witnesses	Yes[20]	No
New Hampshire - Chap. 56	Min. 2 Witnesses	Yes[21]	No[22]

[16] Interested witness may not take under will unless two other non-interested attested the will.

[17] Interested witness will not be permitted to receive bequests under the will.

[18] Interested witness may not take in excess of intestate share unless two other disinterested witnesses also subscribe.

[19] Unless at least one other disinterested witness, interested witness may not receive share exceeding intestate entitlement.

[20] All devises to interested witness void unless two non-interested witnesses also attest the will.

[21] Unless two other disinterested witnesses attest, bequest to interested witness is void.

[22] If court finds compelling reasons for allowing non-resident executor, then such executor may be allowed to serve.

STATE - BY - STATE PROBATE MATRIX (CONTINUED)

State & Applicable Statute	# of Required Witnesses	Witnesses Interested?	Non-Resident Executor?
New Jersey - Chap 3B	Min. 2 Witnesses	Yes	No Direct Reference
New Mexico - Chap. 45	Min. 2 Witnesses	Yes	Yes[23]
New York - Parts 2 & 3	Min. 2 Witnesses	Yes[24]	No Direct Reference
North Carolina - Chap. 31	Min. 2 Witnesses	Yes[25]	Yes
North Dakota - Chap. 30	Min. 2 Witnesses	Yes	Yes[26]
Ohio - Sect. 2107	Min. 2 Witnesses	Yes[27]	No
Oklahoma - Chap. 58 & 84	Min. 2 Witnesses	No Direct Reference	Yes
Oregon - Sect. 112 & 113	Min. 2 Witnesses	Yes	Yes[28]
Pennsylvania - Tit. 20	Min. 2 Witnesses[29]	No Direct Reference	No Direct Reference
Rhode Island - Chap. 33	Min. 2 Witnesses[30]	Yes[31]	Yes[32]

[23] Non-resident executor is allowable so long as they agree to jurisdiction in New Mexico.

[24] Interested witness may only receive share in excess of intestate interest if two additional disinterested witnesses attest to the will.

[25] Interested witnesses will take nothing unless two additional disinterested witnesses attest to the will.

[26] Non-resident executors must consent to jurisdiction within North Dakota.

[27] Interested witnesses shall take only a value equal to the value of their intestate share unless two other disinterested witnesses attest.

[28] Non-resident executor must consent to jurisdiction in Oregon.

[29] Two witnesses are only required, however, if one other than the testator executes the will.

[30] No formal attestation language is required, however.

[31] Interested witnesses may not receive bequests under the will.

[32] Executor may be non-resident as long as he is not a trust administrator.

STATE - BY - STATE PROBATE MATRIX (CONTINUED)

State & Applicable Statute	# of Required Witnesses	Witnesses Interested?	Non-Resident Executor?
South Carolina - Chap. 62	Min. 2 Witnesses	Yes[33]	Yes[34]
South Dakota - Chap. 29A	Min. 2 Witnesses	Yes	Yes[35]
Tennessee - Chap. 32	Min. 2 Witnesses[36]	Yes[37]	Yes[38]
Texas - Tit. IV	Min. 2 Witnesses	Yes[39]	Yes[40]
Utah - Chap. 75	Min. 2 Witnesses	Yes	Yes[41]
Vermont - Chap. 14	Min. 3 Witnesses	Yes[42]	No[43]

[33] Witnesses may be interested in South Carolina though any devise exceeding value of intestate entitlement will be null unless will attested to by two additional disinterested witnesses.

[34] Foreign executor permissible if the executor consents to jurisdiction in South Carolina.

[35] Non-resident executor must consent to jurisdiction within South Dakota.

[36] While two witnesses are required, there is no formal attestation language provided under Tennessee law.

[37] If will is attested to by witnesses, interested witness may not take bequeath valued greater than intestate share unless two additional disinterested witnesses also attest.

[38] Non-resident executors must consent to jurisdiction in Tennessee and may only serve if a resident executor is also named to serve.

[39] Interested witness may take bequeath equal in value to his intestate share unless it can otherwise be established that no undue influence took place.

[40] Executor may be non-resident but must appoint resident to accept service of process and must consent to jurisdiction in Texas.

[41] Non-resident executor must consent to jurisdiction in Utah.

[42] Witnesses may be interested though bequest is void unless will is attested by three or more disinterested witnesses. This provision applies to spouse of interested witnesses as well.

[43] The court may deem that a non-resident executor is allowable if spouse or children of testator so petition.

STATE - BY - STATE PROBATE MATRIX (CONTINUED)

State & Applicable Statute	# of Required Witnesses	Witnesses Interested?	Non-Resident Executor?
Virginia - Chap. 64.1	Min. 2 Witnesses	Yes	Yes[44]
Washington - Chap. 11	Min. 2 Witnesses	Yes[45]	Yes[46]
W. Virginia - Chap. 41 & 44	Min. 2 Witnesses	Yes[47]	Yes[48]
Wisconsin - Sect. 853 & 851	Min. 2 Witnesses	No	Yes[49]
Wyoming - Chap. 2	Min. 2 Witnesses	Yes[50]	Yes[51]

[44] Non-resident may serve as executor only if additional resident executor is named to serve or if non-resident executor is parent, spouse, child, or sibling of the testator.

[45] There will be a rebuttable presumption that witness procured bequests through duress, fraud, or undue influence unless two additional disinterested witnesses also attested. If the presumption is not rebutted, witness shall take share equal to that which he would have been entitled to through intestate succession.

[46] Non-resident executor must consent to jurisdiction in Washington.

[47] Witness may be interested, however, unless the will can be otherwise proved without witness, he shall be entitled only to that which he would have taken under intestate succession.

[48] Non-resident executor must consent to jurisdiction in West Virginia and may be required to post a performance bond.

[49] Non-resident executor is permissible if executor appoints resident to receive service of process in Wisconsin.

[50] Interested witness may not take under the will a value greater than that which he would have received under intestate succession unless there are two additional disinterested witnesses who have attested.

[51] Executor may be a non-resident but he must appoint a resident for service of process.

APPENDIX B

Intestate Succession

To recap from the Friday Evening session, *intestate succession* specifies who is entitled to receive your property when you die without a will. You need to understand how, and to whom, your property will be distributed if you die without a will—for example, in case any of the following occur:

- Your will is deemed invalid. (For example, you did not adhere to your state's requirements when drafting your will.)

- Your will is successfully contested. (Will contests are discussed in detail during the Sunday Evening session.)

- You live in a common law state, and your surviving spouse chooses to take against the will. (I explain common law states and a spouse's right to take against the will in the Saturday Morning session.)

- You do not name a residuary beneficiary in your will. (Residuary beneficiaries are discussed in detail during the Saturday Afternoon session.)

In this appendix, you will learn how states typically handle intestate succession. I have included several examples of who inherits when you die without a will. Who knows, one of the examples may resemble your own situation.

Understanding Intestate Succession

To better understand intestate succession, first look at what a surviving spouse is entitled to inherit under intestate succession laws.

In most states, your surviving spouse receives the following share of your probate estate if you die without a will:

- One-half of the probate estate if you are survived by at least one child or by *issue* of at least one deceased child (that is, your grand-children from a deceased child). Your surviving child or children share the remaining half of the estate.

  For example, say that you die with a spouse and three children. Your spouse will take one-half of your estate, and your three children will share the remaining one-half interest equally (each child receives one-sixth interest).

- Three-fourths of the net probate estate if you have no surviving issue but are survived by one or both parents. Your surviving parent(s) receive the remaining one-fourth of the estate.

- The entire net probate estate if you have no surviving issue or parents.

The conditions outlined in the preceding list are effective only if your surviving spouse is the biological or adoptive parent of your surviving children.

If the surviving spouse is considered a second or subsequent spouse with whom you did not, at any time, have children *and* you left surviving children (or their descendants) from a previous spouse, the surviving subsequent, childless spouse is entitled to only one-third of your real property. However, he or she will receive one-half of your personal property. If you had no children at any time, a second or subsequent spouse is treated like a first spouse.

Again, if you have neither a spouse nor children when you die, your probate estate passes to other close heirs (for example, your parents, siblings, nieces, nephews, grandparents, aunts, uncles, and cousins).

General Intestate Succession Laws

Although states vary slightly in regard to the distribution of probate property upon an intestate's death, all states adhere to the general order of succession shown in Table B-1.

TABLE B-1 HOW MOST STATES HANDLE INTESTATE SUCCESSION

Your Status upon Death	How Your Estate Is Handled
Unmarried, no children, living parent(s) and siblings	Entire estate passes to your parents and siblings equally.*
Unmarried, no children, parents deceased, surviving siblings	Entire estate passes to siblings equally.
Unmarried, no children, parents deceased, no surviving siblings, surviving grandparents	Entire estate passes to living grandparents equally.
Unmarried, no children, parents deceased, no siblings, grandparents deceased	Entire estate passes to living aunts and uncles equally. Any child of a deceased aunt or uncle (cousin) will be entitled to his or her parent's share.
Unmarried, living children, surviving parents	Entire estate passes to children equally.
Unmarried, no relatives within *sixth degree***	Entire estate passes to the state (also known as *escheating*).
Married, no kids, one or more surviving parents	One-fourth of your estate passes to your living parent(s). Three-fourths passes to your spouse.
Married with children	One-half of your estate passes to your surviving spouse. One-half is shared equally among your children.

*Note, however, that in most states, if the intestate had no children, parent(s) never take less than one-fourth of their deceased child's probate estate. For example, if you had three siblings at your death, each surviving parent would be entitled to one-fourth of your estate (one-half the total). Your three siblings would share the remaining one-half (one-sixth each).

**Within the sixth degree means that the intestate left no surviving spouse, children, grandchildren, great-grandchildren, parents, siblings, nieces and nephews, grandparents, aunts, uncles, and cousins. (Jump ahead to Figure B-13 for an illustration of which heirs qualify as being within the sixth degree to the intestate.)

Examples of Intestate Succession

This section includes examples that show how the majority of states handle particular intestate succession issues. For the purpose of these examples, you take a look at Adam and his family. In each example, you assume that Adam dies without a will.

Example One

Adam is married to Eve. They have four adult children named Robert, Wilma, Edward, and Betty. Robert has one child named Naomi. Wilma has two children named Jack and Jill. Edward has no children. Betty has three children named Donald, Kelli, and Nikki. Adam's parents—John and Mary—are both alive; he has one sister, Lucy, and one brother, Charlie (see Figure B-1).

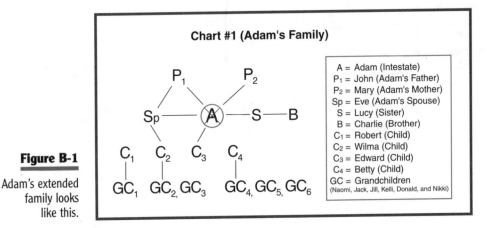

Figure B-1

Adam's extended family looks like this.

NOTE   I know. It's all rather confusing. That's why I provided the illustrations in the figures that follow. Also, please note that in the figures, I use circles with crosses to identify those who have died.

Question: In this example, who will inherit Adam's probate estate?

Answer: In most states, one-half of Adam's probate estate will pass to his surviving spouse (Eve) and the remaining one-half will be shared equally between his four children (Robert, Wilma, Edward, and Betty), with each child receiving one-eighth of Adam's estate.

Example Two

Now, suppose that Adam is a bachelor. He hasn't met Eve, and he has no children. Both parents are still alive, as are his siblings.

Question: Who will inherit Adam's estate at his death? (See Figure B-2.)

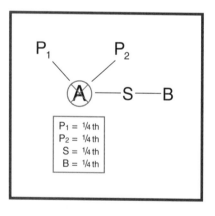

Figure B-2

Note that Adam has neither a spouse nor children at his death.

Answer: In most states, Adam's parents would share his estate equally with his two siblings (Lucy and Charlie).

NOTE

Parents and siblings share equally. However, each parent's share *cannot* be less than one-quarter of the decedent's estate. If Adam had another brother, his parents would share one-half of his estate, and his three siblings would share equally in the remaining one-half estate (each sibling would receive one-sixth of Adam's estate).

Example Three

Now, assume that Adam's parents (John and Mary) both predecease Adam. He is not married, and he has no children. His brother, Charlie, died before Adam, and Charlie left two children (Patty and Cathy).

Question: Who gets what? (See Figure B-3.)

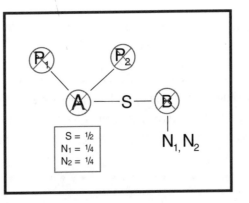

Figure B-3

Adam's brother (Charlie) predeceased Adam, leaving children (Adam's nieces) at his death.

Answer: Adam's sister (Lucy) will receive one-half of Adam's estate. The remaining one-half (which would have gone to Adam's brother, Charlie, had Charlie been alive at the time of Adam's death) will be shared equally between Charlie's children (Patty and Cathy, who are Adam's nieces).

Example Four

In this example, Adam and Eve are married with the aforementioned children (Robert, Wilma, Edward, and Betty). Eve has predeceased Adam. Both of Adam's parents are alive, as are his siblings.

Question: How will Adam's estate be distributed upon his death? (See Figure B-4.)

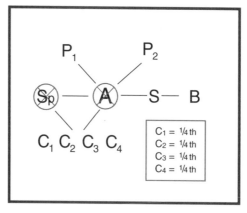

Figure B-4

An intestate's surviving children share his estate only with his surviving spouse.

Answer: Adam's children will share his estate equally, with each child receiving one-fourth of his estate.

NOTE In this example, neither Adam's parents nor his siblings are entitled to a share of his probate estate because he has surviving children at his death. Adam's grandchildren will not inherit a portion of his estate because their parents (Adam's children) are alive at his death.

Example Five

In this example, Adam and Eve are married with the aforementioned children (Robert, Wilma, Edward, and Betty). Eve has predeceased Adam. Both of Adam's parents are alive, as are his siblings. However, Wilma (Adam's daughter) also has predeceased him. Wilma is survived by her two children, Jack and Jill, who are Adam's grandchildren.

Question: What effect does Wilma's death have on Adam's estate? (See Figure B-5.)

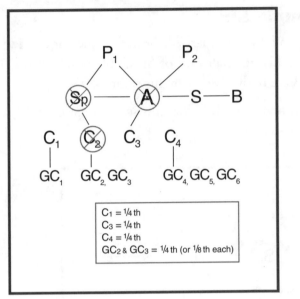

Figure B-5

Grandchildren are entitled to a portion of an intestate's estate only if their parent (the intestate's child) is no longer living.

$C_1 = \frac{1}{4}$ th
$C_3 = \frac{1}{4}$ th
$C_4 = \frac{1}{4}$ th
GC_2 & $GC_3 = \frac{1}{4}$ th (or $\frac{1}{8}$ th each)

Answer: Adam's estate will be split as follows:

✪ One-fourth to his son Robert

✪ One-fourth to his son Edward

✪ One-fourth to his daughter Betty

✪ One-fourth to his grandchildren (Jack and Jill), who will share it equally

NOTE

In this example, Jack and Jill are sharing their mother's one-fourth share of Adam's estate *per stirpes*. *Per stirpes* refers to a distribution whereby the beneficiaries take, by representation, the share that their ancestors would have taken.

You seem to be getting the hang of it! But try a few more, just to be sure.

Example Six

Adam and Eve are married; however, once again, Eve has predeceased Adam. This time, all four of his children also died before him. Adam's parents are both alive, as are his siblings.

Question: What effect does this scenario have on Adam's estate? (See Figure B-6.)

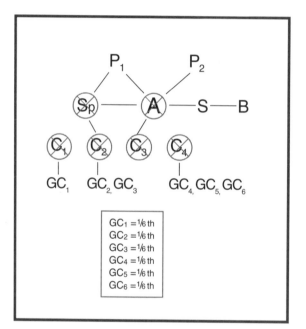

Figure B-6

Descendants of an intestate (children, grandchildren) only share with each other or with an intestate's surviving spouse.

Answer: Adam's living grandchildren will share his estate equally.

NOTE

In this example, Adam's grandchildren are all taking equally (one-sixth each) and not by representation or per stirpes (one-third for Katie, one-sixth each for Jack and Jill, and one-ninth each for Donald, Kelli, and Nikki). This is because Adam left no living children at his death. Thus, all grandchildren are considered the same degree from Adam. If all heirs are of the same degree from the decedent, they take equally. Heirs of different degrees take by representation.

Example Seven

In this example, Adam and Eve are married but they have no children. Adam's mother (Mary) and siblings (Lucy and Charlie) are still alive.

Question: How will Adam's estate be distributed upon his death? (See Figure B-7.)

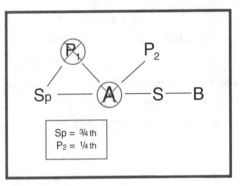

Figure B-7

An intestate's surviving spouse shares only with the intestate's children or parents.

Answer: Eve will receive three-fourths of her husband's probate estate. Adam's surviving parent (Mary) will receive the remaining one-fourth of his estate.

NOTE Even if both of Adam's parents had survived him, in most states, they would be entitled to only one-fourth of his estate—with his surviving spouse still taking three-fourths of the probate estate.

Example Eight

Adam is married to Eve, but they have no children. Both of Adam's parents are dead. His siblings, however, are both alive.

Question: Who will inherit Adam's probate estate at his death? (See Figure B-8.)

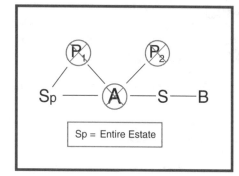

Figure B-8

An intestate's surviving spouse never shares with the intestate's siblings.

Sp = Entire Estate

Answer: Adam's surviving spouse (Eve) will inherit Adam's entire estate. Adam's siblings will not inherit any of his probate estate because only a decedent's surviving issue, or surviving parents, can share with a spouse.

NOTE

Your surviving spouse never takes less than one-half of your net probate estate. Also, your surviving spouse can be entitled to the entire net probate estate if you had no children or grandchildren *and* your parents are dead.

Example Nine

Adam is married to Eve, but they have no children. Eve has predeceased Adam, as have both his parents. His siblings (Lucy and Charlie), however, are both alive.

To make it a bit more interesting, say that Adam's grandmother (Hilda) is still alive (she loves her yogurt!).

Question: How will this affect Adam's probate estate? (See Figure B-9.)

Answer: Adam's siblings (Lucy and Charlie) will share Adam's estate equally. Adam's grandmother (Hilda) will take nothing.

Figure B-9

An intestate's surviving grandparent is further removed from the intestate than his surviving siblings.

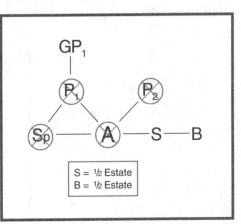

NOTE

In most states, a grandparent never takes under intestate succession laws as long as the decedent is survived by one or more siblings. In this example, Grandma receives a share of Adam's estate only if Adam's siblings (Lucy and Charlie) predecease him *and* leave no issue (Adam's nieces and nephews).

Example Ten

In this example, Adam is a bachelor. (This seems more humane than killing off Eve every time.) Adam has no children, and both his parents died before him. Adam was an only child (so he had no siblings). His grandmother (Hilda) was not so fortunate this time—an expired cup of yogurt did her in. Adam has one living aunt (Gladys) and two uncles (Larry and Moe). Moe died several years ago, leaving two children (Melba and William).

Question: How will Adam's estate be distributed upon his death? (See Figure B-10.)

Answer: Adam's estate will be split equally between his aunt and uncles, with each entitled to a one-third share of his estate. Because his Uncle Moe is deceased, however, his one-third share will be split equally between his children (Melba and William, Adam's cousins).

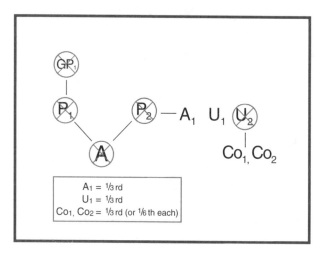

Figure B-10

An intestate's cousin inherits only if his or her parent (the intestate's aunt or uncle) is no longer living.

NOTE In this example, Melba and William are taking, by representation, the share their father would have taken.

Example Eleven

Adam is married to Eve, but they have no children. Eve has yet again predeceased Adam. Both of Adam's parents are also dead. Adam's sister (Lucy) and brother (Charlie) predeceased Adam, but Charlie left two surviving daughters (Patty and Cathy, Adam's nieces.). Adam has one living aunt (Gladys) and two uncles (Larry and Moe). Moe died several years ago, leaving two children (Melba and William, who are Adam's cousins).

Question: How will Adam's estate be distributed upon his death? (See Figure B-11.)

Answer: Adam's nieces (Patty and Cathy) will share Adam's estate equally. His living aunt, uncle, and cousins are not entitled to a portion of his estate because they are legally considered to be further removed from Adam than his nieces. Intestate succession rules always give preference to the heirs of a closer degree to the intestate.

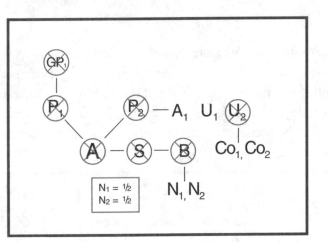

Figure B-11

An intestate's nieces and nephews are considered to be of a closer degree to the intestate than aunts, uncles or cousins.

Example Twelve

Adam is unmarried and has no children. Both Adam's parents and grand-parents are dead. Adam was an only child (he had no siblings), and he had no aunts or uncles (his parents were also "only children").

Question: How will Adam's estate be distributed upon his death?

Answer: Adam's entire estate will pass to the state. Scary, huh?

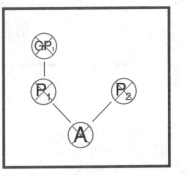

Figure B-12

If an intestate is not survived by heirs within the sixth degree, his or her estate will become property of the state.

No Takers?

Depending on your state laws, if no relatives or heirs are alive at your death, your estate would then *escheat* to the state. Property escheats to the state only if you die without a will and there are no surviving relatives within the sixth degree. (See Figure B-13 for an illustration of which heirs are considered to be within the sixth degree—relationship-wise—of the intestate.)

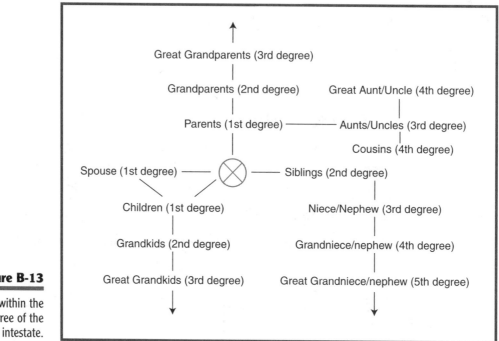

Figure B-13

Heirs within the sixth degree of the intestate.

Take a Break

Okay! Enough about intestate succession for now. It's time to take a short break. Now's a good time to run to the video store and rent that new release that you've been wanting to see.

Intestate Succession Rules for the Illegitimate and Adopted Child

Now that you have a basic understanding of state intestate laws, you might want to look at how certain heirs, specifically illegitimate and adopted children, inherit from a deceased parent who dies without a will.

The following information is a general overview of how states typically deal with such situations. However, it is always best to check your state's law in case you have any questions.

FIND IT ON THE WEB

You can check with a family law or probate attorney in your area or simply log onto Cornell University's Web site at **www.law.cornell.edu/states/listings.html**. Cornell has posted all states' statutes, excluding Louisiana, on its Web site.

Children Born out of Wedlock

Children born out of wedlock—sometimes referred to as *illegitimate children*—are also entitled to a share of their deceased parents' intestate estate. This can be tricky. The general rule followed by most states is that a child born out of wedlock will inherit from, by, and through the mother (maternal side), just as a legitimate child would. A child born out of wedlock will inherit from, by, and through the biological father (paternal side) only in the following instances:

- ✪ Paternity is established in a court action filed during the father's lifetime or within five months following the father's death.
- ✪ The father marries the mother and acknowledges that he fathered the child.

NOTE

The testimony of the mother is admissible during the court proceeding to establish paternity. However, this testimony is not sufficient to prove paternity unless it is corroborated.

BE SURE TO ESTABLISH PATERNITY WHILE DAD IS ALIVE

Question: I have a 12-year-old son whose biological father died last year, leaving no will. Although he had never met his father and his father never acknowledged him as his son, isn't my son entitled to something?

Answer: Most likely, no. In many states, unless paternity was established in a court proceeding during the father's lifetime or within five months following his death, a child born out of wedlock cannot claim a share of the biological father's estate. Most courts interpret this statute to mean that an action to establish paternity must be filed at least within five months from the date of death, although paternity does not actually have to be proven within the five months. Depending on when his biological father died, your son's claim might be barred. Check with an attorney in your state to be sure.

Adopted Children

For purposes of intestate succession, the majority of states treat an adopted child as the natural child of the adopting parents. However, there can be no double dipping—meaning that the child cannot inherit from the adopting parents and from the biological parents *unless* he or she inherits through a will.

 NOTE In most states, once a child is adopted, that child no longer is considered a child of his natural or biological parents—nor is he considered a child of any previous adopting parents.

APPENDIX C

Estate Inventory Worksheet

In this appendix, you will find an Estate Inventory Worksheet to help you record your assets—what you own and how you own it.

You can use the completed worksheet to calculate your estate net worth (that is, your total assets minus your total liabilities). After you determine your estate net worth, you can establish whether and how your estate might be subject to federal estate taxes at your death.

You can also use the worksheet to begin determining to whom (called your *beneficiaries*) you want to leave your property.

Estate Inventory Worksheet

Name: _____

Social Security No.: _____ Birth Date: _____

Address: _____ City: _____ State: _____ Zip: _____

Spouse's Name: _____

Social Security No.: _____ Birth Date: _____

List children's full legal names and birth dates, if applicable:

1. _____

2. _____

3. _____

4. _____

5. _____

List grandchildren's full legal names and birth dates, if applicable:

1. _____

2. _____

3. _____

4. _____

5. _____

ASSETS

Real Estate (home, vacation property, other lands)

Type / Description	Address	How Owned / Held	Purchase Price	Mortgage Amount	Current Value

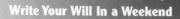

Accounts (checking accounts, savings accounts, certificates of deposit, mutual funds, money markets)

Type of Account	Institution Name	Account Number	How Owned	Current Value

Stocks and Bonds

Company Name	How Owned	Quantity of Stock Held	Cost	Current Value

Business Interests (sole proprietorships, partnerships, corporations)

Business Name	Form of Business	Ownership Interest	How Owned	Value of Interest

Motor Vehicles (automobiles, RVs, planes, boats, motorcycles)

Type / Make	Year / Model	How Owned	Purchase Price	Current Value

Miscellaneous Property (antiques, art, jewelry, home furnishings, clothing, collectibles, tools, sports equipment, pets, etc.)

Type of Property / Description	How Owned	Current Value

Life Insurance

Institution Name	Policy Number	Policy Owner	Name of Insured	Beneficiaries	Face Value	Cash Value

Retirement Benefits (IRA, Keogh, 401(k), pension and profit sharing)

Type of Plan	Company Name	Owner	Beneficiary	Current Value

Other Assets (including inheritances and intangible assets such as copyrights, trademarks, patents)

Type of Assets / Description	How Owned	Current Value

Total Value of Assets: _____

LIABILITIES

(Including credit card debt, owed child support, legal judgments, mortgage(s), bank loans, and other personal loans)

Type of Liability / Description	Who Owes	Amount Owed

Total Liabilities: _____

Estate Net Worth: _____
(total value assets minus total liabilities)

Probate
Forms

The following documents are actual forms from the Probate Division of the Marion County Superior Court in Indiana. Although county forms may vary slightly, the forms in this appendix provide a general overview of the types of documents that may be required of your estate.

In this appendix, you will find the following sample forms:

❖ **Oath of Personal Representative.** A document filed with the probate court in your county, wherein your executor swears to discharge his or her duties faithfully and according to the law in your particular state.

❖ **Letters Testamentary (also commonly referred to as Letters of Administration).** A document issued by the court admitting your will to probate and authorizing your executor to legally administer your estate.

❖ **Letters Testamentary for Unsupervised Administration.** A document issued by the court that admits your will to probate and authorizes your executor to legally administer your estate without court supervision.

❖ **Notice of Administration (sometimes referred to as Notice to Creditors).** The court's official notification to your creditors giving them a certain amount of time to file a claim against your estate.

❖ **Statement of Claimant.** The form that creditors filing claims against your estate are required to file.

❖ **Notice of Final Account.** A court notice informing all interested persons that a final accounting of your estate has been filed and that your executor has petitioned for the estate to be closed and your property to be distributed according to the terms of your will.

STATE OF INDIANA   )   IN THE MARION SUPERIOR COURT
)SS: PROBATE DIVISION
COUNTY OF MARION   )   CAUSE NO. _____

IN THE MATTER OF   )
THE ESTATE OF: .   )
)
_____   )

OATH OF PERSONAL REPRESENTATIVE

I, _____, swear that I will faithfully
discharge my duties as personal representative of the estate, according to law, so help me
God.

_____
Personal Representative

_____
Personal Representative

Subscribed and sworn before me, this _____ day of _____, _____

_____
Clerk, Marion Superior Court, Probate Division

Personal Representative's Address:_____
_____ Zip Code: _____
Personal Representative's Date of Birth: _____-_____-_____ S.S. No. _____

Personal Representative's Address: _____
_____ Zip Code: _____
Personal Representative's Date of Birth: _____-_____-_____ S.S. No. _____

Figure D-1

Your executor may be required to sign an oath with the probate court upon seeking appointment as your personal representative.

LETTERS TESTAMENTARY

Cause No. _____

STATE OF INDIANA, MARION COUNTY, Sct:

I, SARAH M. TAYLOR, Clerk of the Marion Superior Court, Probate Division, State of Indiana, do hereby Certify that the last Will and Testament of _____, deceased, has been duly admitted to probate and recorded in said Court, and _____ _____ having been given bond or Trust Oath and duly qualified as _____ is duly authorized and empowered to take upon _____self the administration of said estate according to law and to carry out the terms of such will.

WITNESS my hand and seal of said Court, at the City of Indianapolis, Indiana, this _____ day of _____, _____

_____, Clerk
Marion Superior Court, Probate Division

STATE OF INDIANA, MARION COUNTY, Sct:

I, SARAH M. TAYLOR, Clerk of the Marion Superior Court, Probate Division, State of Indiana, the same being a Court of Record, and having within Marion County exclusive probate jurisdiction, do hereby certify the foregoing to be a true and complete copy of the LETTERS TESTAMENTARY granted and issued to _____ _____ on the estate of _____ late of said County deceased, and that said Letters Testamentary are still in force, and all the legal acts of said Execut____ entitled to full faith and credit, as fully appears from the records of said Court in my custody as such Clerk, and on file in my office.

IN TESTIMONY WHEREOF, I hereunto affix the seal of said Court and subscribe my name, at the City of Indianapolis, Indiana, this _____ day of _____, _____

_____, Clerk

Figure D-2

A Letters Testamentary gives your executor the legal authority to administer your estate and to carry out the terms of your will.

Estate of _____

Cause No. _____

LETTER TESTAMENTARY (UNSUPERVISED ADMINISTRATION)

State of Indiana, Marion County, Sct:
  To Whom These Presents Shall Come, Greeting:

  I, SARAH M. TAYLOR, Clerk of the Marion Superior Court, Probate Division, within and for said County and State of Indiana, do hereby certify that the last Will and Testament of:
_____ deceased, late of said County, has been duly admitted and recorded in said Court, and _____
_____ qualified as personal representative and is duly authorized and empowered to administer said estate according to law, and to carry out the terms of such will.

  WITNESS my hand and the seal of said Court, at the City of Indianapolis, Indiana, this _____ day of _____, _____

_____
Marion Superior Court, Probate Division

  In accordance with the provisions of Indiana Code sections 29-1-7.5-1, 29-1-7.5-8 the court granted a petition for Administration without court supervision. The personal representative may do all of the things provided for in section 29-1-7.5-3 without order of the Court, which included the following:

1. Acquire or dispose of an asset, including land in this or another state, for cash or on credit, at public or private sale.
2. Vote stocks or other securities in person or by general limited proxy.
3. Hold security in the name of a nominee or in other form without disclosure of the interest of the estate.
4. Sell, mortgage, or lease any real or personal property of the estate or any interest therein for cash, credit, or for part cash and part credit, and with or without security for unpaid balances.
5. Distribute assets of the estate upon such terms as he may impose.
6. Perform any other act necessary or appropriate to administer the estate.
7. These letters of unsupervised administration remain in effect unless revoked by the Court as provided in section 29-1-7.5-2.

Figure D-3

A Letters Testamentary for Unsupervised Administration allows your executor to administer your estate and to carry out the terms of your will without court supervision.

Attorney:

_____

_____

_____

_____

NOTICE OF ADMINISTRATION

In the Marion Superior Court, Probate Division

In the matter of the Estate of _____, deceased.

Cause Number _____

Notice is hereby given that _____ was on the _____ day of _____, _____, appointed personal representative of the estate of _____, deceased.

All persons who have claims against against this estate, whether or not now due, must file the claim in the office of the clerk of this court within five (5) months from the date of the first publication of this notice, or within one (1) year after the decedent's death, whichever is earlier, or the claims will be forever barred.

Dated at Indianapolis, Indiana, this _____ day of _____, _____

_____
Clerk of the Marion Superior Court,
Probate Division

Figure D-4

Legal notice is placed by the court asking creditors to file a claim against the estate within a set period of time, typically five months from notice publication or one year from the decedent's death, whichever is earlier.

STATE OF INDIANA   )   Claim No. _____

County of Marion   )

IN THE MARION SUPERIOR COURT, PROBATE DIVISION

In re the Estate of:

Deceased: _____   Cause No. _____

CLAIM OF: _____

CLAIMANT'S NAME

Statement of Claim:

_____

_____

_____

_____

_____

(Attach additional pages as needed.)

I do solemnly swear that this claim, after deducting all credits, set-offs and deductions to which the estate is entitled, is justly due and wholly unpaid, so help me God.

Claimant's Signature_____

Printed Name_____

Address:_____

Street   Telephone

_____

City   State   Zip

Subscribed and sworn to before me this _____ day of _____, _____

Notary Public or Clerk of the Marion Superior Court, Probate Division

IC 29-1-14-1; All claims against a decedent's estate, other than expenses of administration and claims of the United States, and of the the state and any subdivision thereof, whether due or to become due, absolute or contingent, liquidated or unliquidated, founded on contract or otherwise, shall be forever barred against the estate, ther personal representative, the heirs, devisees and legatees of the decedent, unless filed with the court in which such estate is being administered within:

(1) Five (5) months after the date of the first published notice to creditors; or

(2) Three (3) months after the court has revoked probate of a will, in accordance with

IC 29-1-7-21, if the claimant was named as a beneficiary in that revoked will; whichever is later.

(b) No claim shall be allowed whcih was barred by any statute of limitations at the time of decedent's death.

IC 29-1-14-2; If any claim against the decedent be bounded upon any written instrument, alleged to have been executed by him, the original, or a complete copy thereof, shall be filed with the statement, unless it is lost or destroyed, in which case its loss or destruction must be stated in the claim; the statement shall set forth all credits and deductions to which the estate is entitled and shall be accompanied by the affidavit of the claimant, his agent or attorney, that the claim, after deducting all credits, set-offs and deductions to which the estate is entitled, is justly due and wholly unpaid, or if not yet due, when it will or may become due, and no claim shall be received unless accompanied by such affidavit; if the claim be secured by a lien on any real or personal property, such lien shall be particularly set forth in such statement, and a reference given to where the lien, if of record, will be found.

Name: _____ Attorney ID #: _____

ATTORNEY FOR CLAIMANT

Address: _____ Phone: _____

Figure D-5

Here is a typical proof of claim form required of all creditors filing a claim against an estate.

STATE OF INDIANA)   IN THE MARION SUPERIOR COURT
) SS: PROBATE DIVISION - COURT 8
COUNTY OF MARION)   CHARLES J. DEITER, JUDGE

IN THE MATTER OF   )
)
THE ESTATE OF   )   ESTATE DOCKET
)
_____.) _____

NOTICE OF FINAL ACCOUNT

The Final Account and Petition for Distribution filed by _____

_____, personal representative, is set for hearing on

the _____ day of _____, ____, at _____.

Any objections to the Final Account and Petition for Distribution <u>MUST</u> be filed in

writing on or before the _____ day of _____, ____.

_____
Sarah M. Taylor
Clerk of the Marion Superior Court
Probate Division-Court 8
200 East Washington Street, Room 1741
Indianapolis, Indiana 46204

Attorney:

_____
_____
_____
_____

7-1-97 (No. 67)

Figure D-6

Legal notice is placed by the probate court setting a hearing for a final accounting and petition for distribution of an estate.

Example Wills

In this appendix, you will find five sample wills to review: a living will and four wills created with the WillWriter software, provided by Business Logic Corporation, located on the CD-ROM at the back of this book. The first will *(living will)* gives you an idea of what a living will (also called *directives to physicians*) might look like. As I mention in the Introduction to this book, a living will is a legal document that states your desire to refuse certain medical treatments (such as artificial life support) should you become unable to communicate your wishes.

The remaining four wills were created with WillWriter to give you an idea of what your finished will—created during the Saturday Evening session—may look like. I drafted these wills for Adam A. Adams, a fictional character, based on the following four scenarios:

- Adam is single.
- Adam is single with children.
- Adam is married.
- Adam is married with children.

I included the will for those who are single with children to show how a will takes into account a guardian who is someone other than the minor child's other parent. If this applies to you, you'll want to take a look at the specific language in this will.

At the end of this appendix, you will also find a real-life will provided by Business Logic Corporation, the makers of WillWriter.

Living Will
of Adam A. Adams

Directive made this April 1, 2000.

All other previously dated Living Wills and Codicils are revoked.

TO MY FAMILY, MY PHYSICIAN, MY CLERGYMAN, MY LAWYER:

I, Adam A. Adams, being of sound mind, willfully and voluntarily make known my desire that my life shall not be artificially prolonged pursuant to the following:

If the time comes when I can no longer take part in decisions for my own future, this statement and declaration shall stand as the expression of my wishes.

I recognize that death is as much a reality as birth, growth, maturity, and old age – it is but a phase in the cycle of life and is the only certainty. I do not fear death as much as I fear the indignity of deterioration, dependence, and hopeless pain.

If there is no reasonable expectation of my recovery from physical or mental disability, I wish to be allowed to die and not be kept alive by artificial means or heroic measures, but wish only that drugs be mercifully administered to me for terminal suffering, even if they hasten the moment of my death.

I recognize that my wishes place a heavy burden of responsibility upon you, and I therefore make the following declaration with the intention of sharing this responsibility and the decision with you and of mitigating any feelings of guilt that you may have:

DECLARATION

If at any time I should have an incurable injury, disease, or illness certified to be a terminal condition by a physician, and where the application of life-sustaining procedures would serve only to artificially prolong the moment of my death and where any physician determines that my death is imminent whether or not life-sustaining procedures are utilized, I direct that such procedures be withheld or withdrawn, and that I be permitted to die naturally.

Figure E-1

Sample living will.

In the absence of my ability to give directions regarding the use of such life-sustaining procedures, it is my intention that this directive shall be honored by my family and physicians as the final expression of my legal right to refuse medical or surgical treatment and accept the consequences from such refusal. I understand the full importance of this directive, and I am emotionally and mentally competent to make this directive.

_____

Adam. A. Adams
Crown Point, Lake County, Indiana.

The declarant has been personally known to me, and I believe Adam. A. Adams to be of sound mind.

_____

John Q. Public

_____

Jane W. Doe

Figure E-1

continued

Last Will and Testament
of Adam A. Adams

I, ADAM A. ADAMS, a resident of Crown Point, Indiana, declare that this is my Last Will and Testament.

FIRST

I hereby revoke all previous Wills and Codicils that I have made.

SECOND

I direct for the disposition of my remains in the following manner.

I would like to donate my body or parts of it as follows:

I hereby leave my organs to science, to be used as necessary.

I direct my Executor to carry out such arrangements.

THIRD

I am not married and have no spouse.

I give all my jewelry, clothing, household furniture and furnishings, personal automobiles and other tangible articles of a personal nature, or my interest in any such property along with:

(a) any insurance on the property,
(b) any personal life insurance proceeds,
(c) any registered retirement savings plans, registered retirement income funds, pension plans and annuities,
(d) any income tax deferred assets,

to my mother and father, John and Mary Feder, to be distributed equally among them.

Figure E-2

Sample will for an unmarried testator with no children.

FOURTH

I have no minor child, or children.

FIFTH

To Charles Adams, my brother, I leave my 1999 Land Rover Discovery automobile, my Ski-Doo, and my Harley-Davidson motorcycle.

To Lucy Adams-Baker, my sister, I leave my lake cottage and surrounding property in Lake Wobegon, Minnesota.

No other special gifts are left, and any assets not directly disposed of in this Will shall be given to the surviving members in order of succession.

SIXTH

To The National Association for the Preservation of African Wildlife, I leave $25,000.

SEVENTH

I nominate John Q. Public as Executor of this Will, to serve without bond.

If he shall for any reason fail to qualify as Executor, I nominate Jane W. Doe as Executor or Executrix to serve without bond. The term "my Executor" as used in this Will shall include any personal representative of my estate.

I authorize my Executor to sell, with or without notice, at either public or private sale, and to lease any property belonging to my estate, subject only to such confirmation of court as may be required by law.

I authorize my Executor to invest and reinvest any surplus money in the Executor's hands in every kind of property, real, personal, or mixed and every kind of investment, specifically including but not limited to interest bearing accounts, corporate obligations of every kind, preferred or common stocks, shares of investment trusts, investment companies, mutual funds, or common trust funds, including funds administered by the Executor, and mortgage participations, that persons of prudence, discretion, and intelligence acquire for their own account.

Figure E-2

continued

No bequest provided for in this Will or in any Codicil hereto shall bear interest if not paid or satisfied within any period prescribed by law.

EIGHTH

I direct that all inheritance, estate, or other death taxes that may by reason of my death be attributable to my probate estate or any portion of it, or to any property or transfers of property outside my probate estate, shall be paid by my Executor out of the residue of my estate disposed of by this Will, without adjustment among the residuary beneficiaries, and shall not be charged against or collected from any beneficiary of my probate estate, or from any transferee or beneficiary of any property outside my probate estate.

NINTH

Except as otherwise provided in this Will, I have intentionally failed to provide herein for any of my heirs, and I specifically disinherit any person claiming to be my heir who is not provided for in this Will. If any beneficiary under this Will in any manner, directly or indirectly, contests or attacks this Will or any of its provisions, any gift or other provision I have made to or for that person under this Will is revoked and shall be disposed of in the same manner provided herein as if that contesting beneficiary had predeceased me without issue.

TENTH

As used in this Will, the term "issue" shall refer to lineal descendants of all degrees, and the terms "child," "children," and "issue" shall include adopted persons. However, in no event shall any of these terms include any foster child or stepchild, regardless of the existence of a parent-and-child relationship between that person and myself.

I sign my name to this Will on April 1, 2000, at Crown Point, in the County of Lake, in the State of Indiana.

_____

ADAM A. ADAMS

Figure E-2

continued

On the date written below, ADAM A. ADAMS declared to us, the undersigned, that this instrument, consisting of these few pages including the page signed by us, as witnesses, was his Last Will and Testament and requested us, to act as witnesses to it.

He thereupon signed this Will in our presence, all of us being present at the same time.

We now, at his request, in his presence and in the presence of each other, subscribe our names as witnesses. Each states that the Testator is not a minor and appears to be of sound mind and that we have no knowledge of any facts indicating that the foregoing instrument, or any part of it, was procured by duress, menace, fraud, or undue influence.

We, each for himself or herself, declare that each of us is over the age of majority, and that each of us is, and the others appear to be of sound mind.

We, each for himself or herself, declare under penalty of perjury that the foregoing is true and correct and that this attestation and this declaration are executed on the 1st day of April, 2000 at Crown Point, in the County of Lake, in the State of Indiana.

Witness #1

John Q. Public residing at 123 Madeline Boulevard, Merrillville, Indiana 46410

_____

Print Name

_____

Signature

Dated:_____

Figure E-2

continued

Witness #2

Barbara C. Stolzmann residing at 456 Sweet Water Canyon, Crown Point, Indiana 46037

_____

Print Name

_____

Signature

Dated:_____

Witness #3

Pauline Stolzmann residing at 789 Rocky Pointe Road, Indianapolis, Indiana 46355

_____

Print Name

_____

Signature

Dated:_____

Figure E-2

continued

Last Page of:

THE LAST WILL AND TESTAMENT OF ADAM A. ADAMS

Affidavit of Execution

I, John Q. Public, of the City of Merrillville, in the County of Lake, in the State of Indiana,

Make oath and say:

1. On the 1st day of April, 2000, I was present and saw the paper annexed and marked as LAST WILL AND TESTAMENT of this my affidavit executed by Adam A. Adams.

2. At time of execution, I knew such person(s) who was on that date of the full age of Eighteen (18) years to the best of my knowledge.

3. The said paper writing was executed by such person in the presence of myself, Barbara C. Stolzmann of the City of Crown Point, in the County of Lake, and Pauline Stolzmann of the City of Indianapolis, in the County of Marion. We were all present at the same time, whereupon we did, in the presence of such person, attest and subscribe the said paper writing as witnesses.

_____

John Q. Public

Witness

SWORN BEFORE ME AT THE City of Crown Point in the County of Lake

this _____ day of April, 2000.

_____ Commissioner for Oaths

_____ Notary Public

_____

Commissioner/Notary

Figure E-2

continued

Last Will and Testament
of Adam A. Adams

I, ADAM A. ADAMS, a resident of Crown Point, Indiana, declare that this is my Last Will and Testament.

FIRST

I hereby revoke all previous Wills and Codicils that I have made.

SECOND

I direct for the disposition of my remains in the following manner.

I would like to donate my body or parts of it as follows:

I leave my organs to science, to be used as necessary.

I would like for my body to be cremated and my remains to be scattered over the Atlantic Ocean.

I direct my Executor to carry out such arrangements.

THIRD

I am not married and have no spouse.

I give all my jewelry, clothing, household furniture and furnishings, personal automobiles and other tangible articles of a personal nature, or my interest in any such property not otherwise disposed of by this Will or in any other manner together with:

(a) any insurance on the property,
(b) any personal life insurance proceeds,
(c) any registered retirement savings plans, registered retirement income funds, pension plans and annuities,
(d) any income tax deferred assets,

to all of my children: Robert F. Adams, Wilma F. Williams, Edward R. Adams and Betty Adams-Bettman, to be distributed equally among them.

Figure E-3

Sample will for an unmarried testator with children.

All references in this Will to "my child" or "my children" include any and all children hereinafter born to or adopted by me.

FOURTH

I have a minor child, Edward R. Adams. I leave the child in the custody of Claudette M. Majdak who will act as his official Guardian. Should Claudette M. Majdak not be able to serve as the Guardian for any reason, I nominate Angela Sue Alberts to act as his official Guardian. I direct that no bond be required of any Guardian nominated hereunder.

I specifically request that my ex-wife, Eve N. Adams, the mother of Edward R. Adams, not be granted custody of the minor child. I feel that it would be in the best interest of the minor child for Claudette M. Majdak or Angela Sue Alberts to be serve as his Guardian rather than Eve N. Adams, as she has not provided for, nor had any contact with, the minor child for the past three (3) years.

My Executor shall represent any child who has not reached the age of majority in matters relating to any distribution or selection of assets that shall constitute the child's share, and my Executor in my Executor's discretion, sell for the child's account any part of that child's share.

Any property or its proceeds distributable to a child under the age of majority may be delivered without bond to any suitable person with whom he or she resides or who has the care or control of the minor.

FIFTH

To Mary Feder, my mother, I leave my cottage and surrounding land in Lake Wobegon, Minnesota.

To Charles Adams, my brother, I leave my 1999 Land Rover Discovery automobile, my Ski-Doo, and my Harley-Davidson motorcycle.

To Lucy Adams-Baker, my sister, I leave my collection of British Royalty memorabilia.

No other special gifts are left; any assets not directly disposed of in this Will shall be given to the surviving members in order of succession.

Figure E-3

continued

SIXTH

To the National Association for the Preservation of African Wildlife, I leave $25,000.

SEVENTH

I nominate John Q. Public as Executor of this Will, to serve without bond.

If he shall for any reason fail to qualify as Executor, I nominate Jane W. Doe as Executor or Executrix to serve without bond. The term "my Executor" as used in this Will shall include any personal representative of my estate.

I authorize my Executor to sell, with or without notice, at either public or private sale, and to lease any property belonging to my estate, subject only to such confirmation of court as may be required by law.

I authorize my Executor to invest and reinvest any surplus money in the Executor's hands in every kind of property, real, personal, or mixed and every kind of investment, specifically including but not limited to interest bearing accounts, corporate obligations of every kind, preferred or common stocks, shares of investment trusts, investment companies, mutual funds, or common trust funds, including funds administered by the Executor, and mortgage participations, that persons of prudence, discretion, and intelligence acquire for their own account.

No bequest provided for in this Will or in any Codicil hereto shall bear interest if not paid or satisfied within any period prescribed by law.

EIGHTH

I direct that all inheritance, estate, or other death taxes that may by reason of my death be attributable to my probate estate or any portion of it, or to any property or transfers of property outside my probate estate, shall be paid by my Executor out of the residue of my estate disposed of by this Will, without adjustment among the residuary beneficiaries, and shall not be charged against or collected from any beneficiary of my probate estate, or from any transferee or beneficiary of any property outside my probate estate.

Figure E-3

continued

NINTH

Except as otherwise provided in this Will, I have intentionally failed to provide herein for any of my heirs, and I specifically disinherit any person claiming to be my heir who is not provided for in this Will. If any beneficiary under this Will in any manner, directly or indirectly, contests or attacks this Will or any of its provisions, any gift or other provision I have made to or for that person under this Will is revoked and shall be disposed of in the same manner provided herein as if that contesting beneficiary had predeceased me without issue.

TENTH

As used in this Will, the term "issue" shall refer to lineal descendants of all degrees, and the terms "child," "children," and "issue" shall include adopted persons. However, in no event shall any of these terms include any foster child or stepchild, regardless of the existence of a parent-and-child relationship between that person and myself.

I sign my name to this Will on April 1, 2000, at Crown Point, in the County of Lake, in the State of Indiana.

_____

ADAM A. ADAMS

On the date written below, ADAM A. ADAMS declared to us, the undersigned, that this instrument, consisting of these few pages including the page signed by us, as witnesses, was his Last Will and Testament and requested us, to act as witnesses to it.

He thereupon signed this Will in our presence, all of us being present at the same time.

We now, at his request, in his presence and in the presence of each other, subscribe our names as witnesses. Each states that the Testator is not a minor and appears to be of sound mind and that we have no knowledge of any facts indicating that the foregoing instrument, or any part of it, was procured by duress, menace, fraud, or undue influence.

We, each for himself or herself, declare that each of us is over the age of majority, and that each of us is, and the others appear to be of sound mind.

Figure E-3

continued

We, each for himself or herself, declare under penalty of perjury that the foregoing is true and correct and that this attestation and this declaration are executed on the 1st day of April, 2000 at Crown Point, in the County of Lake, in the State of Indiana.

Witness #1

John Q. Public residing at 123 Madeline Boulevard, Merrillville, Indiana 46410

_____

Print Name

_____

Signature

Dated:_____

Witness #2

Barbara C. Stolzmann residing at 456 Sweet Water Canyon, Crown Point, Indiana 46037

_____

Print Name

_____

Signature

Dated:_____

Witness #3

Pauline Stolzmann residing at 789 Rocky Pointe Road, Indianapolis, Indiana 46355

_____

Print Name

_____

Signature

Dated:_____

Figure E-3

continued

Last Page of:

THE LAST WILL AND TESTAMENT OF ADAM A. ADAMS

Affidavit of Execution

I, John Q. Public, of the City of Merrillville, in the County of Lake, in the State of Indiana,

Make oath and say:

1. On the 1st day of April, 2000, I was present and saw the paper annexed and marked as LAST WILL AND TESTAMENT of this my affidavit executed by Adam A. Adams.

2. At time of execution, I knew such person(s) who was on that date of the full age of Eighteen (18) years to the best of my knowledge.

3. The said paper writing was executed by such person in the presence of myself, Barbara C. Stolzmann of the City of Crown Point, in the County of Lake, and Pauline Stolzmann of the City of Indianapolis, in the County of Marion. We were all present at the same time, whereupon we did, in the presence of such person, attest and subscribe the said paper writing as witnesses.

_____

John Q. Public

Witness

SWORN BEFORE ME AT THE City of Crown Point in the County of Lake

this _____ day of April, 2000.

_____ Commissioner for Oaths

_____ Notary Public

_____

Commissioner/Notary

Figure E-3

continued

Last Will and Testament
of Adam A. Adams

I, ADAM A. ADAMS, a resident of Crown Point, Indiana, declare that this is my Last Will and Testament.

FIRST

I hereby revoke all previous Wills and Codicils that I have made.

SECOND

I direct for the disposition of my remains in the following manner.

I would like to donate my body or parts of it as follows:

I leave my organs to science, to be used as necessary.

I would like for my body to be cremated and for my remains to be scattered over the Atlantic Ocean.

I direct my Executor to carry out such arrangements.

THIRD

I am married to Eve N. Adams, and all references in this Will to my "wife" or "my spouse" are to her.

I give all my jewelry, clothing, household furniture and furnishings, personal automobiles and other tangible articles of a personal nature, or my interest in any such property not otherwise disposed of by this Will or in any other manner together with:

(a) any insurance on the property,
(b) any personal life insurance proceeds,
(c) any registered retirement savings plans, registered retirement income funds, pension plans and annuities,
(d) any income tax deferred assets,

to my spouse, Eve N. Adams.

Figure E-4

Sample will for a married testator with no children.

FOURTH

I have no minor child, or children.

FIFTH

To Mary Feder, my mother, I leave my cottage and surrounding land in Lake Wobegon, Minnesota.

To Charles Adams, my brother, I leave my 1999 Land Rover Discovery automobile, my Ski-Doo, and my Harley-Davidson motorcycle.

To Lucy Adams-Baker, my sister, I leave my collection of British Royalty memorabilia.

No other special gifts are left; any assets not directly disposed of in this Will shall be given to the surviving members in order of succession.

SIXTH

To National Association for the Preservation of African Wildlife, I leave $25,000.

SEVENTH

I nominate John Q. Public as Executor of this Will, to serve without bond.

If he shall for any reason fail to qualify as Executor, I nominate Jane W. Doe as Executor or Executrix to serve without bond. The term "my Executor" as used in this Will shall include any personal representative of my estate.

I authorize my Executor to sell, with or without notice, at either public or private sale, and to lease any property belonging to my estate, subject only to such confirmation of court as may be required by law.

I authorize my Executor to invest and reinvest any surplus money in the Executor's hands in every kind of property, real, personal, or mixed and every kind of investment, specifically including but not limited to interest bearing accounts, corporate obligations of every kind, preferred or common stocks, shares of investment trusts, investment companies, mutual funds, or common trust funds,

Figure E-4

continued

including funds administered by the Executor, and mortgage participations, that persons of prudence, discretion, and intelligence acquire for their own account.

No bequest provided for in this Will or in any Codicil hereto shall bear interest if not paid or satisfied within any period prescribed by law.

EIGHTH

I direct that all inheritance, estate, or other death taxes that may by reason of my death be attributable to my probate estate or any portion of it, or to any property or transfers of property outside my probate estate, shall be paid by my Executor out of the residue of my estate disposed of by this Will, without adjustment among the residuary beneficiaries, and shall not be charged against or collected from any beneficiary of my probate estate, or from any transferee or beneficiary of any property outside my probate estate.

NINTH

Except as otherwise provided in this Will, I have intentionally failed to provide herein for any of my heirs, and I specifically disinherit any person claiming to be my heir who is not provided for in this Will. If any beneficiary under this Will in any manner, directly or indirectly, contests or attacks this Will or any of its provisions, any gift or other provision I have made to or for that person under this Will is revoked and shall be disposed of in the same manner provided herein as if that contesting beneficiary had predeceased me without issue.

TENTH

As used in this Will, the term "issue" shall refer to lineal descendants of all degrees, and the terms "child," "children," and "issue" shall include adopted persons. However, in no event shall any of these terms include any foster child or stepchild, regardless of the existence of a parent-and-child relationship between that person and myself.

I sign my name to this Will on April 1, 2000, at Crown Point, in the County of Lake, in the State of Indiana.

_____

ADAM A. ADAMS

Figure E-4

continued

On the date written below, ADAM A. ADAMS declared to us, the undersigned, that this instrument, consisting of these few pages including the page signed by us, as witnesses, was his Last Will and Testament and requested us, to act as witnesses to it.

He thereupon signed this Will in our presence, all of us being present at the same time.

We now, at his request, in his presence and in the presence of each other, subscribe our names as witnesses. Each states that the Testator is not a minor and appears to be of sound mind and that we have no knowledge of any facts indicating that the foregoing instrument, or any part of it, was procured by duress, menace, fraud, or undue influence.

We, each for himself or herself, declare that each of us is over the age of majority, and that each of us is, and the others appear to be of sound mind.

We, each for himself or herself, declare under penalty of perjury that the foregoing is true and correct and that this attestation and this declaration are executed on the 1st day of April, 2000 at Crown Point, in the County of Lake, in the State of Indiana.

Witness #1

John Q. Public residing at 123 Madeline Boulevard, Merrillville, Indiana 46410

_____

Print Name

_____

Signature

Dated:_____

Figure E-4

continued

Witness #2

Barbara C. Stolzmann residing at 456 Sweet Water Canyon, Crown Point, Indiana 46037

_____

Print Name

_____

Signature

Dated:_____

Witness #3

Pauline Stolzmann residing at 789 Rocky Pointe Road, Indianapolis, Indiana 46355

_____

Print Name

_____

Signature

Dated:_____

Figure E-4

continued

Last Page of:

THE LAST WILL AND TESTAMENT OF ADAM A. ADAMS

Affidavit of Execution

I, John Q. Public, of the City of Merrillville, in the County of Lake, in the State of Indiana,

Make oath and say:

1. On the 1st day of April, 2000, I was present and saw the paper annexed and marked as LAST WILL AND TESTAMENT of this my affidavit executed by Adam A. Adams.

2. At time of execution, I knew such person(s) who was on that date of the full age of Eighteen (18) years to the best of my knowledge.

3. The said paper writing was executed by such person in the presence of myself, Barbara C. Stolzmann of the City of Crown Point, in the County of Lake, and Pauline Stolzmann of the City of Indianapolis, in the County of Marion. We were all present at the same time, whereupon we did, in the presence of such person, attest and subscribe the said paper writing as witnesses.

_____

John Q. Public

Witness

SWORN BEFORE ME AT THE City of Crown Point in the County of Lake

this _____ day of April, 2000.

_____ Commissioner for Oaths

_____ Notary Public

_____

Commissioner/Notary

Figure E-4

continued

Last Will and Testament
of Adam A. Adams

I, ADAM A. ADAMS, a resident of Crown Point, Indiana, declare that this is my Last Will and Testament.

FIRST

I hereby revoke all previous Wills and Codicils that I have made.

SECOND

I direct for the disposition of my remains in the following manner.

I would like to donate my body or parts of it as follows:

I leave my organs to science, to be used as necessary.

I would like for my body to be cremated and for my remains to be scattered over the Atlantic Ocean.

I direct my Executor to carry out such arrangements.

THIRD

I am married to Eve N. Adams, and all references in this Will to my "wife" or "my spouse" are to her.

I give all my jewelry, clothing, household furniture and furnishings, personal automobiles and other tangible articles of a personal nature, or my interest in any such property not otherwise disposed of by this Will or in any other manner together with:

(a) any insurance on the property,
(b) any personal life insurance proceeds,
(c) any registered retirement savings plans, registered retirement income funds, pension plans and annuities,
(d) any income tax deferred assets,

to my spouse, Eve N. Adams.

Figure E-5

Sample will for a
married testator
with children.

If, however, my spouse fails to survive me by thirty (30) days, then I direct that her share shall be distributed equally to all of my following children: Robert F. Adams, Wilma F. Williams, Robert R. Adams, and Betty Adams-Bettman.

All references in this Will to "my child" or "my children" include any and all children hereinafter born to or adopted by me.

FOURTH

I have a minor child, Robert R. Adams, and if the other parent of this child does not survive me by thirty (30) days, I leave the child in the custody of Claudette M. Majdak, who will act as his official Guardian. In case Claudette M. Majdak should not be able to serve for any reason, I nominate Angela Sue Alberts to act as the minor child's guardian. I direct that no bond be required of any Guardian nominated herein.

My Executor shall represent any child who has not reached the age of majority in matters relating to any distribution or selection of assets that shall constitute the child's share, and my Executor in my Executor's discretion, sell for the child's account any part of that child's share.

Any property or its proceeds distributable to a child under the age of majority may be delivered without bond to any suitable person with whom he or she resides or who has the care or control of the minor.

FIFTH

To Mary Feder, my mother, I leave my cottage and surrounding land in Lake Wobegon, Minnesota.

To Charles Adams, my brother, I leave my 1999 Land Rover Discovery automobile, my Ski-Doo, and my Harley-Davidson motorcycle.

To Lucy Adams-Baker, my sister, I leave my collection of British Royalty memorabilia.

No other special gifts are left, any assets not directly disposed of in this Will shall be given to the surviving members in order of succession.

Figure E-5

continued

SIXTH

To the National Association for the Preservation of African Wildlife, I leave $25,000.

SEVENTH

I nominate John Q. Public as Executor of this Will, to serve without bond.

If he shall for any reason fail to qualify as Executor, I nominate Jane W. Doe as Executor or Executrix to serve without bond. The term "my Executor" as used in this Will shall include any personal representative of my estate.

I authorize my Executor to sell, with or without notice, at either public or private sale, and to lease any property belonging to my estate, subject only to such confirmation of court as may be required by law.

I authorize my Executor to invest and reinvest any surplus money in the Executor's hands in every kind of property, real, personal, or mixed and every kind of investment, specifically including but not limited to interest bearing accounts, corporate obligations of every kind, preferred or common stocks, shares of investment trusts, investment companies, mutual funds, or common trust funds, including funds administered by the Executor, and mortgage participations, that persons of prudence, discretion, and intelligence acquire for their own account.

No bequest provided for in this Will or in any Codicil hereto shall bear interest if not paid or satisfied within any period prescribed by law.

EIGHTH

I direct that all inheritance, estate, or other death taxes that may by reason of my death be attributable to my probate estate or any portion of it, or to any property or transfers of property outside my probate estate, shall be paid by my Executor out of the residue of my estate disposed of by this Will, without adjustment among the residuary beneficiaries, and shall not be charged against or collected from any beneficiary of my probate estate, or from any transferee or beneficiary of any property outside my probate estate.

Figure E-5

continued

NINTH

Except as otherwise provided in this Will, I have intentionally failed to provide herein for any of my heirs, and I specifically disinherit any person claiming to be my heir who is not provided for in this Will. If any beneficiary under this Will in any manner, directly or indirectly, contests or attacks this Will or any of its provisions, any gift or other provision I have made to or for that person under this Will is revoked and shall be disposed of in the same manner provided herein as if that contesting beneficiary had predeceased me without issue.

TENTH

As used in this Will, the term "issue" shall refer to lineal descendants of all degrees, and the terms "child," "children," and "issue" shall include adopted persons. However, in no event shall any of these terms include any foster child or stepchild, regardless of the existence of a parent-and-child relationship between that person and myself.

I sign my name to this Will on April 1, 2000, at Crown Point, in the County of Lake, in the State of Indiana.

_____

ADAM A. ADAMS

On the date written below, ADAM A. ADAMS declared to us, the undersigned, that this instrument, consisting of these few pages including the page signed by us, as witnesses, was his Last Will and Testament and requested us, to act as witnesses to it.

He thereupon signed this Will in our presence, all of us being present at the same time.

We now, at his request, in his presence and in the presence of each other, subscribe our names as witnesses. Each states that the Testator is not a minor and appears to be of sound mind and that we have no knowledge of any facts indicating that the foregoing instrument, or any part of it, was procured by duress, menace, fraud, or undue influence.

We, each for himself or herself, declare that each of us is over the age of majority, and that each of us is, and the others appear to be of sound mind.

Figure E-5

continued

We, each for himself or herself, declare under penalty of perjury that the foregoing is true and correct and that this attestation and this declaration are executed on the 1st day of April, 2000 at Crown Point, in the County of Lake, in the State of Indiana.

Witness #1

John Q. Public residing at 123 Madeline Boulevard, Merrillville, Indiana 46410

_____

Print Name

_____

Signature

Dated:_____

Witness #2

Barbara C. Stolzmann residing at 456 Sweet Water Canyon, Crown Point, Indiana 46037

_____

Print Name

_____

Signature

Dated:_____

Witness #3

Pauline Stolzmann residing at 789 Rocky Pointe Road, Indianapolis, Indiana 46355

_____

Print Name

_____

Signature

Dated:_____

Figure E-5

continued

Last Page of:

THE LAST WILL AND TESTAMENT OF ADAM A. ADAMS

Affidavit of Execution

I, John Q. Public, of the City of Merrillville, in the County of Lake, in the State of Indiana,

Make oath and say:

1. On the 1st day of April, 2000, I was present and saw the paper annexed and marked as LAST WILL AND TESTAMENT of this my affidavit executed by Adam A. Adams.

2. At time of execution, I knew such person(s) who was on that date of the full age of Eighteen (18) years to the best of my knowledge.

3. The said paper writing was executed by such person in the presence of myself, Barbara C. Stolzmann of the City of Crown Point, in the County of Lake, and Pauline Stolzmann of the City of Indianapolis, in the County of Marion. We were all present at the same time, whereupon we did, in the presence of such person, attest and subscribe the said paper writing as witnesses.

_____

John Q. Public

Witness

SWORN BEFORE ME AT THE City of Crown Point in the County of Lake

this _____ day of April, 2000.

_____ Commissioner for Oaths

_____ Notary Public

_____

Commissioner/Notary

Figure E-5

continued

WILL OF JEROME J. GARCIA

I, JEROME J. GARCIA, also known as JERRY GARCIA, a resident of Marin County, California, hereby make, publish and declare this to be my Last Will and Testament.

FIRST
REVOCATION OF PRIOR WILLS

I revoke all Wills and Codicils heretofore made by me.

SECOND
DECLARATIONS

I declare that I am married; my wife's name is DEBORAH KOONS. We have no children by our marriage. I have four children now living from prior relationships, namely HEATHER GARCIA KATZ, born December 8, 1963, ANNABELLE WLAKER GARCIA, born February 2, 1970, THERESA ADAMS GARCIA, born September 21, 1974, and KEELIN GARCIA, born December 20, 1987. I have no deceased children leaving issue, and I have not adopted any children. The terms ``child'' or ``children'' as used in this Will shall refer only to my children and if any person shall claim and establish any right to participate in my estate other than as provided in this Will, whether as heir or in any other capacity whatsoever, I give and bequeath to each such person the sum of One Dollar ($1.00).

THIRD
COMMUNITY PROPERTY

I declare my intention to dispose of all property, real and personal, of which I have the right to dispose by Will, including any and all property as to which I may have at the time of my death a power of appointment by Will. I confirm to my wife her interest in our community property. It is my intention by this Will to dispose of all my separate Property and of my one-half (1/2) interest in our community property.

FOURTH
PERSONAL PROPERTY

Except as specifically provided hereinbelow, I give my jewelry, clothing, household furniture and furnishings, personal automobiles, books, pictures, objects of art and other tangible articles of a personal nature, or my interest in such property, which I may have at the time of my death, not otherwise specifically disposed of by this Will or in any other manner, together with any insurance on such property, to my wife, if she survives me for sixty (60)

Figure E-6

Jerry Garcia's will

days, and if she does not, then to such of my children, by representation, who survive me for sixty (60) days in equal shares as they shall agree, or as my Executor shall, in my Executor's discretion, determine if my children do not agree within one hundred fifty (150) days of my death.

In the absence of a conflict of interest, my Executor shall represent any child under age eighteen (18) in matter relating to any distribution under this Article FOURTH, including selection of the assets that shall constitute that child's share, and my Executor may, in my Executor's discretion, sell for the child's account any part of that child's share. Any property or its proceeds distributable to a child under age eighteen (18) pursuant to this Paragraph may be delivered without bond to the guardian of such child or to any suitable person with whom he or she resides or who has the care or control of him or her.

If neither my wife nor any of my children shall survive me, then this gift shall lapse and such property, and any insurance thereon, shall become part of the residue of my estate.

FIFTH
GUITARS

I give all my guitars made by DOUGLAS ERWIN, to DOUGLAS ERWIN, or to his estate if he predeceases me.

SIXTH
DISTRIBUTION OF RESIDUE OF ESTATE

After payment of all my debts, my last illness and funeral expenses, and provision for my child support obligations for KEELIN GARCIS, my marital settlement agreement with CAROLYN ADAMS GARCIA which is being drafted at the time of signing this will, and my agreement with MANASHA MATHESON regarding the house to be owned one-half by her and one-half by the trust established for KEELIN GARCIA which is being drafted at the time of signing this will, my Executor shall divide and distribute the remainder of my estate for my wife/husband and children as follows:

A. If my wife survives me for sixty (60) days, I give her one-third (1/3) of my estate outright and free of trust. If my wife fails to survice me for sixty days this bequest shall lapse and the amount shall be included with the remainder of my estate under paragraph B.

B. I give the remaining two-thirds (2/3) of my estate, or if my wife fails to survive me, my entire remaining estate, to my daughters, my friends, and my brother as follows:

Figure E-6

continued

1. The following shares shall be distributed outright and free of trust, by right of representation, to the persons indicated:

HEATHER GARCIA KATZ ONE-FIFTH (1/5)

ANNABELLE WALKER GARCIA ONE-FIFTH (1/5)

SUNSHINE MAY WALKER KESEY ONE-TENTH (1/10)

CLIFFORD GARCIA ONE-TENTH (1/10)

2. I give to the Trustee hereinafter named, IN TRUST, for the benefit of my younger daughters, THERESA ADAMS GARCIA and KEELIN GARCIA, one-fifth (1/5) of my estate for each,
to be held, administered and distributed as a separate trust for each child as follows:

a. So long as my child is living and is under age twenty-one (21), the Trustee shall pay to
or apply for her benefit, as much of the net income and principal of the Trust as the
Trustee, in the Trustee's absolute discretion, shall deem necessary for her proper support,
health, maintenance and education, after taking into consideration, to the extent the
Trustee shall deem advisable, any other income or resources of my child, known to the
Trustee. Any net income not distributed shall be accumulated and added to principal.

b. When the child attains the age of twenty-one (21), the trust share allocated on account
of such child shall thereupon be distributed free of trust to that child.

c. If my child dies prior to receipt of her entire share of principal and income provided
herein, and that child is survived by issue, then the remaining principal and income shall
be held in trust for those issue under the terms of this subparagraph 2. If my child is not
survived by issue, then the remaining principal and income shall be distributed free of
trust to the other residual beneficiaries receiving fractional interests in my estate under
this paragraph B in proporation to those fractional interests, by right of representation;
provided, however, if a part of that balance would otherwise be distributed to aperson for
whose benefit a trust is then being administered under this Will, that part shall instead be
added to that trust and shall thereafter be administered according to its terms.

d. Whenever provision is made in this Article SIXTH for payment for the ``education'' of a
beneficiary, the term ``education'' shall be construed to include college and postgraduate
study, so long as pursued to advantage by the beneficiary at an institution of the beneficiary's choice; and in determining payments to be made for such college of post-graduate
education, the Trustee shall take into consideration the beneficary's related living expenses
to the extent that they are reasonable.

Figure E-6

continued

e. Notwithstanding the directions given as to the distribution of income and principal in this Article SIXTH, any trusts established by this Article shall terminate, if they have not previously terminated, twenty-one (21) years after the death of the survivor of the class composed of my wife/husband and all my issue living at my death, and the then remaining principal and undistributed income of such trusts shall be paid to my issue or other beneficiaries then living to whom income payments could be made under such trusts immediately prior to its termination under this clause, such issue to take by right of representation.

SEVENTH
ULTIMATE DISTRIBUTION

If at the time of my death, or at any later time before full distribution of any Trust established under Article SIXTH, all my issue are deceased, and no other disposition of the property is directed by this Will, the estate or the portion of it then remaining shall there upon be distributed to those persons who would then by my heirs, their identities and respective shares to be determined as though my death had then occurred and according to the laws of the State of California then in effect relating to the succession of separate property not acquired from a predeceased spous.

EIGHTH
TRUSTEE'S POWERS

I give to the Trustee of all of the Trusts established under this Will the following powers, in addition to and not in limitation of the common-law and statutory powers, and without application or permission of any court.

A. To retain any property, real or personal, which the Trustee may receive, even though such property (by reason of its character, amount, proportion to the total Trust Estate or otherwise) would not be considered appropriate for a Trustee apart from this provision.

B. To sell, exchange, give options upon, partition, or otherwise dispose of any property which the Trustee may hold from time to time at public or private sale or otherwise, for cash or other consideration or on credit, and upon such terms and for such consideration as the Trustee shall think fit, and to transfer and convey the same free of all trust.

C. To invest and reinvest the Trust Estate from time to time in any property, real or personal, including (without limiting the generality of the foregoing language) securities of domestic and foreign corporations and investment trusts, common trust funds, including those established by any successor corporate fiduciary which acts as Executor and Trustee hereunder, bonds, preferred stocks, common stocks, mortgages, mortgage participation,

Figure E-6

continued

even though such investment (by reason of its character, amount, proportion to the total Trust Estate or otherwise) would not be considered appropriate for a Trustee apart from this provision, and even though such investment causes a greater proportion of the principal to be invested in investment of one type or of one company than would be considered appropriate for a Trustee apart from this provision; to lend money to any and all persons, including any or all of the beneficiaries hereof, upon such terms and conditions as the Trustee in the Trustee's sole discretion deems proper; in connection with such loans the Trustee may or may not demand security therefor or interest thereon as the Trustee in the Trustee's sole discretion deems proper.

D. To improve any real estate held in the Trust Estate, including the power to demolish any buildings in whole or in part and to erect buildings; to lease real estate on such terms as the Trustee thinks fit, including leases for periods that my extend beyond the duration of the Trusts, and to grant renewals thereof; and to foreclose, extend, assign, partially release and discharge mortgages.

E. To borrow money from any lender even though a successor fiduciary hereunder, execute promissory notes therefor, and to secure said obligations by mortgage or pledge of any of the Trust property.

F. To compromise or arbitrate any claim in favor of or against the Trust Estate; to commence or defend any litigation concerning the Trust Estate which the Trustee in the Trustee's absolutie discretion considers prudent, and costs and expenses of such, including reasonable attorney's fees, to be borne by the Trust Estate; to give or receive consideration in any settlement to reduce the rate of return on any investment, with or without consideration; to prepay or accept prepayment of any debt; to enforce, abstain from enforcing, release or modify, with or without consideration, any right, obligation, or claim; to extend and renew any obligation or hold the same after maturity without extension or renewal; to accept deeds in lieu of foreclosure and pay consideration for the same; to determine that any property is worthless or of insufficient value to warrant keeping or protecting, and to abandon any such property or convey the same with or without consideration; and to use any portion of the Trust Estate to protect any other portion of the Trust Estate.

G. To vote all securities held as a part of the Trust Estate, or to join in a voting trust or other lawful form of stockholders' agreements respecting the voting of shares for such period as the Trustee deems proper; to pay all assessments on such securities, to exercise options, subscriptions and conversion rights on such securities, with respect thereto; to

Figure E-6

continued

employ such brokers, banks, counsel, custodians, attorneys or other agents, and to delegate to them such powers (including, among others, the right to vote shares of stock held in trust) or join in a voting trust or other lawful form of stockholders' agreements respecting the voting of shares for such periods as the Trustee deems proper; and to cause securities held from time to time to be registered in the name of the Trustee, or in the name of the Trustee's nominee with or without mention of the Trust in any instrument of ownership, and to keep the same unregistered or to retain them in condition that they will pass by delivery.

H. To incur and pay all taxes, assessments, costs, charges, fees and other expenses of every kind which the Trustee deems necessary or advisable in connection with the administration of the Trust created hereby, including reasonable Trustee's fees.

I. To join in or oppose any reorganization, recapitalization, consolidation ormerger, liquidation or foreclosure, or any plan therefor; to deposit property with, and delegate discretionary power to any committee or depository; to pay assessments, expenses and compensation; and to retain any property issued therein; to exercise or sell conversion or subscription rights, and to retain the property received.

J. To hold, manage, invest and account for the several shares which may be held in trust, either as separate funds or as a single fund, as the Trustee deems proper; if as a single fund, making the division thereof only upon the Trustee's books of account and allocating to each share its proportionate part of the principal and income of the common fund and charging against each share its proportionate part of the common expenses.

K. To keep any or all of the Trust property at any place or places in California or elsewhere in the United States or abroad, or with a depository or custodian at such place or places.

L. In dividing the Trust Estate into shares or in distributing the same, to divide or distribute in cash or in kind as the Trustee thinks fit. For purposes of division or distribution, to value the Trust Estate reasonably and in good faith, and such valuation shall be conclusive on all parties. Where distribution or division is made in kind, the Trustee shall, so far as the Trustee finds practicable, allocate to the beneficiaries proportionate amounts of each kind or security; or other property of the Trust Estate.

M. The Trustee is authorized in the Trustee's discretion to retain from income distributable to any beneficiary an amount equal to the income tax (Federal and State) the Trustee estimates will be imposed upon such income; any sums so withheld shall be applied to the tax liability of such beneficiary. Nothing herein shall be construed as imposing an obligation

Figure E-6

continued

upon the Trustee to retain any sums for the purpose mentioned, nor that said tax shall be assumed or borne by the assets held for such beneficiary. No liability shall attach to the Trustee if the Trustee acts or fails to act as authorized in Subparagraph M.

N. To partition, without sale, any real or personal property held jointly or in common with others or distributable to one or more persons hereunder; to pay or receive consideration to effect equality of partition; to unite with any other owner in the management, leasing, use of improvement of any property.

O. To determine, as to all property received, whether and to what extent the same shall be deemed to be principal or income and as to all charges or expenses paid, whether and to what extent the same shall be charged against principal or against income, including, without limiting the generality of the foregoing language, power to apportion any receipt or expense between principal and income and to determine what part, if any, of the actual income received upon any wasting investment or upon any security purchased or acquired at a premium shall be retained and added to principal to prevent diminution of principal upon exhaustion or maturity thereof. In this regard, the Trustee in the Trustee's absolute discretion, may, but shall not be required to, if the Trustees deems it proper, allocate receipts or charges and expenses to income or principal according to the Principal and Income Law of the State of California as it may from time to time exist. All allocation of receipts or charges and expenses shall be conclusive on all persons interested in any trusts created hereby.

P. In all matters to administer and invest the Trust Estate as fully and freely as an individual owner might do, without any restrictions to which fiduciaries are ordinarily subject, except the duty to act in good faith and with reasonable care.

Q. The Trustee shall also have the power to do all things necessary to continue any business enterprise, in whatever form, owned or controlled by me upon my death for such period as the Trustee shall deem to be in the best interests of the Trust Estate.

R. The Trustee is authorized to employ attorneys, accountants, investment advisors, specialists and such other agents as he shall deeme necessary or desirable. The Trustee shall have the authority to appoint an investment manager or managers to manage all or any part of the assets of the Trust Estate, appointments shall include the power to acquire and dispose of such assets. The Trustee may charge the compensation of such attorneys, accountants, investment advisors, specialists and other agents and any other expenses against the Trust Estate.

Figure E-6

continued

NINTH
PAYMENT OF TAXES AND EXPENSES

I direct that all estate, succession or other death taxes, duties, charges or assessments that may by reaso of my death be attributable to my probate estate or any portion of it, or to any property or transfers of property outside my probate estate, including but not limited to burial expenses, expenses of last illness, attorney's fees, executor's fees, appraiser's fees, accountant's fees and other expenses of administering my estate shall be paid by the Executor from the estate in the same manner as if said taxes were a debt of my estate, without apportionment, deduction, or reimbursement thereof and without adjustment thereof among my beneficiaries. Provided, however, if there is inadequate cash in my estate to pay such taxes and expenses, then my executor may borrow such funds as I have given authority in Article TWELFTH below.

TENTH
NO CONTEST CLAUSE

If any beneficiary of my Will or any Codicil hereto or of the Trusts created hereunder before or after the admission of this Will to probate, directly or indirectly, contests or aids in the contest of the same or any provision thereof, or contests the distribution of my estate in accordance with my Will or any Codicil, the provisions herein made to or for the benefit of such contestant or contestants are hereby revoked and for the purpose of my Will and any Codicil, said contestant or contestants shall be deemed to have predeceases me.

ELEVENTH
SPENDTHRIFT PROVISION

Each and every beneficiary under the Trust or Trusts created by this Will is hereby restrained from and is and shall be without right, power, or authority to sell, transfer, pledge, hypothecate, mortgage, alienate, anticipate, or in any other manner affect or impair his, her or their beneficial and legal rights, titles, interests, claims and estates in and to the income and/or principal of said trusts, and the rights, titles, interests and estate of any beneficiary thereunder shall not be subject nor liable to any process of law or court, and all of the income and/or principal under said trusts shall be paid over to the beneficiary in person, or, in the event of the minority or incompetency of any beneficiary, to the guardian of that beneficiary in such manner as in the Trustee's discretion seems most advisable at the time and in the manner provided by the terms of the Trust.

Figure E-6

continued

TWELFTH
EXECUTOR'S APPOINTMENT AND POWERS

I hereby nominate and appoint my wife DEBORAH KOONS, and my attorney DAVID M. HELLMAN, as Executor of this Will. If either of them shall be, or become unable or unwilling to act, then the survivor shall act with JEFFREY E. EHLENBACH. No bond or other security shall be required of any person who acts as Executor hereunder.

A. I hereby expressly authorize and empower my Executor to sell and dispose of the whole or any portion of my estate, real or personal, and wherever situate, as and when and upon such terms as my Executor deems proper, at public or private sale, with or without notice, and without first securing any order or court therefor. I further grant to my Executor all the powers granted to the Trustee under Article EIGHTH hereof, insofar as such powers are appropriate for the administration of my estate and the probate of my Will;

B. If my Executor in good faith decides that there is uncertainty as to the inclusion of particular property in my gross estate for federal estate tax purposes, my Executor shall exclude such property from my gross estate in the estate tax return. My Executor shall not be liable for any loss to my estate or to any beneficary, which loss results from the decision made in good faith that there is uncertainty as to the inclusion of particular property in my gross estate.

C. The decision of my Executor as to the date which should be selected for the valuation of property in my gross estate for federal estate tax purposes shal be conclusive on al concerned;

D. When a choice is available as to whether certain deductions shall be taken as income tax deductions or estate tax deductions, the decision of my Executor in this regard shall be conclusive on all concerned and no adjustment of income and principal account shall be made as a result of such decision;

E. Beginning as of the date of my death and until the establishment of the trusts provided for herein, my Executor shall make such payments of estate income, which is allocable to trust assets, as would be required if the trusts had actually been established at the date of my death.

F. My Executor is authorized to execute and deliver disclaimers under Internal Revenue Code X2518 and California Probate Code XX260 through 295 or any successor statute.

Figure E-6

continued

THIRTEENTH
TRUSTEE'S APPOINTMENT AND COMPENSATION

I hereby nominate and appoint my wife DEBORAH KOONS, and my attorney DAVID M. HELLMAN, as Trustee of this Will. If either of them shall be, or become unable or unwilling to act, then the survivor shall act with JEFFREY E. EHLENBACH. No bond or other security shall be required of any person who acts as Trustee hereunder.

The individual Trustees shall be entitled to receive reasonable commissions similar to those charged by corporate Trustees in the San Francisco Bay Area. Any successor Trustee shall be entitled to reasonable compensation for its services.

FOURTEENTH
GUARDIAN

If MANASHA MATHESON does not survive me, I hereby nominate and appoint SUNSHINE MAY WALKER KESEY, as the guardian of KEELIN GARCIA, if she is then a minor. No bond shal be required of any person who acts as guardian hereunder.

FIFTEENTH
DELAYED DISTRIBUTION

I direct that no interest shall be payable on account of any delary in distributing any devise, bequest, or legacy under my Will or any Codicial thereto.

SIXTEENTH
DEFINITIONS

The words ``Executor,'' ``Trustee,'' ``child,'' ``children,'' and ``beneficiary,'' as used herein, shall comprehend both the singular and the plural, and the masculine or feminine shall be deemed to include the other wherever the context of this Will requires. This Will and any Codicil shall be interpreted under the California law as in effect at the date of signature of such document.

IN WITNESS WHEREOF, I have hereunto set my hand this May 12, 1994.

Jerome J. Garcia

On the date indicated below, JEROME J. GARCIA, declared to us, the undersigned, that this instrument, consisting of sixteen (16) pages, including the page signed by us as witnesses, was the testator's Will and requested us to act as witnesses to it. The testator thereupon

Figure E-6

continued

signed this Will in our presence, all of us being present at the same time. We now, at the testator's request, in the testator's presence and in the presence of each other, subscribe our names as witnesses.

It is our belief that the testator is of sound mind and memory and is under no constraint or undue influence whatsoever.

We declare under penalty of perjury that the foregoing is true and correct and that this declaration was executed on May 12, 1994, at San Rafael, California.

David M. Hellman residing at 523 4th St. #102, San Rafael, CA 94901

Tanna Burcher residing at 523 4th St. #102, San Rafael, CA 94901

ATTACHMENT 8

Name	Relationship	Age	Address
Deborah Koons Garcia	Spouse	Adult	c/o Max Gutierrez, Jr., Esq. Brobeck, Phleger & Harrison One Market Plaza, 27th Floor Spear Street Tower San Francisco, CA 94105
Heather Garcia Katz	Daughter	Adult	c/o Michael Rubenstein, Esq. Rubenstein & Bohachek 200 California Street, 5th Floor San Francisco, CA 94111
Annabelle Walker Garcia	Daughter	Adult	c/o David C. Phillips, Esq. Goldstein & Phillips One Embarcadero Center Eighth Floor San Francisco, CA 94111
Theresa Adams Garcia	Daughter	Adult	c/o David C. Phillips, Esq. Goldstein & Phillips One Embarcadero Center Eighth Floor San Francisco, CA 94111

Figure E-6

continued

Keelin Garcia	Daughter	Minor	c/o Manasha Matheson c/o Esther R. Lerner, Esq. Lerner Law Offices 88 Kearny Street, Ste. 1750 San Francisco, CA 94108
Douglas Erwin	Friend	Adult	P.O. Box 2232 Sonoma, CA 95476
Carolyn Adams Garcia	Former Spouse	Adult	c/o David C. Phillips, Esq. Goldstein & Phillips One Embarcadero Center Eighth Floor San Francisco, CA 94111
Manasha Matheson	Friend	Adult	c/o Esther R. Lerner, Esq. Lerner Law Offices 88 Kearny Street, Ste. 1750 San Francisco, CA 94108
Sunshine May Walker	Friend	Adult	c/o David C. Phillips, Esq. Goldstein & Phillips One Embarcadero Center Eighth Floor San Francisco, CA 94111
Clifford Garcia	Brother	Adult	91 Laura Lane Fairfax, CA 94930

Figure E-6

continued

Tax
Forms

The following documents are actual tax forms from the United States Department of the Treasury–Internal Revenue Service (IRS).

In this appendix, you will find the following tax forms:

○ **Form 706: United States Estate (and Generation-Skipping Transfer) Tax Return.** The executor of a decedent's estate uses form 706 to determine the estate tax imposed by the IRS. Form 706 is also used to compute the generation-skipping transfer tax imposed by the IRS. This form must be filed (within nine months of the date of a decedent's death) by the executors for the estates of all U.S. citizens or residents whose gross estates (including taxable gifts made during the decedents' lifetimes), less specific exemptions, are more than $675,000 in 2000. For dates of death after 2000, the executor must file Form 706 for all estates with values exceeding the applicable exclusion amount for that year. (See Table 2.3 in the Saturday Morning session for the applicable exclusion amounts.)

○ **Form 709: United States Gift (and Generation-Skipping Transfer) Tax Return.** This form must be filed annually for taxable gifts made during the calendar year. (For more information on what constitutes a taxable gift, see "Don't Forget Your Uncle Sam" in the Saturday Morning session)

○ **Form 709(A): United States Gift (and Generation-Skipping Transfer) Tax Return–Short Form.** This form is an annual short form gift tax return that certain married couples may use instead of Form 709 to report nontaxable gifts that they consent to split.

○ **Form 1041: U.S. Income Tax Return for Estates and Trusts.** This form must be filed by the executor of a decedent's estate when the estate generates income during the probate administration proceeding. (For more information regarding when an income tax return for an estate must be filed, see the Sunday Evening session.)

For more information or questions regarding these forms, contact the Internal Revenue Service (IRS). You can access the IRS's Internet Web site at **www.irs.gov** to download forms, instructions, and publications, or you can order forms and publications 24 hours a day, seven days a week, by calling 1-800-TAX-FORM (1-800-829-3676). You can also obtain copies of most forms at your local IRS office.

Form **706** (Rev. July 1999) Department of the Treasury Internal Revenue Service	**United States Estate (and Generation-Skipping Transfer) Tax Return** Estate of a citizen or resident of the United States (see separate instructions). To be filed for decedents dying after December 31, 1998. For Paperwork Reduction Act Notice, see page 1 of the separate instructions.	OMB No. 1545-0015

Part 1.—Decedent and Executor

1a	Decedent's first name and middle initial (and maiden name, if any)	1b	Decedent's last name	2	Decedent's Social Security No.
3a	Legal residence (domicile) at time of death (county, state, and ZIP code, or foreign country)	3b Year domicile established	4 Date of birth	5 Date of death	
6a	Name of executor (see page 4 of the instructions)	6b Executor's address (number and street including apartment or suite no. or rural route; city, town, or post office; state; and ZIP code)			
6c	Executor's social security number (see page 4 of the instructions)				
7a	Name and location of court where will was probated or estate administered			7b Case number	

8 If decedent died testate, check here ▶ ☐ and attach a certified copy of the will. **9** If Form 4768 is attached, check here ▶ ☐

10 If Schedule R-1 is attached, check here ▶ ☐

Part 2.—Tax Computation

1	Total gross estate less exclusion (from Part 5, Recapitulation, page 3, item 12)	1	
2	Total allowable deductions (from Part 5, Recapitulation, page 3, item 23)	2	
3	Taxable estate (subtract line 2 from line 1)	3	
4	Adjusted taxable gifts (total taxable gifts (within the meaning of section 2503) made by the decedent after December 31, 1976, other than gifts that are includible in decedent's gross estate (section 2001(b)))	4	
5	Add lines 3 and 4	5	
6	Tentative tax on the amount on line 5 from Table A on page 12 of the instructions	6	
7a	If line 5 exceeds $10,000,000, enter the lesser of line 5 or $17,184,000. If line 5 is $10,000,000 or less, skip lines 7a and 7b and enter -0- on line 7c . **7a**		
b	Subtract $10,000,000 from line 7a **7b**		
c	Enter 5% (.05) of line 7b	7c	
8	Total tentative tax (add lines 6 and 7c)	8	
9	Total gift tax payable with respect to gifts made by the decedent after December 31, 1976. Include gift taxes by the decedent's spouse for such spouse's share of split gifts (section 2513) only if the decedent was the donor of these gifts and they are includible in the decedent's gross estate (see instructions)	9	
10	Gross estate tax (subtract line 9 from line 8)	10	
11	Maximum unified credit (applicable credit amount) against estate tax . **11**		
12	Adjustment to unified credit (applicable credit amount). (This adjustment may not exceed $6,000. See page 4 of the instructions.) **12**		
13	Allowable unified credit (applicable credit amount) (subtract line 12 from line 11).	13	
14	Subtract line 13 from line 10 (but do not enter less than zero)	14	
15	Credit for state death taxes. Do not enter more than line 14. Figure the credit by using the amount on line 3 less $60,000. See Table B in the instructions and **attach credit evidence** (see instructions)	15	
16	Subtract line 15 from line 14	16	
17	Credit for Federal gift taxes on pre-1977 gifts (section 2012) (attach computation) **17**		
18	Credit for foreign death taxes (from Schedule(s) P). (Attach Form(s) 706-CE.) **18**		
19	Credit for tax on prior transfers (from Schedule Q). **19**		
20	Total (add lines 17, 18, and 19)	20	
21	Net estate tax (subtract line 20 from line 16)	21	
22	Generation-skipping transfer taxes (from Schedule R, Part 2, line 10)	22	
23	Total transfer taxes (add lines 21 and 22)	23	
24	Prior payments. Explain in an attached statement **24**		
25	United States Treasury bonds redeemed in payment of estate tax . **25**		
26	Total (add lines 24 and 25).	26	
27	Balance due (or overpayment) (subtract line 26 from line 23)	27	

Under penalties of perjury, I declare that I have examined this return, including accompanying schedules and statements, and to the best of my knowledge and belief, it is true, correct, and complete. Declaration of preparer other than the executor is based on all information of which preparer has any knowledge.

Signature(s) of executor(s)   Date

Signature of preparer other than executor   Cat. No. 20548R   Address (and ZIP code)   Date

Figure F-1

Form 706, page 1

Form 706 (Rev. 7-99)

Estate of:

Part 3—Elections by the Executor

Please check the "Yes" or "No" box for each question. (See instructions beginning on page 5.)

			Yes	No
1	Do you elect alternate valuation?	1		
2	Do you elect special use valuation? If "Yes," you must complete and attach Schedule A–1.	2		
3	Do you elect to pay the taxes in installments as described in section 6166? If "Yes," you must attach the additional information described on page 8 of the instructions.	3		
4	Do you elect to postpone the part of the taxes attributable to a reversionary or remainder interest as described in section 6163?	4		

Part 4—General Information (Note: *Please attach the necessary supplemental documents. You must attach the death certificate.*)
(See instructions on page 9.)

Authorization to receive confidential tax information under Regs. sec. 601.504(b)(2)(i); to act as the estate's representative before the IRS; and to make written or oral presentations on behalf of the estate if return prepared by an attorney, accountant, or enrolled agent for the executor:

Name of representative (print or type)	State	Address (number, street, and room or suite no., city, state, and ZIP code)

I declare that I am the ☐ attorney/ ☐ certified public accountant/ ☐ enrolled agent (you must check the applicable box) for the executor and prepared this return for the executor. I am not under suspension or disbarment from practice before the Internal Revenue Service and am qualified to practice in the state shown above.

Signature	CAF number	Date	Telephone number

1 Death certificate number and issuing authority (attach a copy of the death certificate to this return).

2 Decedent's business or occupation. If retired, check here ▶ ☐ and state decedent's former business or occupation.

3 Marital status of the decedent at time of death:
☐ Married
☐ Widow or widower—Name, SSN, and date of death of deceased spouse ▶ ------------------------------------

☐ Single
☐ Legally separated
☐ Divorced—Date divorce decree became final ▶

4a Surviving spouse's name	**4b** Social security number	**4c** Amount received (see page 9 of the instructions)

5 Individuals (other than the surviving spouse), trusts, or other estates who receive benefits from the estate (do not include charitable beneficiaries shown in Schedule O) (see instructions). For Privacy Act Notice (applicable to individual beneficiaries only), see the Instructions for Form 1040.

Name of individual, trust, or estate receiving $5,000 or more	Identifying number	Relationship to decedent	Amount (see instructions)
All unascertainable beneficiaries and those who receive less than $5,000 ▶			

Total

Please check the "Yes" or "No" box for each question.

		Yes	No
6	Does the gross estate contain any section 2044 property (qualified terminable interest property (QTIP) from a prior gift or estate) (see page 9 of the instructions)?		

(continued on next page)

Page 2

Figure F-1

Form 706,
page 2

Form 706 (Rev. 7-99)

Part 4—General Information *(continued)*

Please check the "Yes" or "No" box for each question.	Yes	No
7a Have Federal gift tax returns ever been filed?		
If "Yes," please attach copies of the returns, if available, and furnish the following information:		

7b Period(s) covered	**7c** Internal Revenue office(s) where filed

If you answer "Yes" to any of questions 8–16, you must attach additional information as described in the instructions.

		Yes	No
8a	Was there any insurance on the decedent's life that is not included on the return as part of the gross estate?		
b	Did the decedent own any insurance on the life of another that is not included in the gross estate?		
9	Did the decedent at the time of death own any property as a joint tenant with right of survivorship in which **(a)** one or more of the other joint tenants was someone other than the decedent's spouse, and **(b)** less than the full value of the property is included on the return as part of the gross estate? If "Yes," you must complete and attach Schedule E		
10	Did the decedent, at the time of death, own any interest in a partnership or unincorporated business or any stock in an inactive or closely held corporation?		
11	Did the decedent make any transfer described in section 2035, 2036, 2037, or 2038 (see the instructions for Schedule G beginning on page 11 of the separate instructions)? If "Yes," you must complete and attach Schedule G		
12	Were there in existence at the time of the decedent's death:		
a	Any trusts created by the decedent during his or her lifetime?		
b	Any trusts not created by the decedent under which the decedent possessed any power, beneficial interest, or trusteeship?		
13	Did the decedent ever possess, exercise, or release any general power of appointment? If "Yes," you must complete and attach Schedule H		
14	Was the marital deduction computed under the transitional rule of Public Law 97-34, section 403(e)(3) (Economic Recovery Tax Act of 1981)? If "Yes," attach a separate computation of the marital deduction, enter the amount on item 20 of the Recapitulation, and note on item 20 "computation attached."		
15	Was the decedent, immediately before death, receiving an annuity described in the "General" paragraph of the instructions for Schedule I? If "Yes," you must complete and attach Schedule I		
16	Was the decedent ever the beneficiary of a trust for which a deduction was claimed by the estate of a pre-deceased spouse under section 2056(b)(7) and which is not reported on this return? If "Yes," attach an explanation.		

Part 5—Recapitulation

Item number	Gross estate		Alternate value	Value at date of death
1	Schedule A—Real Estate	1		
2	Schedule B—Stocks and Bonds	2		
3	Schedule C—Mortgages, Notes, and Cash	3		
4	Schedule D—Insurance on the Decedent's Life (attach Form(s) 712) . . .	4		
5	Schedule E—Jointly Owned Property (attach Form(s) 712 for life insurance) .	5		
6	Schedule F—Other Miscellaneous Property (attach Form(s) 712 for life insurance)	6		
7	Schedule G—Transfers During Decedent's Life (att. Form(s) 712 for life insurance)	7		
8	Schedule H—Powers of Appointment	8		
9	Schedule I—Annuities	9		
10	Total gross estate (add items 1 through 9).	10		
11	Schedule U—Qualified Conservation Easement Exclusion	11		
12	Total gross estate less exclusion (subtract item 11 from item 10). Enter here and on line 1 of Part 2—Tax Computation	12		

Item number	Deductions		Amount
13	Schedule J—Funeral Expenses and Expenses Incurred in Administering Property Subject to Claims . . .	13	
14	Schedule K—Debts of the Decedent	14	
15	Schedule K—Mortgages and Liens	15	
16	Total of items 13 through 15	16	
17	Allowable amount of deductions from item 16 (see the instructions for item 17 of the Recapitulation) .	17	
18	Schedule L—Net Losses During Administration	18	
19	Schedule L—Expenses Incurred in Administering Property Not Subject to Claims	19	
20	Schedule M—Bequests, etc., to Surviving Spouse	20	
21	Schedule O—Charitable, Public, and Similar Gifts and Bequests	21	
22	Schedule T—Qualified Family-Owned Business Interest Deduction	22	
23	Total allowable deductions (add items 17 through 22). Enter here and on line 2 of the Tax Computation	23	

Page 3

Figure F-1

Form 706, page 3

Form 706 (Rev. 7-99)

Estate of:

SCHEDULE A—Real Estate

- For jointly owned property that must be disclosed on Schedule E, see the instructions on the reverse side of Schedule E.
- Real estate that is part of a sole proprietorship should be shown on Schedule F.
- Real estate that is included in the gross estate under section 2035, 2036, 2037, or 2038 should be shown on Schedule G.
- Real estate that is included in the gross estate under section 2041 should be shown on Schedule H.
- If you elect section 2032A valuation, you must complete Schedule A and Schedule A-1.

Item number	Description	Alternate valuation date	Alternate value	Value at date of death
1				

Total from continuation schedules or additional sheets attached to this schedule . . .

TOTAL. (Also enter on Part 5, Recapitulation, page 3, at item 1.) . . . .

(If more space is needed, attach the continuation schedule from the end of this package or additional sheets of the same size.)

(See the instructions on the reverse side.)

Schedule A—Page 4

Figure F-1

Form 706, page 4

Instructions for Schedule A—Real Estate

If the total gross estate contains any real estate, you must complete Schedule A and file it with the return. On Schedule A list real estate the decedent owned or had contracted to purchase. Number each parcel in the left-hand column.

Describe the real estate in enough detail so that the IRS can easily locate it for inspection and valuation. For each parcel of real estate, report the area and, if the parcel is improved, describe the improvements. For city or town property, report the street and number, ward, subdivision, block and lot, etc. For rural property, report the township, range, landmarks, etc.

If any item of real estate is subject to a mortgage for which the decedent's estate is liable; that is, if the indebtedness may be charged against other property of the estate that is not subject to that mortgage, or if the decedent was personally liable for that mortgage, you must report the full value of the property in the value column. Enter the amount of the mortgage under "Description" on this schedule. The unpaid amount of the mortgage may be deducted on Schedule K.

If the decedent's estate is NOT liable for the amount of the mortgage, report only the value of the equity of redemption (or value of the property less the indebtedness) in the value column as part of the gross estate. Do not enter any amount less than zero. Do not deduct the amount of indebtedness on Schedule K.

Also list on Schedule A real property the decedent contracted to purchase. Report the full value of the property and not the equity in the value column. Deduct the unpaid part of the purchase price on Schedule K.

Report the value of real estate without reducing it for homestead or other exemption, or the value of dower, curtesy, or a statutory estate created instead of dower or curtesy.

Explain how the reported values were determined and attach copies of any appraisals.

Schedule A Examples

In this example, alternate valuation is not adopted; the date of death is January 1, 1999.

Item number	Description	Alternate valuation date	Alternate value	Value at date of death
1	House and lot, 1921 William Street NW, Washington, DC (lot 6, square 481). Rent of $2,700 due at end of each quarter, February 1, May 1, August 1, and November 1. Value based on appraisal, copy of which is attached			$108,000
	Rent due on item 1 for quarter ending November 1, 1998, but not collected at date of death			2,700
	Rent accrued on item 1 for November and December 1998			1,800
2	House and lot, 304 Jefferson Street, Alexandria, VA (lot 18, square 40). Rent of $600 payable monthly. Value based on appraisal, copy of which is attached			96,000
	Rent due on item 2 for December 1998, but not collected at date of death			600

In this example, alternate valuation is adopted; the date of death is January 1, 1999.

Item number	Description	Alternate valuation date	Alternate value	Value at date of death
1	House and lot, 1921 William Street NW, Washington, DC (lot 6, square 481). Rent of $2,700 due at end of each quarter, February 1, May 1, August 1, and November 1. Value based on appraisal, copy of which is attached. Not disposed of within 6 months following death	7/1/99	90,000	$108,000
	Rent due on item 1 for quarter ending November 1, 1998, but not collected until February 1, 1999	2/1/99	2,700	2,700
	Rent accrued on item 1 for November and December 1998, collected on February 1, 1999	2/1/99	1,800	1,800
2	House and lot, 304 Jefferson Street, Alexandria, VA (lot 18, square 40). Rent of $600 payable monthly. Value based on appraisal, copy of which is attached. Property exchanged for farm on May 1, 1999	5/1/99	90,000	96,000
	Rent due on item 2 for December 1998, but not collected until February 1, 1999	2/1/99	600	600

Schedule A—Page 5

Figure F-1

Form 706,
page 5

Form 706 (Rev. 7-99)

Instructions for Schedule A-1. Section 2032A Valuation

The election to value certain farm and closely held business property at its special use value is made by checking "Yes" to line 2 of Part 3, Elections by the Executor, Form 706. Schedule A-1 is used to report the additional information that must be submitted to support this election. In order to make a valid election, you must complete Schedule A-1 and attach all of the required statements and appraisals.

For definitions and additional information concerning special use valuation, see section 2032A and the related regulations.

Part 1. Type of Election

Estate and GST Tax Elections. If you elect special use valuation for the estate tax, you must also elect special use valuation for the GST tax and vice versa.

You must value each specific property interest at the same value for GST tax purposes that you value it at for estate tax purposes.

Protective Election. To make the protective election described in the separate instructions for line 2 of Part 3, Elections by the Executor, you must check this box, enter the decedent's name and social security number in the spaces provided at the top of Schedule A-1, and complete line 1 and column A of lines 3 and 4 of Part 2. For purposes of the protective election, list on line 3 all of the real property that passes to the qualified heirs even though some of the property will be shown on line 2 when the additional notice of election is subsequently filed. You need not complete columns B–D of lines 3 and 4. You need not complete any other line entries on Schedule A-1. Completing Schedule A-1 as described above constitutes a Notice of Protective Election as described in Regulations section 20.2032A-8(b).

Part 2. Notice of Election

Line 10. Because the special use valuation election creates a potential tax liability for the recapture tax of section 2032A(c), you must list each person who receives an interest in the specially valued property on Schedule A-1. If there are more than eight persons who receive interests, use an additional sheet that follows the format of line 10. In the columns "Fair market value" and "Special use value," you should enter the total respective values of all the specially valued property interests received by each person.

GST Tax Savings

To compute the additional GST tax due upon disposition (or cessation of qualified use) of the property, each "skip person" (as defined in the instructions to Schedule R) who receives an interest in the specially valued property must know the total GST tax savings on all of the interests in specially valued property received. This GST tax savings is the difference between the total GST tax that was imposed on all of the interests in specially valued property received by the skip person valued at their special use value and the total GST tax that would have been imposed on the same interests received by the skip person had they been valued at their fair market value.

Because the GST tax depends on the executor's allocation of the GST exemption and the grandchild exclusion, the skip person who receives the interests is unable to compute this GST tax savings. Therefore, for each skip person who receives an interest in specially valued property, you must attach worksheets showing the total GST tax savings attributable to all of that person's interests in specially valued property.

How To Compute the GST Tax Savings. Before computing each skip person's GST tax savings, you must complete Schedules R and R-1 for the entire estate (using the special use values).

For each skip person, you must complete two Schedules R (Parts 2 and 3 only) as worksheets, one showing the interests in

specially valued property received by the skip person at their special use value and one showing the same interests at their fair market value.

If the skip person received interests in specially valued property that were shown on Schedule R-1, show these interests on the Schedule R, Parts 2 and 3 worksheets, as appropriate. Do not use Schedule R-1 as a worksheet.

Completing the Special Use.Value Worksheets. On lines 2–4 and 6, enter -0-.

Completing the Fair Market Value Worksheets. *Lines 2 and 3, fixed taxes and other charges.* If valuing the interests at their fair market value (instead of special use value) causes any of these taxes and charges to increase, enter the increased amount (only) on these lines and attach an explanation of the increase. Otherwise, enter -0-.

Line 6—GST exemption. If you completed line 10 of Schedule R, Part 1, enter on line 6 the amount shown for the skip person on the *line 10 special use allocation schedule* you attached to Schedule R. If you did not complete line 10 of Schedule R, Part 1, enter -0- on line 6.

Total GST Tax Savings. For each skip person, subtract the tax amount on line 10, Part 2 of the special use value worksheet from the tax amount on line 10, Part 2 of the fair market value worksheet. This difference is the skip person's total GST tax savings.

Part 3. Agreement to Special Valuation Under Section 2032A

The agreement to special valuation by persons with an interest in property is required under section 2032A(a)(1)(B) and (d)(2) and must be signed by all parties who have any interest in the property being valued based on its qualified use as of the date of the decedent's death.

An interest in property is an interest that, as of the date of the decedent's death, can be asserted under applicable local law so as to affect the disposition of the specially valued property by the estate. Any person who at the decedent's death has any such interest in the property, whether present or future, or vested or contingent, must enter into the agreement. Included are owners of remainder and executory interests; the holders of general or special powers of appointment; beneficiaries of a gift over in default of exercise of any such power; joint tenants and holders of similar undivided interests when the decedent held only a joint or undivided interest in the property or when only an undivided interest is specially valued; and trustees of trusts and representatives of other entities holding title to, or holding any interests in the property. An heir who has the power under local law to caveat (challenge) a will and thereby affect disposition of the property is not, however, considered to be a person with an interest in property under section 2032A solely by reason of that right. Likewise, creditors of an estate are not such persons solely by reason of their status as creditors.

If any person required to enter into the agreement either desires that an agent act for him or her or cannot legally bind himself or herself due to infancy or other incompetency, or due to death before the election under section 2032A is timely exercised, a representative authorized by local law to bind the person in an agreement of this nature may sign the agreement on his or her behalf.

The Internal Revenue Service will contact the agent designated in the agreement on all matters relating to continued qualification under section 2032A of the specially valued real property and on all matters relating to the special lien arising under section 6324B. It is the duty of the agent as attorney-in-fact for the parties with interests in the specially valued property to furnish the IRS with any requested information and to notify the IRS of any disposition or cessation of qualified use of any part of the property.

Schedule A-1—Page 6

Figure F-1

Form 706, page 6

Checklist for Section 2032A Election. *If you are going to make the special use valuation election on Schedule A-1, please use this checklist to ensure that you are providing everything necessary to make a valid election.*

To have a valid special use valuation election under section 2032A, you must file, in addition to the Federal estate tax return, **(a)** a notice of election (Schedule A-1, Part 2), and **(b)** a fully executed agreement (Schedule A-1, Part 3). You must include certain information in the notice of election. To ensure that the notice of election includes all of the information required for a valid election, use the following checklist. The checklist is for your use only. Do not file it with the return.

1. Does the notice of election include the decedent's name and social security number as they appear on the estate tax return?

2. Does the notice of election include the relevant qualified use of the property to be specially valued?

3. Does the notice of election describe the items of real property shown on the estate tax return that are to be specially valued and identify the property by the Form 706 schedule and item number?

4. Does the notice of election include the fair market value of the real property to be specially valued and also include its value based on the qualified use (determined without the adjustments provided in section 2032A(b)(3)(B))?

5. Does the notice of election include the adjusted value (as defined in section 2032A(b)(3)(B)) of **(a)** all real property that both passes from the decedent and is used in a qualified use, without regard to whether it is to be specially valued, and **(b)** all real property to be specially valued?

6. Does the notice of election include **(a)** the items of personal property shown on the estate tax return that pass from the decedent to a qualified heir and that are used in qualified use and **(b)** the total value of such personal property adjusted under section 2032A(b)(3)(B)?

7. Does the notice of election include the adjusted value of the gross estate? (See section 2032A(b)(3)(A).)

8. Does the notice of election include the method used to determine the special use value?

9. Does the notice of election include copies of written appraisals of the fair market value of the real property?

10. Does the notice of election include a statement that the decedent and/or a member of his or her family has owned all of the specially valued property for at least 5 years of the 8 years immediately preceding the date of the decedent's death?

11. Does the notice of election include a statement as to whether there were any periods during the 8-year period preceding the decedent's date of death during which the decedent or a member of his or her family did not **(a)** own the property to be specially valued, **(b)** use it in a qualified use, or **(c)** materially participate in the operation of the farm or other business? (See section 2032A(e)(6).)

12. Does the notice of election include, for each item of specially valued property, the name of every person taking an interest in that item of specially valued property and the following information about each such person: **(a)** the person's address, **(b)** the person's taxpayer identification number, **(c)** the person's relationship to the decedent, and **(d)** the value of the property interest passing to that person based on both fair market value and qualified use?

13. Does the notice of election include affidavits describing the activities constituting material participation and the identity of the material participants?

14. Does the notice of election include a legal description of each item of specially valued property?

(In the case of an election made for qualified woodlands, the information included in the notice of election must include the reason for entitlement to the woodlands election.)

Any election made under section 2032A will not be valid unless a properly executed agreement (Schedule A-1, Part 3) is filed with the estate tax return. To ensure that the agreement satisfies the requirements for a valid election, use the following checklist.

1. Has the agreement been signed by each and every qualified heir having an interest in the property being specially valued?

2. Has every qualified heir expressed consent to personal liability under section 2032A(c) in the event of an early disposition or early cessation of qualified use?

3. Is the agreement that is actually signed by the qualified heirs in a form that is binding on all of the qualified heirs having an interest in the specially valued property?

4. Does the agreement designate an agent to act for the parties to the agreement in all dealings with the IRS on matters arising under section 2032A?

5. Has the agreement been signed by the designated agent and does it give the address of the agent?

Figure F-1

Form 706,
page 7

Form 706 (Rev. 7-99)

Estate of:

Decedent's Social Security Number
:

SCHEDULE A-1—Section 2032A Valuation

Part 1. Type of Election (Before making an election, see the checklist on page 7.):

☐ **Protective election (Regulations section 20.2032A-8(b)).** Complete Part 2, line 1, and column A of lines 3 and 4. (See instructions.)
☐ **Regular election.** Complete all of Part 2 (including line 11, if applicable) and Part 3. (See instructions.)

Before completing Schedule A-1, see the checklist on page 7 for the information and documents that must be included to make a valid election.

The election is not valid unless the agreement (i.e., Part 3—Agreement to Special Valuation Under Section 2032A)—
• Is signed by each and every qualified heir with an interest in the specially valued property, and
• Is attached to this return when it is filed.

Part 2. Notice of Election (Regulations section 20.2032A-8(a)(3))
    Note: *All real property entered on lines 2 and 3 must also be entered on Schedules A, E, F, G, or H, as applicable.*

1   Qualified use—check one ▶ ☐ Farm used for farming, or
                    ▶ ☐ Trade or business other than farming
2   Real property used in a qualified use, passing to qualified heirs, and to be specially valued on this Form 706.

A	B	C	D
Schedule and item number from Form 706	Full value (without section 2032A(b)(3)(B) adjustment)	Adjusted value (with section 2032A(b)(3)(B) adjustment)	Value based on qualified use (without section 2032A(b)(3)(B) adjustment)

Totals . . . .

Attach a legal description of all property listed on line 2.
Attach copies of appraisals showing the column B values for all property listed on line 2.

3   Real property used in a qualified use, passing to qualified heirs, but not specially valued on this Form 706.

A	B	C	D
Schedule and item number from Form 706	Full value (without section 2032A(b)(3)(B) adjustment)	Adjusted value (with section 2032A(b)(3)(B) adjustment)	Value based on qualified use (without section 2032A(b)(3)(B) adjustment)

Totals . . . .
If you checked "Regular election," you must attach copies of appraisals showing the column B values for all property listed on line 3.

(continued on next page)   Schedule A-1—Page 8

Figure F-1

Form 706,
page 8

Form 706 (Rev. 7-99)

4 Personal property used in a qualified use and passing to qualified heirs.

A Schedule and item number from Form 706	B Adjusted value (with section 2032A(b)(3)(B) adjustment)	A (continued) Schedule and item number from Form 706	B (continued) Adjusted value (with section 2032A(b)(3)(B) adjustment)
		"Subtotal" from Col. B, below left	....

Subtotal . . . .   **Total adjusted value** . . .

5 Enter the value of the total gross estate as adjusted under section 2032A(b)(3)(A). ▶ _____

6 Attach a description of the method used to determine the special value based on qualified use.

7 Did the decedent and/or a member of his or her family own all property listed on line 2 for at least 5 of the 8 years immediately preceding the date of the decedent's death? . . . . □ Yes □ No

8 Were there any periods during the 8-year period preceding the date of the decedent's death during which the decedent or a member of his or her family:

	Yes	No
a Did not own the property listed on line 2 above?		
b Did not use the property listed on line 2 above in a qualified use?		
c Did not materially participate in the operation of the farm or other business within the meaning of section 2032A(e)(6)?.		

If "Yes" to any of the above, you must attach a statement listing the periods. If applicable, describe whether the exceptions of sections 2032A(b)(4) or (5) are met.

9 Attach affidavits describing the activities constituting material participation and the identity and relationship to the decedent of the material participants.

10 Persons holding interests. Enter the requested information for each party who received any interest in the specially valued property. **(Each of the qualified heirs receiving an interest in the property must sign the agreement, and the agreement must be filed with this return.)**

	Name	Address
A		
B		
C		
D		
E		
F		
G		
H		

	Identifying number	Relationship to decedent	Fair market value	Special use value
A				
B				
C				
D				
E				
F				
G				
H				

You must attach a computation of the GST tax savings attributable to direct skips for each person listed above who is a skip person. (See instructions.)

11 Woodlands election. Check here ▶ □ if you wish to make a woodlands election as described in section 2032A(e)(13). Enter the Schedule and item numbers from Form 706 of the property for which you are making this election ▶.................................... You must attach a statement explaining why you are entitled to make this election. The IRS may issue regulations that require more information to substantiate this election. You will be notified by the IRS if you must supply further information.

Schedule A-1—Page 9

Figure F-1

Form 706,
page 9

Form 706 (Rev. 7-99)

Part 3. Agreement to Special Valuation Under Section 2032A

Estate of:	Date of Death	Decedent's Social Security Number

There cannot be a valid election unless:

- The agreement is executed by each and every one of the qualified heirs, and
- The agreement is included with the estate tax return when the estate tax return is filed.

We (list all qualified heirs and other persons having an interest in the property required to sign this agreement)

_____

_____ ,

being all the qualified heirs and _____

_____ ,

being all other parties having interests in the property which is qualified real property and which is valued under section 2032A of the Internal Revenue Code, do hereby approve of the election made by _____ ,

Executor/Administrator of the estate of _____ ,

pursuant to section 2032A to value said property on the basis of the qualified use to which the property is devoted and do hereby enter into this agreement pursuant to section 2032A(d).

The undersigned agree and consent to the application of subsection (c) of section 2032A of the Code with respect to all the property described on line 2 of Part 2 of Schedule A-1 of Form 706, attached to this agreement. More specifically, the undersigned heirs expressly agree and consent to personal liability under subsection (c) of 2032A for the additional estate and GST taxes imposed by that subsection with respect to their respective interests in the above-described property in the event of certain early dispositions of the property or early cessation of the qualified use of the property. It is understood that if a qualified heir disposes of any interest in qualified real property to any member of his or her family, such member may thereafter be treated as the qualified heir with respect to such interest upon filing a Form 706-A and a new agreement.

The undersigned interested parties who are not qualified heirs consent to the collection of any additional estate and GST taxes imposed under section 2032A(c) of the Code from the specially valued property.

If there is a disposition of any interest which passes, or has passed to him or her, or if there is a cessation of the qualified use of any specially valued property which passes or passed to him or her, each of the undersigned heirs agrees to file a **Form 706-A,** United States Additional Estate Tax Return, and pay any additional estate and GST taxes due within 6 months of the disposition or cessation.

It is understood by all interested parties that this agreement is a condition precedent to the election of special use valuation under section 2032A of the Code and must be executed by every interested party even though that person may not have received the estate (or GST) tax benefits or be in possession of such property.

Each of the undersigned understands that by making this election, a lien will be created and recorded pursuant to section 6324B of the Code on the property referred to in this agreement for the adjusted tax differences with respect to the estate as defined in section 2032A(c)(2)(C).

As the interested parties, the undersigned designate the following individual as their agent for all dealings with the Internal Revenue Service concerning the continued qualification of the specially valued property under section 2032A of the Code and on all issues regarding the special lien under section 6324B. The agent is authorized to act for the parties with respect to all dealings with the Service on matters affecting the qualified real property described earlier. This authority includes the following:

- To receive confidential information on all matters relating to continued qualification under section 2032A of the specially valued real property and on all matters relating to the special lien arising under section 6324B.
- To furnish the Internal Revenue Service with any requested information concerning the property.
- To notify the Internal Revenue Service of any disposition or cessation of qualified use of any part of the property.
- To receive, but not to endorse and collect, checks in payment of any refund of Internal Revenue taxes, penalties, or interest.
- To execute waivers (including offers of waivers) of restrictions on assessment or collection of deficiencies in tax and waivers of notice of disallowance of a claim for credit or refund.
- To execute closing agreements under section 7121.

(continued on next page)

Schedule A-1— Page 10

Figure F-1

Form 706,
page 10

Part 3. Agreement to Special Valuation Under Section 2032A *(Continued)*

Estate of:	Date of Death	Decedent's Social Security Number

● Other acts (specify) ▶ _____

By signing this agreement, the agent agrees to provide the Internal Revenue Service with any requested information concerning this property and to notify the Internal Revenue Service of any disposition or cessation of the qualified use of any part of this property.

_____	_____	_____
Name of Agent	Signature	Address

The property to which this agreement relates is listed in Form 706, United States Estate (and Generation-Skipping Transfer) Tax Return, and in the Notice of Election, along with its fair market value according to section 2031 of the Code and its special use value according to section 2032A. The name, address, social security number, and interest (including the value) of each of the undersigned in this property are as set forth in the attached Notice of Election.

IN WITNESS WHEREOF, the undersigned have hereunto set their hands at _____ ,

this _____ day of _____ .

SIGNATURES OF EACH OF THE QUALIFIED HEIRS:

_____   _____
Signature of qualified heir   Signature of qualified heir

_____   _____
Signature of qualified heir   Signature of qualified heir

_____   _____
Signature of qualified heir   Signature of qualified heir

_____   _____
Signature of qualified heir   Signature of qualified heir

_____   _____
Signature of qualified heir   Signature of qualified heir

_____   _____
Signature of qualified heir   Signature of qualified heir

_____
Signatures of other interested parties

_____
Signatures of other interested parties

Schedule A-1—Page 11

Figure F-1

Form 706,
page 11

Form 706 (Rev. 7-99)

Estate of:

SCHEDULE B—Stocks and Bonds

(For jointly owned property that must be disclosed on Schedule E, see the instructions for Schedule E.)

Item number	Description including face amount of bonds or number of shares and par value where needed for identification. Give 9-digit CUSIP number.	Unit value	Alternate valuation date	Alternate value	Value at date of death
	CUSIP number				
1					

Total from continuation schedules (or additional sheets) attached to this schedule . . .

TOTAL. (Also enter on Part 5, Recapitulation, page 3, at item 2.) . . . .

(If more space is needed, attach the continuation schedule from the end of this package or additional sheets of the same size.)
(The instructions to Schedule B are in the separate instructions.)

Schedule B—Page 12

Figure F-1

Form 706, page 12

Form 706 (Rev. 7-99)

Estate of:

SCHEDULE C—Mortgages, Notes, and Cash
(For jointly owned property that must be disclosed on Schedule E, see the instructions for Schedule E.)

Item number	Description	Alternate valuation date	Alternate value	Value at date of death
1				

Total from continuation schedules (or additional sheets) attached to this schedule . .

TOTAL. (Also enter on Part 5, Recapitulation, page 3, at item 3.). . . . .

(If more space is needed, attach the continuation schedule from the end of this package or additional sheets of the same size.)
(See the instructions on the reverse side.)

Schedule C—Page 13

Figure F-1

Form 706,
page 13

Form 706 (Rev. 7-99)

Instructions for Schedule C.— Mortgages, Notes, and Cash

Complete Schedule C and file it with your return if the total gross estate contains any:

- mortgages,
- notes, or
- cash.

List on Schedule C:

- Mortgages and notes payable **to the decedent** at the time of death.
- Cash the decedent had at the date of death.

Do not list on Schedule C:

- Mortgages and notes payable **by the decedent.** (If these are deductible, list them on Schedule K.)

List the items on Schedule C in the following order:

- mortgages,
- promissory notes,
- contracts by decedent to sell land,
- cash in possession, and
- cash in banks, savings and loan associations, and other types of financial organizations.

What to enter in the "Description" column:

For mortgages, list:

- face value,
- unpaid balance,
- date of mortgage,
- date of maturity,
- name of maker,
- property mortgaged,
- interest dates, and
- interest rate.

Example to enter in "Description" column:

"Bond and mortgage of $50,000, unpaid balance: $24,000; dated: January 1, 1981; John Doe to Richard Roe; premises: 22 Clinton Street, Newark, NJ; due: January 1, 1999; interest payable at 10% a year--January 1 and July 1."

For promissory notes, list:

- in the same way as mortgages.

For contracts by the decedent to sell land, list:

- name of purchaser,
- contract date,
- property description,
- sale price,
- initial payment,
- amounts of installment payment,
- unpaid balance of principal, and
- interest rate.

For cash in possession, list:

- such cash separately from bank deposits.

For cash in banks, savings and loan associations, and other types of financial organizations, list:

- name and address of each financial organization,
- amount in each account,
- serial or account number,
- nature of account--checking, savings, time deposit, etc., and
- unpaid interest accrued from date of last interest payment to the date of death.

Important: If you obtain statements from the financial organizations, keep them for IRS inspection.

Schedule C—Page 14

Figure F-1

Form 706,
page 14

Form 706 (Rev. 7-99)

Estate of:

SCHEDULE D—Insurance on the Decedent's Life

You must list **all** policies on the life of the decedent and attach a Form 712 for each policy.

Item number	Description	Alternate valuation date	Alternate value	Value at date of death
1				

Total from continuation schedules (or additional sheets) attached to this schedule . .

TOTAL. (Also enter on Part 5, Recapitulation, page 3, at item 4.). . . . .

(If more space is needed, attach the continuation schedule from the end of this package or additional sheets of the same size.)

(See the instructions on the reverse side.)

Schedule D—Page 15

Figure F-1

Form 706,
page 15

Form 706 (Rev. 7-99)

Instructions for Schedule D—Insurance on the Decedent's Life

If you are required to file Form 706 and there was any insurance on the decedent's life, whether or not included in the gross estate, you must complete Schedule D and file it with the return.

Insurance you must include on Schedule D. Under section 2042 you must include in the gross estate:

- Insurance on the decedent's life receivable by or for the benefit of the estate; and
- Insurance on the decedent's life receivable by beneficiaries other than the estate, as described below.

The term "insurance" refers to life insurance of every description, including death benefits paid by fraternal beneficiary societies operating under the lodge system, and death benefits paid under no-fault automobile insurance policies if the no-fault insurer was unconditionally bound to pay the benefit in the event of the insured's death.

Insurance in favor of the estate. Include on Schedule D the full amount of the proceeds of insurance on the life of the decedent receivable by the executor or otherwise payable to or for the benefit of the estate. Insurance in favor of the estate includes insurance used to pay the estate tax, and any other taxes, debts, or charges that are enforceable against the estate. The manner in which the policy is drawn is immaterial as long as there is an obligation, legally binding on the beneficiary, to use the proceeds to pay taxes, debts, or charges. You must include the full amount even though the premiums or other consideration may have been paid by a person other than the decedent.

Insurance receivable by beneficiaries other than the estate. Include on Schedule D the proceeds of all insurance on the life of the decedent not receivable by or for the benefit of the decedent's estate if the decedent possessed at death any of the incidents of ownership, exercisable either alone or in conjunction with any person.

Incidents of ownership in a policy include:

- The right of the insured or estate to its economic benefits;
- The power to change the beneficiary;

- The power to surrender or cancel the policy;
- The power to assign the policy or to revoke an assignment;
- The power to pledge the policy for a loan;
- The power to obtain from the insurer a loan against the surrender value of the policy;
- A reversionary interest if the value of the reversionary interest was more than 5% of the value of the policy immediately before the decedent died. (An interest in an insurance policy is considered a reversionary interest if, for example, the proceeds become payable to the insured's estate or payable as the insured directs if the beneficiary dies before the insured.)

Life insurance not includible in the gross estate under section 2042 may be includible under some other section of the Code. For example, a life insurance policy could be transferred by the decedent in such a way that it would be includible in the gross estate under section 2036, 2037, or 2038. (See the instructions to Schedule G for a description of these sections.)

Completing the Schedule

You must list every policy of insurance on the life of the decedent, whether or not it is included in the gross estate.

Under "Description" list:

- Name of the insurance company and
- Number of the policy.

For every policy of life insurance listed on the schedule, you must request a statement on **Form 712,** Life Insurance Statement, from the company that issued the policy. Attach the Form 712 to the back of Schedule D.

If the policy proceeds are paid in one sum, enter the net proceeds received (from Form 712, line 24) in the value (and alternate value) columns of Schedule D. If the policy proceeds are not paid in one sum, enter the value of the proceeds as of the date of the decedent's death (from Form 712, line 25).

If part or all of the policy proceeds are not included in the gross estate, you must explain why they were not included.

Schedule D—Page 16

Figure F-1

Form 706,
page 16

Form 706 (Rev. 7-99)

Estate of:

SCHEDULE E—Jointly Owned Property
(If you elect section 2032A valuation, you must complete Schedule E and Schedule A-1.)

PART 1.—Qualified Joint Interests—Interests Held by the Decedent and His or Her Spouse as the Only Joint Tenants (Section 2040(b)(2))

Item number	Description For securities, give CUSIP number.	Alternate valuation date	Alternate value	Value at date of death

Total from continuation schedules (or additional sheets) attached to this schedule . . . . .

1a	Totals	**1a**	
1b	Amounts included in gross estate (one-half of line **1a**)	**1b**	

PART 2.—All Other Joint Interests

2a State the name and address of each surviving co-tenant. If there are more than three surviving co-tenants, list the additional co-tenants on an attached sheet.

Name	Address (number and street, city, state, and ZIP code)
A.	
B.	
C.	

Item number	Enter letter for co-tenant	Description (including alternate valuation date if any) For securities, give CUSIP number.	Percentage includible	Includible alternate value	Includible value at date of death

Total from continuation schedules (or additional sheets) attached to this schedule . . . . . .

2b	Total other joint interests		
3	**Total includible joint interests** (add lines 1b and 2b). Also enter on Part 5, Recapitulation, page 3, at item 5		

(If more space is needed, attach the continuation schedule from the end of this package or additional sheets of the same size.)
(See the instructions on the reverse side.)

Schedule E—Page 17

Figure F-1

Form 706, page 17

Form 706 (Rev. 7-99)

Instructions for Schedule E. Jointly Owned Property

If you are required to file Form 706, you must complete Schedule E and file it with the return if the decedent owned any joint property at the time of death, whether or not the decedent's interest is includible in the gross estate.

Enter on this schedule all property of whatever kind or character, whether real estate, personal property, or bank accounts, in which the decedent held at the time of death an interest either as a joint tenant with right to survivorship or as a tenant by the entirety.

Do not list on this schedule property that the decedent held as a tenant in common, but report the value of the interest on Schedule A if real estate, or on the appropriate schedule if personal property. Similarly, community property held by the decedent and spouse should be reported on the appropriate Schedules A through I. The decedent's interest in a partnership should not be entered on this schedule unless the partnership interest itself is jointly owned. Solely owned partnership interests should be reported on Schedule F, "Other Miscellaneous Property."

Part 1—Qualified joint interests held by decedent and spouse. Under section 2040(b)(2), a joint interest is a qualified joint interest if the decedent and the surviving spouse held the interest as:

- Tenants by the entirety, or
- Joint tenants with right of survivorship if the decedent and the decedent's spouse are the only joint tenants.

Interests that meet either of the two requirements above should be entered in Part 1. Joint interests that do not meet either of the two requirements above should be entered in Part 2.

Under "Description," describe the property as required in the instructions for Schedules A, B, C, and F for the type of property involved. For example, jointly held stocks and bonds should be described using the rules given in the instructions to Schedule B.

Under "Alternate value" and "Value at date of death," enter the full value of the property.

Note: *You cannot claim the special treatment under section 2040(b) for property held jointly by a decedent and a surviving spouse who is not a U.S. citizen. You must report these joint interests on Part 2 of Schedule E, not Part 1.*

Part 2—Other joint interests. All joint interests that were not entered in Part 1 must be entered in Part 2.

For each item of property, enter the appropriate letter A, B, C, etc., from line 2a to indicate the name and address of the surviving co-tenant.

Under "Description," describe the property as required in the instructions for Schedules A, B, C, and F for the type of property involved.

In the "Percentage includible" column, enter the percentage of the total value of the property that you intend to include in the gross estate.

Generally, you must include the full value of the jointly owned property in the gross estate. However, the full value should not be included if you can show that a part of the property originally belonged to the other tenant or tenants and was never received or acquired by the other tenant or tenants from the decedent for less than adequate and full consideration in money or money's worth, or unless you can show that any part of the property was acquired with consideration originally belonging to the surviving joint tenant or tenants. In this case, you may exclude from the value of the property an amount proportionate to the consideration furnished by the other tenant or tenants. Relinquishing or promising to relinquish dower, curtesy, or statutory estate created instead of dower or curtesy, or other marital rights in the decedent's property or estate is not consideration in money or money's worth. See the Schedule A instructions for the value to show for real property that is subject to a mortgage.

If the property was acquired by the decedent and another person or persons by gift, bequest, devise, or inheritance as joint tenants, and their interests are not otherwise specified by law, include only that part of the value of the property that is figured by dividing the full value of the property by the number of joint tenants.

If you believe that less than the full value of the entire property is includible in the gross estate for tax purposes, you must establish the right to include the smaller value by attaching proof of the extent, origin, and nature of the decedent's interest and the interest(s) of the decedent's co-tenant or co-tenants.

In the "Includible alternate value" and "Includible value at date of death" columns, you should enter only the values that you believe are includible in the gross estate.

Schedule E—Page 18

Figure F-1

Form 706, page 18

Estate of:

SCHEDULE F—Other Miscellaneous Property Not Reportable Under Any Other Schedule

(For jointly owned property that must be disclosed on Schedule E, see the instructions for Schedule E.)
(If you elect section 2032A valuation, you must complete Schedule F and Schedule A-1.)

		Yes	No
1	Did the decedent at the time of death own any articles of artistic or collectible value in excess of $3,000 or any collections whose artistic or collectible value combined at date of death exceeded $10,000? . . . . If "Yes," submit full details on this schedule and attach appraisals.		
2	Has the decedent's estate, spouse, or any other person, received (or will receive) any bonus or award as a result of the decedent's employment or death? . . . . If "Yes," submit full details on this schedule.		
3	Did the decedent at the time of death have, or have access to, a safe deposit box? . . . . If "Yes," state location, and if held in joint names of decedent and another, state name and relationship of joint depositor.		

If any of the contents of the safe deposit box are omitted from the schedules in this return, explain fully why omitted.

Item number	Description For securities, give CUSIP number.	Alternate valuation date	Alternate value	Value at date of death
1				

Total from continuation schedules (or additional sheets) attached to this schedule . .

TOTAL. (Also enter on Part 5, Recapitulation, page 3, at item 6.) . . . .

(If more space is needed, attach the continuation schedule from the end of this package or additional sheets of the same size.)
(See the instructions on the reverse side.)

Schedule F—Page 19

Figure F-1

Form 706,
page 19

Form 706 (Rev. 7-99)

Instructions for Schedule F—Other Miscellaneous Property

You must complete Schedule F and file it with the return.

On Schedule F list all items that must be included in the gross estate that are not reported on any other schedule, including:

- Debts due the decedent (other than notes and mortgages included on Schedule C)
- Interests in business
- Insurance on the life of another (obtain and attach **Form 712,** Life Insurance Statement, for each policy)

Note for single premium or paid-up policies: *In certain situations, for example where the surrender value of the policy exceeds its replacement cost, the true economic value of the policy will be greater than the amount shown on line 56 of Form 712. In these situations, you should report the full economic value of the policy on Schedule F. See Rev. Rul. 78-137, 1978-1 C.B. 280 for details.*

- Section 2044 property (see **Decedent Who Was a Surviving Spouse** below)
- Claims (including the value of the decedent's interest in a claim for refund of income taxes or the amount of the refund actually received)
- Rights
- Royalties
- Leaseholds
- Judgments
- Reversionary or remainder interests
- Shares in trust funds (attach a copy of the trust instrument)
- Household goods and personal effects, including wearing apparel
- Farm products and growing crops
- Livestock
- Farm machinery
- Automobiles

If the decedent owned any interest in a partnership or unincorporated business, attach a statement of assets and liabilities for the valuation date and for the 5 years before the valuation date. Also attach statements of the net earnings for the same 5 years.

You must account for goodwill in the valuation. In general, furnish the same information and follow the methods used to value close corporations. See the instructions for Schedule B.

All partnership interests should be reported on Schedule F unless the partnership interest, itself, is jointly owned. Jointly owned partnership interests should be reported on Schedule E.

If real estate is owned by the sole proprietorship, it should be reported on Schedule F and not on Schedule A. Describe the real estate with the same detail required for Schedule A.

Line 1. If the decedent owned at the date of death articles with artistic or intrinsic value (e.g., jewelry, furs, silverware, books, statuary, vases, oriental rugs, coin or stamp collections), check the "Yes" box on line 1 and provide full details. If any one article is valued at more than $3,000, or any collection of similar articles is valued at more than $10,000, attach an appraisal by an expert under oath and the required statement regarding the appraiser's qualifications (see Regulations section 20.2031-6(b)).

Decedent Who Was a Surviving Spouse

If the decedent was a surviving spouse, he or she may have received qualified terminable interest property (QTIP) from the predeceased spouse for which the marital deduction was elected either on the predeceased spouse's estate tax return or on a gift tax return, Form 709. The election was available for gifts made and decedents dying after December 31, 1981. List such property on Schedule F.

If this election was made and the surviving spouse retained his or her interest in the QTIP property at death, the full value of the QTIP property is includible in his or her estate, even though the qualifying income interest terminated at death. It is valued as of the date of the surviving spouse's death, or alternate valuation date, if applicable. Do not reduce the value by any annual exclusion that may have applied to the transfer creating the interest.

The value of such property included in the surviving spouse's gross estate is treated as passing from the surviving spouse. It therefore qualifies for the charitable and marital deductions on the surviving spouse's estate tax return if it meets the other requirements for those deductions.

For additional details, see Regulations section 20.2044-1.

Schedule F—Page 20

Figure F-1

Form 706, page 20

Form 706 (Rev. 7-99)

Estate of:

SCHEDULE G—Transfers During Decedent's Life

(If you elect section 2032A valuation, you must complete Schedule G and Schedule A-1.)

Item number	Description For securities, give CUSIP number.	Alternate valuation date	Alternate value	Value at date of death
A.	Gift tax paid by the decedent or the estate for all gifts made by the decedent or his or her spouse within 3 years before the decedent's death (section 2035(b))	X X X X X		
B.	Transfers includible under section 2035(a), 2036, 2037, or 2038:			
1				
	Total from continuation schedules (or additional sheets) attached to this schedule . .			
	TOTAL. (Also enter on Part 5, Recapitulation, page 3, at item 7.).			

SCHEDULE H—Powers of Appointment

(Include "5 and 5 lapsing" powers (section 2041(b)(2)) held by the decedent.)

(If you elect section 2032A valuation, you must complete Schedule H and Schedule A-1.)

Item number	Description	Alternate valuation date	Alternate value	Value at date of death
1				
	Total from continuation schedules (or additional sheets) attached to this schedule . .			
	TOTAL. (Also enter on Part 5, Recapitulation, page 3, at item 8.).			

(If more space is needed, attach the continuation schedule from the end of this package or additional sheets of the same size.)
(The instructions to Schedules G and H are in the separate instructions.)

Schedules G and H—Page 21

Figure F-1

Form 706, page 21

Form 706 (Rev. 7-99)

Estate of:

SCHEDULE I—Annuities

Note: *Generally, no exclusion is allowed for the estates of decedents dying after December 31, 1984 (see page 15 of the instructions).*

A Are you excluding from the decedent's gross estate the value of a lump-sum distribution described in section 2039(f)(2)? . . . . **Yes** | **No**
If "Yes," you must attach the information required by the instructions.

Item number	Description Show the entire value of the annuity before any exclusions.	Alternate valuation date	Includible alternate value	Includible value at date of death
1				

Total from continuation schedules (or additional sheets) attached to this schedule . .

TOTAL. (Also enter on Part 5, Recapitulation, page 3, at item 9.) . . . .
(If more space is needed, attach the continuation schedule from the end of this package or additional sheets of the same size.)

Schedule I—Page 22   (The instructions to Schedule I are in the separate instructions.)

Figure F-1

Form 706,
page 22

Estate of:

SCHEDULE J—Funeral Expenses and Expenses Incurred in Administering Property Subject to Claims

Note: *Do not list on this schedule expenses of administering property not subject to claims. For those expenses, see the instructions for Schedule L.*

If executors' commissions, attorney fees, etc., are claimed and allowed as a deduction for estate tax purposes, they are not allowable as a deduction in computing the taxable income of the estate for Federal income tax purposes. They are allowable as an income tax deduction on Form 1041 if a waiver is filed to waive the deduction on Form 706 (see the Form 1041 instructions).

Item number	Description	Expense amount	Total amount
1	**A. Funeral expenses:**		
	Total funeral expenses . . . . ▶		
	B. Administration expenses:		
1	Executors' commissions—amount estimated/agreed upon/paid. (Strike out the words that do not apply.)		
2	Attorney fees—amount estimated/agreed upon/paid. (Strike out the words that do not apply.) . .		
3	Accountant fees—amount estimated/agreed upon/paid. (Strike out the words that do not apply.).		

		Expense amount
4	Miscellaneous expenses:	
	Total miscellaneous expenses from continuation schedules (or additional sheets) attached to this schedule	
	Total miscellaneous expenses . . . . ▶	

TOTAL. (Also enter on Part 5, Recapitulation, page 3, at item 13.) . . . . ▶

(If more space is needed, attach the continuation schedule from the end of this package or additional sheets of the same size.)
(See the instructions on the reverse side.)

Schedule J—Page 23

Figure F-1

Form 706, page 23

Form 706 (Rev. 7-99)

Instructions for Schedule J—Funeral Expenses and Expenses Incurred in Administering Property Subject to Claims

General. You must complete and file Schedule J if you claim a deduction on item 13 of Part 5, Recapitulation.

On Schedule J, itemize funeral expenses and expenses incurred in administering property subject to claims. List the names and addresses of persons to whom the expenses are payable and describe the nature of the expense. **Do not list expenses incurred in administering property not subject to claims on this schedule. List them on Schedule L instead.**

The deduction is limited to the amount paid for these expenses that is allowable under local law but may not exceed:

1. The value of property subject to claims included in the gross estate, plus

2. The amount paid out of property included in the gross estate but not subject to claims. This amount must actually be paid by the due date of the estate tax return.

The applicable local law under which the estate is being administered determines which property is and is not subject to claims. If under local law a particular property interest included in the gross estate would bear the burden for the payment of the expenses, then the property is considered property subject to claims.

Unlike certain claims against the estate for debts of the decedent (see the instructions for Schedule K in the separate instructions), you cannot deduct expenses incurred in administering property subject to claims on both the estate tax return and the estate's income tax return. If you choose to deduct them on the estate tax return, you cannot deduct them on a Form 1041 filed for the estate. Funeral expenses are only deductible on the estate tax return.

Funeral Expenses. Itemize funeral expenses on line A. Deduct from the expenses any amounts that were reimbursed, such as death benefits payable by the Social Security Administration and the Veterans Administration.

Executors' Commissions. When you file the return, you may deduct commissions that have actually been paid to you or that you expect will be paid. You may not deduct commissions if none will be collected. If the amount of the commissions has not been fixed by decree of the proper court, the deduction will be allowed on the final examination of the return, provided that:

● The District Director is reasonably satisfied that the commissions claimed will be paid;

● The amount entered as a deduction is within the amount allowable by the laws of the jurisdiction where the estate is being administered;

● It is in accordance with the usually accepted practice in that jurisdiction for estates of similar size and character.

If you have not been paid the commissions claimed at the time of the final examination of the return, you must

support the amount you deducted with an affidavit or statement signed under the penalties of perjury that the amount has been agreed upon and will be paid.

You may not deduct a bequest or devise made to you instead of commissions. If, however, the decedent fixed by will the compensation payable to you for services to be rendered in the administration of the estate, you may deduct this amount to the extent it is not more than the compensation allowable by the local law or practice.

Do not deduct on this schedule amounts paid as trustees' commissions whether received by you acting in the capacity of a trustee or by a separate trustee. If such amounts were paid in administering property not subject to claims, deduct them on Schedule L.

Note: Executors' commissions are taxable income to the executors. Therefore, be sure to include them as income on your individual income tax return.

Attorney Fees. Enter the amount of attorney fees that have actually been paid or that you reasonably expect to be paid. If on the final examination of the return the fees claimed have not been awarded by the proper court and paid, the deduction will be allowed provided the District Director is reasonably satisfied that the amount claimed will be paid and that it does not exceed a reasonable payment for the services performed, taking into account the size and character of the estate and the local law and practice. If the fees claimed have not been paid at the time of final examination of the return, the amount deducted must be supported by an affidavit, or statement signed under the penalties of perjury, by the executor or the attorney stating that the amount has been agreed upon and will be paid.

Do not deduct attorney fees incidental to litigation incurred by the beneficiaries. These expenses are charged against the beneficiaries personally and are not administration expenses authorized by the Code.

Interest Expense. Interest expenses incurred after the decedent's death are generally allowed as a deduction if they are reasonable, necessary to the administration of the estate, and allowable under local law.

Interest incurred as the result of a Federal estate tax deficiency is a deductible administrative expense. Penalties are not deductible even if they are allowable under local law.

*Note: If you elect to pay the tax in installments under section 6166, you may **not** deduct the interest payable on the installments.*

Miscellaneous Expenses. Miscellaneous administration expenses necessarily incurred in preserving and distributing the estate are deductible. These expenses include appraiser's and accountant's fees, certain court costs, and costs of storing or maintaining assets of the estate.

The expenses of selling assets are deductible only if the sale is necessary to pay the decedent's debts, the expenses of administration, or taxes, or to preserve the estate or carry out distribution.

Schedule J—Page 24

Figure F-1

Form 706, page 24

Form 706 (Rev. 7-99)

Estate of:

SCHEDULE K—Debts of the Decedent, and Mortgages and Liens

Item number	Debts of the Decedent—Creditor and nature of claim, and allowable death taxes	Amount unpaid to date	Amount in contest	Amount claimed as a deduction
1				

Total from continuation schedules (or additional sheets) attached to this schedule . . . .

TOTAL. (Also enter on Part 5, Recapitulation, page 3, at item 14.) . . . .

Item number	Mortgages and Liens—Description	Amount
1		

Total from continuation schedules (or additional sheets) attached to this schedule . . . .

TOTAL. (Also enter on Part 5, Recapitulation, page 3, at item 15.) . . . .

(If more space is needed, attach the continuation schedule from the end of this package or additional sheets of the same size.)
(The instructions to Schedule K are in the separate instructions.)

Schedule K—Page 25

Figure F-1

Form 706, page 25

Form 706 (Rev. 7-99)

Estate of:

SCHEDULE L—Net Losses During Administration and Expenses Incurred in Administering Property Not Subject to Claims

Item number	Net losses during administration (**Note:** *Do not deduct losses claimed on a Federal income tax return.*)	Amount
1		

Total from continuation schedules (or additional sheets) attached to this schedule . . . .

TOTAL. (Also enter on Part 5, Recapitulation, page 3, at item 18.) . . . .

Item number	Expenses incurred in administering property not subject to claims (Indicate whether estimated, agreed upon, or paid.)	Amount
1		

Total from continuation schedules (or additional sheets) attached to this schedule . . . .

TOTAL. (Also enter on Part 5, Recapitulation, page 3, at item 19.) . . . .

(If more space is needed, attach the continuation schedule from the end of this package or additional sheets of the same size.)

Schedule L—Page 26 (The instructions to Schedule L are in the separate instructions.)

Figure F-1

Form 706, page 26

Form 706 (Rev. 7-99)

Estate of:

SCHEDULE M—Bequests, etc., to Surviving Spouse

Election To Deduct Qualified Terminable Interest Property Under Section 2056(b)(7). If a trust (or other property) meets the requirements of qualified terminable interest property under section 2056(b)(7), and

    a. The trust or other property is listed on Schedule M, and

    b. The value of the trust (or other property) is entered in whole or in part as a deduction on Schedule M,

then unless the executor specifically identifies the trust (all or a fractional portion or percentage) or other property to be excluded from the election, the executor shall be deemed to have made an election to have such trust (or other property) treated as qualified terminable interest property under section 2056(b)(7).

    If less than the entire value of the trust (or other property) that the executor has included in the gross estate is entered as a deduction on Schedule M, the executor shall be considered to have made an election only as to a fraction of the trust (or other property). The numerator of this fraction is equal to the amount of the trust (or other property) deducted on Schedule M. The denominator is equal to the total value of the trust (or other property).

Election To Deduct Qualified Domestic Trust Property Under Section 2056A. If a trust meets the requirements of a qualified domestic trust under section 2056A(a) and this return is filed no later than 1 year after the time prescribed by law (including extensions) for filing the return, and

    a. The entire value of a trust or trust property is listed on Schedule M, and

    b. The entire value of the trust or trust property is entered as a deduction on Schedule M,

then unless the executor specifically identifies the trust to be excluded from the election, the executor shall be deemed to have made an election to have the entire trust treated as qualified domestic trust property.

		Yes	No
1	Did any property pass to the surviving spouse as a result of a qualified disclaimer? **1**		
	If "Yes," attach a copy of the written disclaimer required by section 2518(b).		
2a	In what country was the surviving spouse born? _____		
b	What is the surviving spouse's date of birth? _____		
c	Is the surviving spouse a U.S. citizen? **2c**		
d	If the surviving spouse is a naturalized citizen, when did the surviving spouse acquire citizenship? _____		
e	If the surviving spouse is not a U.S. citizen, of what country is the surviving spouse a citizen? _____		
3	**Election Out of QTIP Treatment of Annuities—**Do you elect under section 2056(b)(7)(C)(ii) **not** to treat as qualified terminable interest property any joint and survivor annuities that are included in the gross estate and would otherwise be treated as qualified terminable interest property under section 2056(b)(7)(C)? (see instructions) **3**		

Item number	Description of property interests passing to surviving spouse	Amount
1		

Total from continuation schedules (or additional sheets) attached to this schedule . . . .

4	**Total** amount of property interests listed on Schedule M	**4**	
5a	Federal estate taxes payable out of property interests listed on Schedule M . .	**5a**	
b	Other death taxes payable out of property interests listed on Schedule M . . .	**5b**	
c	Federal and state GST taxes payable out of property interests listed on Schedule M	**5c**	
d	Add items 5a, b, and c	**5d**	
6	Net amount of property interests listed on Schedule M (subtract 5d from 4). Also enter on Part 5, Recapitulation, page 3, at item 20	**6**	

(If more space is needed, attach the continuation schedule from the end of this package or additional sheets of the same size.)
(See the instructions on the reverse side.)

Schedule M—Page 27

Figure F-1

Form 706,
page 27

Form 706 (Rev. 7-99)

Examples of Listing of Property Interests on Schedule M

Item number	Description of property interests passing to surviving spouse	Amount
1	One-half the value of a house and lot, 256 South West Street, held by decedent and surviving spouse as joint tenants with right of survivorship under deed dated July 15, 1957 (Schedule E, Part I, item 1)	$132,500
2	Proceeds of Gibraltar Life Insurance Company policy No. 104729, payable in one sum to surviving spouse (Schedule D, item 3)	200,000
3	Cash bequest under Paragraph Six of will	100,000

Instructions for Schedule M—Bequests, etc., to Surviving Spouse (Marital Deduction)

General

You must complete Schedule M and file it with the return if you claim a deduction on item 20 of Part 5, Recapitulation.

The marital deduction is authorized by section 2056 for certain property interests that pass from the decedent to the surviving spouse. You may claim the deduction only for property interests that are included in the decedent's gross estate (Schedules A through I).

Note: *The marital deduction is generally not allowed if the surviving spouse is **not** a U.S. citizen. The marital deduction is allowed for property passing to such a surviving spouse in a "qualified domestic trust" or if such property is transferred or irrevocably assigned to such a trust before the estate tax return is filed. The executor must elect qualified domestic trust status on this return. See the instructions that follow, on pages 29–30, for details on the election.*

Property Interests That You May List on Schedule M

Generally, you may list on Schedule M all property interests that pass from the decedent to the surviving spouse and are included in the gross estate. However, you should not list any "Nondeductible terminable interests" (described below) on Schedule M unless you are making a QTIP election. The property for which you make this election must be included on Schedule M. See "Qualified terminable interest property" on the following page.

For the rules on common disaster and survival for a limited period, see section 2056(b)(3).

You may list on Schedule M only those interests that the surviving spouse takes:

1. As the decedent's legatee, devisee, heir, or donee;

2. As the decedent's surviving tenant by the entirety or joint tenant;

3. As an appointee under the decedent's exercise of a power or as a

taker in default at the decedent's nonexercise of a power;

4. As a beneficiary of insurance on the decedent's life;

5. As the surviving spouse taking under dower or curtesy (or similar statutory interest); and

6. As a transferee of a transfer made by the decedent at any time.

Property Interests That You May Not List on Schedule M

You should not list on Schedule M:

1. The value of any property that does not pass from the decedent to the surviving spouse;

2. Property interests that are not included in the decedent's gross estate;

3. The full value of a property interest for which a deduction was claimed on Schedules J through L. The value of the property interest should be reduced by the deductions claimed with respect to it;

4. The full value of a property interest that passes to the surviving spouse subject to a mortgage or other encumbrance or an obligation of the surviving spouse. Include on Schedule M only the net value of the interest after reducing it by the amount of the mortgage or other debt;

5. Nondeductible terminable interests (described below); or

6. Any property interest disclaimed by the surviving spouse.

Terminable Interests

Certain interests in property passing from a decedent to a surviving spouse are referred to as *terminable interests.* These are interests that will terminate or fail after the passage of time, or on the occurrence or nonoccurrence of some contingency. Examples are: life estates, annuities, estates for terms of years, and patents.

The ownership of a bond, note, or other contractual obligation, which when discharged would not have the effect of an annuity for life or for a term, is not considered a terminable interest.

Nondeductible terminable interests. A terminable interest is *nondeductible,* and should not be entered on Schedule M (unless you are making a QTIP election) if:

1. Another interest in the same property passed from the decedent to some other person for less than adequate and full consideration in money or money's worth; and

2. By reason of its passing, the other person or that person's heirs may enjoy part of the property after the termination of the surviving spouse's interest.

This rule applies even though the interest that passes from the decedent to a person other than the surviving spouse is not included in the gross estate, and regardless of when the interest passes. The rule also applies regardless of whether the surviving spouse's interest and the other person's interest pass from the decedent at the same time.

Property interests that are considered to pass to a person other than the surviving spouse are any property interest that: **(a)** passes under a decedent's will or intestacy; **(b)** was transferred by a decedent during life; or **(c)** is held by or passed on to any person as a decedent's joint tenant, as appointee under a decedent's exercise of a power, as taker in default at a decedent's release or nonexercise of a power, or as a beneficiary of insurance on the decedent's life.

For example, a decedent devised real property to his wife for life, with remainder to his children. The life interest that passed to the wife does not qualify for the marital deduction because it will terminate at her death and the children will thereafter possess or enjoy the property.

However, if the decedent purchased a joint and survivor annuity for himself and his wife who survived him, the value of the survivor's annuity, to the extent that it is included in the gross estate, qualifies for the marital deduction because even though the interest will terminate on the wife's death, no one else will possess or enjoy any part of the property.

The marital deduction is not allowed for an interest that the decedent directed the executor or a trustee to convert, after death, into a terminable interest for the surviving spouse. The marital deduction is not allowed for such an interest even if there was no interest

Page 28

Figure F-1

Form 706, page 28

Form 706 (Rev. 7-99)

in the property passing to another person and even if the terminable interest would otherwise have been deductible under the exceptions described below for life estate and life insurance and annuity payments with powers of appointment. For more information, see Regulations sections 20.2056(b)-1(f) and 20.2056(b)-1(g), Example (7).

If any property interest passing from the decedent to the surviving spouse may be paid or otherwise satisfied out of any of a group of assets, the value of the property interest is, for the entry on Schedule M, reduced by the value of any asset or assets that, if passing from the decedent to the surviving spouse, would be nondeductible terminable interests. Examples of property interests that may be paid or otherwise satisfied out of any of a group of assets are a bequest of the residue of the decedent's estate, or of a share of the residue, and a cash legacy payable out of the general estate.

Example: A decedent bequeathed $100,000 to the surviving spouse. The general estate includes a term for years (valued at $10,000 in determining the value of the gross estate) in an office building, which interest was retained by the decedent under a deed of the building by gift to a son. Accordingly, the value of the specific bequest entered on Schedule M is $90,000.

Life Estate With Power of Appointment in the Surviving Spouse. A property interest, whether or not in trust, will be treated as passing to the surviving spouse, and will not be treated as a nondeductible terminable interest if: **(a)** the surviving spouse is entitled for life to all of the income from the entire interest; **(b)** the income is payable annually or at more frequent intervals; **(c)** the surviving spouse has the power, exercisable in favor of the surviving spouse or the estate of the surviving spouse, to appoint the entire interest; **(d)** the power is exercisable by the surviving spouse alone and (whether exercisable by will or during life) is exercisable by the surviving spouse in all events; and **(e)** no part of the entire interest is subject to a power in any other person to appoint any part to any person other than the surviving spouse (or the surviving spouse's legal representative or relative if the surviving spouse is disabled. See Rev. Rul. 85-35, 1985-1 C.B. 328). If these five conditions are satisfied only for a specific portion of the entire interest, see the section 2056(b) regulations to determine the amount of the marital deduction.

Life Insurance, Endowment, or Annuity Payments, With Power of Appointment in Surviving Spouse. A property interest consisting of the entire proceeds under

a life insurance, endowment, or annuity contract is treated as passing from the decedent to the surviving spouse, and will not be treated as a nondeductible terminable interest if: **(a)** the surviving spouse is entitled to receive the proceeds in installments, or is entitled to interest on them, with all amounts payable during the life of the spouse, payable only to the surviving spouse; **(b)** the installment or interest payments are payable annually, or more frequently, beginning not later than 13 months after the decedent's death; **(c)** the surviving spouse has the power, exercisable in favor of the surviving spouse or of the estate of the surviving spouse, to appoint all amounts payable under the contract; **(d)** the power is exercisable by the surviving spouse alone and (whether exercisable by will or during life) is exercisable by the surviving spouse in all events; and **(e)** no part of the amount payable under the contract is subject to a power in any other person to appoint any part to any person other than the surviving spouse. If these five conditions are satisfied only for a specific portion of the proceeds, see the section 2056(b) regulations to determine the amount of the marital deduction.

Charitable Remainder Trusts. An interest in a charitable remainder trust will **not** be treated as a nondeductible terminable interest if:

1. The interest in the trust passes from the decedent to the surviving spouse; and

2. The surviving spouse is the only beneficiary of the trust other than charitable organizations described in section 170(c).

A "charitable remainder trust" is either a charitable remainder annuity trust or a charitable remainder unitrust. (See section 664 for descriptions of these trusts.)

Election To Deduct Qualified Terminable Interests (QTIP)

You may elect to claim a marital deduction for qualified terminable interest property or property interests. You make the QTIP election simply by listing the qualified terminable interest property on Schedule M and deducting its value. You are presumed to have made the QTIP election if you list the property and deduct its value on Schedule M. If you make this election, the surviving spouse's gross estate will include the value of the "qualified terminable interest property." See the instructions for line 6 of General Information for more details. **The election is irrevocable.**

If you file a Form 706 in which you do not make this election, you may not file an amended return to make the election

unless you file the amended return on or before the due date for filing the original Form 706.

The effect of the election is that the property (interest) will be treated as passing to the surviving spouse and will not be treated as a nondeductible terminable interest. All of the other marital deduction requirements must still be satisfied before you may make this election. For example, you may not make this election for property or property interests that are not included in the decedent's gross estate.

Qualified terminable interest property is property **(a)** that passes from the decedent, and **(b)** in which the surviving spouse has a qualifying income interest for life.

The surviving spouse has a *qualifying income interest for life* if the surviving spouse is entitled to all of the income from the property payable annually or at more frequent intervals, or has a usufruct interest for life in the property, and during the surviving spouse's lifetime no person has a power to appoint any part of the property to any person other than the surviving spouse. An annuity is treated as an income interest regardless of whether the property from which the annuity is payable can be separately identified.

Amendments to Regulations sections 20.2044-1, 20.2056(b)-7 and 20.2056(b)-10 clarify that an interest in property is eligible for QTIP treatment if the income interest is contingent upon the executor's election even if that portion of the property for which no election is made will pass to or for the benefit of beneficiaries other than the surviving spouse.

The QTIP election may be made for all or any part of qualified terminable interest property. A partial election must relate to a fractional or percentile share of the property so that the elective part will reflect its proportionate share of the increase or decline in the whole of the property when applying sections 2044 or 2519. Thus, if the interest of the surviving spouse in a trust (or other property in which the spouse has a qualified life estate) is qualified terminable interest property, you may make an election for a part of the trust (or other property) only if the election relates to a defined fraction or percentage of the entire trust (or other property). The fraction or percentage may be defined by means of a formula.

Qualified Domestic Trust Election (QDOT)

The marital deduction is allowed for transfers to a surviving spouse who is not a U.S. citizen only if the property passes to the surviving spouse in a "qualified domestic trust" (QDOT) or if

Page 29

Figure F-1

Form 706, page 29

Form 706 (Rev. 7-99)

such property is transferred or irrevocably assigned to a QDOT before the decedent's estate tax return is filed.

A QDOT is any trust:

1. That requires at least one trustee to be either an individual who is a citizen of the United States or a domestic corporation;

2. That requires that no distribution of corpus from the trust can be made unless such a trustee has the right to withhold from the distribution the tax imposed on the QDOT;

3. That meets the requirements of any applicable regulations; and

4. For which the executor has made an election on the estate tax return of the decedent.

Note: *For trusts created by an instrument executed before November 5, 1990, paragraphs 1 and 2 above will be treated as met if the trust instrument requires that all trustees be individuals who are citizens of the United States or domestic corporations.*

You make the QDOT election simply by listing the qualified domestic trust or the **entire value** of the trust property on Schedule M and deducting its value. You are presumed to have made the QDOT election if you list the trust or trust property and deduct its value on Schedule M. **Once made, the election is irrevocable.**

If an election is made to deduct qualified domestic trust property under section 2056A(d), the following information should be provided for each qualified domestic trust on an attachment to this schedule:

1. The name and address of every trustee;

2. A description of each transfer passing from the decedent that is the source of the property to be placed in trust; and

3. The employer identification number (EIN) for the trust.

The election must be made for an entire QDOT trust. In listing a trust for which you are making a QDOT election, unless you specifically identify the trust as not subject to the election, the election will be considered made for the entire trust.

The determination of whether a trust qualifies as a QDOT will be made as of the date the decedent's Form 706 is filed. If, however, judicial proceedings are brought before the Form 706's due date (including extensions) to have the trust revised to meet the QDOT requirements, then the determination will not be made until the court-ordered changes to the trust are made.

Line 1

If property passes to the surviving spouse as the result of a qualified disclaimer, check "Yes" and attach a copy of the written disclaimer required by section 2518(b).

Line 3

Section 2056(b)(7) creates an automatic QTIP election for certain joint and survivor annuities that are includible in the estate under section 2039. To qualify, only the surviving spouse can have the right to receive payments before the death of the surviving spouse.

The executor can elect out of QTIP treatment, however, by checking the "Yes" box on line 3. Once made, the election is irrevocable. If there is more than one such joint and survivor annuity, you are not required to make the election for all of them.

If you make the election out of QTIP treatment by checking "Yes" on line 3, you cannot deduct the amount of the annuity on Schedule M. If you do not make the election out, you must list the joint and survivor annuities on Schedule M.

Listing Property Interests on Schedule M

List each property interest included in the gross estate that passes from the decedent to the surviving spouse and for which a marital deduction is claimed. This includes otherwise nondeductible terminable interest property for which you are making a QTIP election. Number each item in sequence and describe each item in detail. Describe the instrument (including any clause or paragraph number) or provision of law under which each item passed to the surviving spouse. If possible, show where each item appears (number and schedule) on Schedules A through I.

In listing otherwise nondeductible property for which you are making a QTIP election, unless you specifically identify a fractional portion of the trust or other property as not subject to the election, the election will be considered made for all of the trust or other property.

Enter the value of each interest before taking into account the Federal estate tax or any other death tax. The valuation dates used in determining the value of the gross estate apply also on Schedule M.

If Schedule M includes a bequest of the residue or a part of the residue of the decedent's estate, attach a copy of the computation showing how the value of the residue was determined. Include a statement showing:

● The value of all property that is included in the decedent's gross estate (Schedules A through I) but is not a part of the decedent's probate estate, such as lifetime transfers, jointly owned property that passed to the survivor on decedent's death, and the insurance payable to specific beneficiaries.

● The values of all specific and general legacies or devises, with reference to the applicable clause or paragraph of the decedent's will or codicil. (If legacies are made to each member of a class; for example, $1,000 to each of decedent's employees, only the number in each class and the total value of property received by them need be furnished.)

● The date of birth of all persons, the length of whose lives may affect the value of the residuary interest passing to the surviving spouse.

● Any other important information such as that relating to any claim to any part of the estate not arising under the will.

Lines 5a, b, and c—The total of the values listed on Schedule M must be reduced by the amount of the Federal estate tax, the Federal GST tax, and the amount of state or other death and GST taxes paid out of the property interest involved. If you enter an amount for state or other death or GST taxes on lines 5b or 5c, identify the taxes and attach your computation of them.

Attachments. If you list property interests passing by the decedent's will on Schedule M, attach a certified copy of the order admitting the will to probate. If, when you file the return, the court of probate jurisdiction has entered any decree interpreting the will or any of its provisions affecting any of the interests listed on Schedule M, or has entered any order of distribution, attach a copy of the decree or order. In addition, the District Director may request other evidence to support the marital deduction claimed.

Figure F-1

Page 30

Form 706, page 30

Form 706 (Rev. 7-99)

Estate of:

SCHEDULE O—Charitable, Public, and Similar Gifts and Bequests

	Yes	No
1a If the transfer was made by will, has any action been instituted to have interpreted or to contest the will or any of its provisions affecting the charitable deductions claimed in this schedule? . . . . If "Yes," full details must be submitted with this schedule.		
b According to the information and belief of the person or persons filing this return, is any such action planned? If "Yes," full details must be submitted with this schedule.		
2 Did any property pass to charity as the result of a qualified disclaimer? . . . . If "Yes," attach a copy of the written disclaimer required by section 2518(b).		

Item number	Name and address of beneficiary	Character of institution	Amount
1			

Total from continuation schedules (or additional sheets) attached to this schedule . . . .

3 Total		**3**
4a Federal estate tax payable out of property interests listed above	4a	
b Other death taxes payable out of property interests listed above	4b	
c Federal and state GST taxes payable out of property interests listed above	4c	
d Add items 4a, b, and c		**4d**
5 Net value of property interests listed above (subtract 4d from 3). Also enter on Part 5, Recapitulation, page 3, at item 21		**5**

(If more space is needed, attach the continuation schedule from the end of this package or additional sheets of the same size.)
(The instructions to Schedule O are in the separate instructions.)

Schedule O—Page 31

Figure F-1

Form 706,
page 31

Form 706 (Rev. 7-99)

Estate of:

SCHEDULE P—Credit for Foreign Death Taxes

List all foreign countries to which death taxes have been paid and for which a credit is claimed on this return.

If a credit is claimed for death taxes paid to more than one foreign country, compute the credit for taxes paid to one country on this sheet and attach a separate copy of Schedule P for each of the other countries.

The credit computed on this sheet is for the ....
(Name of death tax or taxes)

.... imposed in ....
(Name of country)

Credit is computed under the ....
(Insert title of treaty or "statute")

Citizenship (nationality) of decedent at time of death

(All amounts and values must be entered in United States money.)

1 Total of estate, inheritance, legacy, and succession taxes imposed in the country named above attributable to property situated in that country, subjected to these taxes, and included in the gross estate (as defined by statute)	**1**
2 Value of the gross estate (adjusted, if necessary, according to the instructions for item 2)	**2**
3 Value of property situated in that country, subjected to death taxes imposed in that country, and included in the gross estate (adjusted, if necessary, according to the instructions for item 3)	**3**
4 Tax imposed by section 2001 reduced by the total credits claimed under sections 2010, 2011, and 2012 (see instructions).	**4**
5 Amount of Federal estate tax attributable to property specified at item 3. (Divide item 3 by item 2 and multiply the result by item 4.)	**5**
6 Credit for death taxes imposed in the country named above (the smaller of item 1 or item 5). Also enter on line 18 of Part 2, Tax Computation	**6**

SCHEDULE Q—Credit for Tax on Prior Transfers

Part 1—Transferor Information

	Name of transferor	Social security number	IRS office where estate tax return was filed	Date of death
A				
B				
C				

Check here ▶ ☐ if section 2013(f) (special valuation of farm, etc., real property) adjustments to the computation of the credit were made (see page 18 of the instructions).

Part 2—Computation of Credit (see instructions beginning on page 18)

Item	Transferor A	Transferor B	Transferor C	Total A, B, & C
1 Transferee's tax as apportioned (from worksheet, (line 7 ÷ line 8) × line 35 for each column) . .				
2 Transferor's tax (from each column of worksheet, line 20)				
3 Maximum amount before percentage requirement (for each column, enter amount from line 1 or 2, whichever is smaller)				
4 Percentage allowed (each column) (see instructions)	%	%	%	
5 Credit allowable (line 3 × line 4 for each column)				
6 TOTAL credit allowable (add columns A, B, and C of line 5). Enter here and on line 19 of Part 2, Tax Computation				

Schedules P and Q—Page 32   (The instructions to Schedules P and Q are in the separate instructions.)

Figure F-1

Form 706, page 32

Form 706 (Rev. 7-99)

SCHEDULE R—Generation-Skipping Transfer Tax

Note: *To avoid application of the deemed allocation rules, Form 706 and Schedule R should be filed to allocate the GST exemption to trusts that may later have taxable terminations or distributions under section 2612 even if the form is not required to be filed to report estate or GST tax.*

The GST tax is imposed on taxable transfers of interests in property located **outside the United States** *as well as property located inside the United States.*

See instructions beginning on page 19.

Part 1—GST Exemption Reconciliation (Section 2631) and Section 2652(a)(3) (Special QTIP) Election

You no longer need to check a box to make a section 2652(a)(3) (special QTIP) election. If you list qualifying property in Part 1, line 9, below, you will be considered to have made this election. See page 21 of the separate instructions for details.

1	Maximum allowable GST exemption	1
2	Total GST exemption allocated by the decedent against decedent's lifetime transfers	2
3	Total GST exemption allocated by the executor, using Form 709, against decedent's lifetime transfers	3
4	GST exemption allocated on line 6 of Schedule R, Part 2	4
5	GST exemption allocated on line 6 of Schedule R, Part 3	5
6	Total GST exemption allocated on line 4 of Schedule(s) R-1	6
7	Total GST exemption allocated to intervivos transfers and direct skips (add lines 2–6)	7
8	GST exemption available to allocate to trusts and section 2032A interests (subtract line 7 from line 1)	8

9 Allocation of GST exemption to trusts (as defined for GST tax purposes):

A	B	C	D	E
Name of trust	Trust's EIN (if any)	GST exemption allocated on lines 2–6, above (see instructions)	Additional GST exemption allocated (see instructions)	Trust's inclusion ratio (optional—see instructions)

9D Total. May not exceed line 8, above **9D**

10 GST exemption available to allocate to section 2032A interests received by individual beneficiaries (subtract line 9D from line 8). You must attach special use allocation schedule (see instructions) | **10**

(The instructions to Schedule R are in the separate instructions.)

Schedule R—Page 33

Figure F-1

Form 706, page 33

Form 706 (Rev. 7-99)

Estate of:

Part 2—Direct Skips Where the Property Interests Transferred Bear the GST Tax on the Direct Skips

Name of skip person	Description of property interest transferred	Estate tax value

1 Total estate tax values of all property interests listed above	1	
2 Estate taxes, state death taxes, and other charges borne by the property interests listed above .	2	
3 GST taxes borne by the property interests listed above but imposed on direct skips other than those shown on this Part 2 (see instructions)	3	
4 Total fixed taxes and other charges (add lines 2 and 3).	4	
5 Total tentative maximum direct skips (subtract line 4 from line 1)	5	
6 GST exemption allocated	6	
7 Subtract line 6 from line 5	7	
8 GST tax due (divide line 7 by 2.818182).	8	
9 Enter the amount from line 8 of Schedule R, Part 3	9	
10 **Total GST taxes payable by the estate** (add lines 8 and 9). Enter here and on line 22 of Part 2—Tax Computation, on page 1.	10	

Schedule R—Page 34

Figure F-1

Form 706, page 34

Form 706 (Rev. 7-99)

Estate of:

Part 3—Direct Skips Where the Property Interests Transferred Do Not Bear the GST
Tax on the Direct Skips

Name of skip person	Description of property interest transferred	Estate tax value

1 Total estate tax values of all property interests listed above **1**

2 Estate taxes, state death taxes, and other charges borne by the property interests listed above . **2**

3 GST taxes borne by the property interests listed above but imposed on direct skips other than
those shown on this Part 3 (see instructions) **3**

4 Total fixed taxes and other charges (add lines 2 and 3). **4**

5 Total tentative maximum direct skips (subtract line 4 from line 1) **5**

6 GST exemption allocated **6**

7 Subtract line 6 from line 5 . . . . **7**

8 GST tax due (multiply line 7 by .55). Enter here and on Schedule R, Part 2, line 9 . . . . . **8**

Schedule R—Page 35

Figure F-1

Form 706,
page 35

SCHEDULE R-1
(Form 706)
(Rev. July 1999)
Department of the Treasury
Internal Revenue Service

Generation-Skipping Transfer Tax
Direct Skips From a Trust
Payment Voucher

OMB No. 1545-0015

Executor: File one copy with Form 706 and send two copies to the fiduciary. Do not pay the tax shown. See the separate instructions.
Fiduciary: See instructions on the following page. Pay the tax shown on line 6.

Name of trust	Trust's EIN
Name and title of fiduciary	Name of decedent
Address of fiduciary (number and street)	Decedent's SSN	Service Center where Form 706 was filed
City, state, and ZIP code	Name of executor
Address of executor (number and street)	City, state, and ZIP code
Date of decedent's death	Filing due date of Schedule R, Form 706 (with extensions)

Part 1—Computation of the GST Tax on the Direct Skip

Description of property interests subject to the direct skip	Estate tax value

1	Total estate tax value of all property interests listed above	1
2	Estate taxes, state death taxes, and other charges borne by the property interests listed above.	2
3	Tentative maximum direct skip from trust (subtract line 2 from line 1)	3
4	GST exemption allocated	4
5	Subtract line 4 from line 3	5
6	**GST tax due from fiduciary** (divide line 5 by 2.818182) **(See instructions if property will not bear the GST tax.)**	6

Under penalties of perjury, I declare that I have examined this return, including accompanying schedules and statements, and to the best of my knowledge and belief, it is true, correct, and complete.

Signature(s) of executor(s) _____   Date _____

_____   Date _____

Signature of fiduciary or officer representing fiduciary _____   Date _____

Schedule R-1 (Form 706)—Page 36

Figure F-1

Form 706,
page 36

Instructions for the Trustee

Introduction

Schedule R-1 (Form 706) serves as a payment voucher for the Generation-Skipping Transfer (GST) tax imposed on a direct skip from a trust, which you, the trustee of the trust, must pay. The executor completes the Schedule R-1 (Form 706) and gives you 2 copies. File one copy and keep one for your records.

How to pay

You can pay by check or money order.
- Make it payable to the "United States Treasury."
- Make the check or money order for the amount on line 6 of Schedule R-1.
- Write "GST Tax" and the trust's EIN on the check or money order.

Signature

You must sign the Schedule R-1 in the space provided.

What to mail

Mail your check or money order and the copy of Schedule R-1 that you signed.

Where to mail

Mail to the Service Center shown on Schedule R-1.

When to pay

The GST tax is due and payable 9 months after the decedent's date of death (shown on the Schedule R-1). You will owe interest on any GST tax not paid by that date.

Automatic extension

You have an automatic extension of time to file Schedule R-1 and pay the GST tax. The automatic extension allows you to file and pay by 2 months after the due date (with extensions) for filing the decedent's Schedule R (shown on the Schedule R-1).

If you pay the GST tax under the automatic extension, you will be charged interest (but no penalties).

Additional information

For more information, see Code section 2603(a)(2) and the instructions for Form 706, United States Estate (and Generation-Skipping Transfer) Tax Return.

Figure F-1

Form 706,
page 37

Form 706 (Rev. 7-99)

Estate of:

SCHEDULE T—Qualified Family-Owned Business Interest Deduction

For details on the deduction, including trades and businesses that do not qualify, see page 22 of the separate Instructions for Form 706.

Part 1—Election

Note: *The executor is deemed to have made the election under section 2057 if he or she files Schedule T and deducts any qualifying business interests from the gross estate.*

Part 2—General Qualifications

1. Did the decedent and/or a member of the decedent's family own the business interests listed on line 5 of this schedule for at least 5 of the 8 years immediately preceding the date of the decedent's death? ☐ **Yes** ☐ **No**

2. Were there any periods during the 8-year period preceding the date of the decedent's death during which the decedent or a member of his or her family:

	Yes	No
a Did not own the business interests listed on this schedule?		
b Did not materially participate, within the meaning of section 2032A(e)(6), in the operation of the business to which such interests relate?.		

If "Yes" to either of the above, you must attach a statement listing the periods. If applicable, describe whether the exceptions of sections 2032A(b)(4) or (5) are met.

Attach affidavits describing the activities constituting material participation and the identity and relationship to the decedent of the material participants.

3. Check the applicable box(es). The qualified family-owned business interest(s) is:
   - ☐ An interest as a proprietor in a trade or business carried on as a proprietorship.
   - ☐ An interest in an entity, at least 50% of which is owned (directly or indirectly) by the decedent and members of the decedent's family.
   - ☐ An interest in an entity, at least 70% of which is owned (directly or indirectly) by members of 2 families and at least 30% of which is owned (directly or indirectly) by the decedent and members of the decedent's family.
   - ☐ An interest in an entity, at least 90% of which is owned (directly or indirectly) by members of 3 families and at least 30% of which is owned (directly or indirectly) by the decedent and members of the decedent's family.

4. Persons holding interests. Enter the requested information for each party who received any interest in the family-owned business. If any qualified heir is not a U.S. citizen, see the line 4 instructions beginning on page 23 of the separate instructions.

   (Each of the qualified heirs receiving an interest in the business must sign the agreement that begins on the following page 40, and the agreement must be filed with this return.)

	Name	Address
A		
B		
C		
D		
E		
F		
G		
H		

	Identifying number	Relationship to decedent	Value of interest
A			
B			
C			
D			
E			
F			
G			
H			

Schedule T (Form 706)—Page 38

Figure F-1

Form 706, page 38

Form 706 (Rev. 7-99)

Part 3—Adjusted Value of Qualified Family-Owned Business Interests

5 Qualified family-owned business interests reported on this return.
Note: *All property listed on line 5 must also be entered on Schedules A, B, C, E, F, G, or H, as applicable.*

A Schedule and item number from Form 706	B Description of business interest and principal place of business	C Reported value

6	**Total** reported value	**6**	
7	Amount of claims or mortgages deductible under section 2053(a)(3) or (4) (see separate instructions).	**7**	
8a	Enter the amount of any indebtedness on qualified residence of the decedent (see separate instructions)	**8a**	
b	Enter the amount of any indebtedness used for educational or medical expenses (see separate instructions)	**8b**	
c	Enter the amount of any indebtedness other than that listed on line 8a or 8b, but do not enter more than $10,000 (see separate instructions)	**8c**	
d	Total (add lines 8a through 8c).	**8d**	
9	Subtract line 8d from line 7.	**9**	
10	Adjusted value of qualified family-owned business interests (subtract line 9 from line 6) . .	**10**	

Part 4—Qualifying Estate

11	Includible gifts of qualified family-owned business interests (see separate instructions):		
a	Amount of gifts taken into account under section 2001(b)(1)(B) .	**11a**	
b	Amount of such gifts excluded under section 2503(b)	**11b**	
c	Add lines 11a and 11b	**11c**	
12	Add lines 10 and 11c.	**12**	
13	Adjusted gross estate (see separate instructions):		
a	Amount of gross estate	**13a**	
b	Enter the amount from line 7 . . .	**13b**	
c	Subtract line 13b from line 13a	**13c**	
d	Enter the amount from line 11c . .	**13d**	
e	Enter the amount of transfers, if any, to the decedent's spouse (see inst.)	**13e**	
f	Enter the amount of other gifts (see inst.)	**13f**	
g	Add the amounts on lines 13d, 13e, and 13f	**13g**	
h	Enter any amounts from line 13g that are otherwise includible in the gross estate	**13h**	
i	Subtract line 13h from line 13g	**13i**	
j	Adjusted gross estate (add lines 13c and 13i).	**13j**	
14	Enter one-half of the amount on line 13j	**14**	
	Note: *If line 12 does not exceed line 14, stop here; the estate does not qualify for the deduction. Otherwise, complete line 15.*		
15	Net value of qualified family-owned business interests you elect to deduct (line 10 reduced by any marital or other deductions)—**DO NOT** enter more than $675,000—(see instructions) (attach schedule)—enter here and on Part 5, Recapitulation, page 3, at item 22	**15**	

Schedule T—Page 39

Figure F-1

Form 706,
page 39

Form 706 (Rev. 7-99)

Part 5—Agreement to Family-Owned Business Interest Deduction Under Section 2057

Estate of:	Date of Death	Decedent's Social Security Number

There cannot be a valid election unless:

• The agreement is executed by each and every one of the qualified heirs, and

• The agreement is included with the estate tax return when the estate tax return is filed.

We (list all qualified heirs and other persons having an interest in the business required to sign this agreement)

_____ ,

being all the qualified heirs and _____

_____ ,

being all other parties having interests in the business(es) which are deducted under section 2057 of the Internal Revenue Code, do hereby approve of the election made by _____ ,

Executor/Administrator of the estate of _____ ,

pursuant to section 2057 to deduct said interests from the gross estate and do hereby enter into this agreement pursuant to section 2057(h).

The undersigned agree and consent to the application of subsection (f) of section 2057 of the Code with respect to all the qualified family-owned business interests deducted on Schedule T of Form 706, attached to this agreement. More specifically, the undersigned heirs expressly agree and consent to personal liability under subsection (c) of 2032A (as made applicable by section 2057(i)(3)(F) of the Code) for the additional estate tax imposed by that subsection with respect to their respective interests in the above-described business interests in the event of certain early dispositions of the interests or the occurrence of any of the disqualifying acts described in section 2057(f)(1) of the Code. It is understood that if a qualified heir disposes of any deducted interest to any member of his or her family, such member may thereafter be treated as the qualified heir with respect to such interest upon filing a new agreement and any other form required by the Internal Revenue Service.

The undersigned interested parties who are not qualified heirs consent to the collection of any additional estate tax imposed under section 2057(f) of the Code from the deducted interests.

If there is a disposition of any interest which passes or has passed to him or her, each of the undersigned heirs agrees to file the appropriate form and pay any additional estate tax due within 6 months of the disposition or other disqualifying act.

It is understood by all interested parties that this agreement is a condition precedent to the election of the qualified family-owned business deduction under section 2057 of the Code and must be executed by every interested party even though that person may not have received the estate tax benefits or be in possession of such property.

Each of the undersigned understands that by making this election, a lien will be created and recorded pursuant to section 6324B of the Code on the interests referred to in this agreement for the applicable percentage of the adjusted tax differences with respect to the estate as defined in section 2057(f)(2)(C).

As the interested parties, the undersigned designate the following individual as their agent for all dealings with the Internal Revenue Service concerning the continued qualification of the deducted property under section 2057 of the Code and on all issues regarding the special lien under section 6324B. The agent is authorized to act for all the parties with respect to all dealings with the Service on matters affecting the qualified interests described earlier. This authority includes the following:

• To receive confidential information on all matters relating to continued qualification under section 2057 of the deducted interests and on all matters relating to the special lien arising under section 6324B.

• To furnish the Service with any requested information concerning the interests.

• To notify the Service of any disposition or other disqualifying events specified in section 2057(f)(1) of the Code.

• To receive, but not to endorse and collect, checks in payment of any refund of Internal Revenue taxes, penalties, or interest.

• To execute waivers (including offers of waivers) of restrictions on assessment or collection of deficiencies in tax and waivers of notice of disallowance of a claim for credit or refund.

• To execute closing agreements under section 7121.

(continued on next page)

Schedule T, Part 5—Page 40

Figure F-1

Form 706, page 40

Form 706 (Rev. 7-99)

Part 5. Agreement to Family-Owned Business Interest Deduction Under Section 2057 (continued)

Estate of:	Date of Death	Decedent's Social Security Number

● Other acts (specify) ▶ _____

By signing this agreement, the agent agrees to provide the Internal Revenue Service with any requested information concerning the qualified business interests and to notify the Internal Revenue Service of any disposition or other disqualifying events with regard to said interests.

Name of Agent	Signature	Address

The interests to which this agreement relates are listed in Form 706, United States Estate (and Generation-Skipping Transfer) Tax Return, along with their fair market value according to section 2031 (or, if applicable, section 2032A) of the Code. The name, address, social security number, and interest (including the value) of each of the undersigned in this business(es) are as set forth in the attached Schedule T.

IN WITNESS WHEREOF, the undersigned have hereunto set their hands at _____ ,

this _____ day of _____ .

SIGNATURES OF EACH OF THE QUALIFIED HEIRS:

Signature of qualified heir	Signature of qualified heir
Signature of qualified heir	Signature of qualified heir
Signature of qualified heir	Signature of qualified heir
Signature of qualified heir	Signature of qualified heir
Signature of qualified heir	Signature of qualified heir
Signature of qualified heir	Signature of qualified heir

Signature(s) of other interested parties

Signature(s) of other interested parties

Figure F-1

Form 706, page 41

Schedule T, Part 5—Page 41

Form 706 (Rev. 7-99)

Estate of:

SCHEDULE U. Qualified Conservation Easement Exclusion

Part 1—Election

Note: *The executor is deemed to have made the election under section 2031(c)(6) if he or she files Schedule U and excludes any qualifying conservation easements from the gross estate.*

Part 2—General Qualifications

1 Describe the land subject to the qualified conservation easement (see separate instructions) _____

2 Did the decedent or a member of the decedent's family own the land described above during the 3-year period ending on the date of the decedent's death? . . . . ☐ **Yes** ☐ **No**

3 The land described above is located (check whichever applies) (see separate instructions):
  ☐ In or within 25 miles of an area which, on the date of the decedent's death, is a metropolitan area.
  ☐ In or within 25 miles of an area which, on the date of the decedent's death, is a national park or wilderness area.
  ☐ In or within 10 miles of an area which, on the date of the decedent's death, is an Urban National Forest.

4 Describe the conservation easement with regard to which the exclusion is being claimed (see separate instructions). _____

Part 3—Computation of Exclusion

5	Estate tax value of the land subject to the qualified conservation easement (see separate instructions)	**5**	
6	Date of death value of any easements granted prior to decedent's death and included on line 11 below (see instructions)	**6**	
7	Add lines 5 and 6	**7**	
8	Value of retained development rights on the land (see instructions)	**8**	
9	Subtract line 8 from line 7	**9**	
10	Multiply line 9 by 30% (.30)	**10**	
11	Value of qualified conservation easement for which the exclusion is being claimed (see instructions)	**11**	
	Note: *If line 11 is less than line 10, continue with line 12. If line 11 is equal to or more than line 10, skip lines 12 through 14, enter ".40" on line 15, and complete the schedule.*		
12	Divide line 11 by line 9. Figure to 3 decimal places (e.g., .123) . .	**12**	
	If line 12 is equal to or less than .100, stop here; the estate does not qualify for the conservation easement exclusion.		
13	Subtract line 12 from .300. Enter the answer in hundredths by rounding any thousandths up to the next higher hundredth (i.e., .030 = .03; but .031 = .04).	**13**	
14	Multiply line 13 by 2	**14**	
15	Subtract line 14 from .40	**15**	
16	Deduction under section 2055(f) for the conservation easement (see separate instructions)	**16**	
17	Amount of indebtedness on the land (see separate instructions)	**17**	
18	Total reductions in value (add lines 8, 16, and 17)	**18**	
19	Net value of land (subtract line 18 from line 5)	**19**	
20	Multiply line 19 by line 15	**20**	
21	Enter the smaller of line 20 or the exclusion limitation (see instructions). Also enter this amount on item 11, Part 5, Recapitulation, Page 3.	**21**	

Schedule U—Page 42

Figure F-1

Form 706, page 42

(Make copies of this schedule before completing it if you will need more than one schedule.)

Estate of:

CONTINUATION SCHEDULE

Continuation of Schedule _____

(Enter letter of schedule you are continuing.)

Item number	Description For securities, give CUSIP number.	Unit value (Sch. B, E, or G only)	Alternate valuation date	Alternate value	Value at date of death or amount deductible

TOTAL. (Carry forward to main schedule.) . . . .

See the instructions on the reverse side.

Figure F-1

Form 706, page 43

Form 706 (Rev. 7-99)

Instructions for Continuation Schedule

When you need to list more assets or deductions than you have room for on one of the main schedules, use the Continuation Schedule on page 43. It provides a uniform format for listing additional assets from Schedules A through I and additional deductions from Schedules J, K, L, M, and O.

Please keep the following points in mind:

● Use a separate Continuation Schedule for each main schedule you are continuing. Do not combine assets or deductions from different schedules on one Continuation Schedule.

● Make copies of the blank schedule before completing it if you expect to need more than one.

● Use as many Continuation Schedules as needed to list all the assets or deductions.

● Enter the letter of the schedule you are continuing in the space at the top of the Continuation Schedule.

● Use the *Unit value* column <u>only</u> if continuing Schedule B, E, or G. For all other schedules, use this space to continue the description.

● Carry the total from the Continuation Schedules forward to the appropriate line on the main schedule.

If continuing	Report	Where on Continuation Schedule
Schedule E, Pt. 2	*Percentage includible*	*Alternate valuation date*
Schedule K	*Amount unpaid to date*	*Alternate valuation date*
Schedule K	*Amount in contest*	*Alternate value*
Schedules J, L, M	*Description of deduction continuation*	*Alternate valuation date* **and** *Alternate value*
Schedule O	*Character of institution*	*Alternate valuation date* **and** *Alternate value*
Schedule O	*Amount of each deduction*	*Amount deductible*

Figure F-1

Form 706, page 44

Continuation Schedule—Page 44

⊕ *Printed on recycled paper*

Form **709**	**United States Gift (and Generation-Skipping Transfer) Tax Return**	OMB No. 1545-0020
	(Section 6019 of the Internal Revenue Code) (For gifts made during calendar year 1999)	**19**99
Department of the Treasury Internal Revenue Service	▶ **See separate instructions. For Privacy Act Notice, see the Instructions for Form 1040.**	

1 Donor's first name and middle initial	2 Donor's last name	3 Donor's social security number
4 Address (number, street, and apartment number)	5 Legal residence (domicile) (county and state)
6 City, state, and ZIP code	7 Citizenship

Part 1—General Information

		Yes	No
8	If the donor died during the year, check here ▶ ☐ and enter date of death..........................		
9	If you received an extension of time to file this Form 709, check here ▶ ☐ and attach the Form 4868, 2688, 2350, or extension letter		
10	Enter the total number of separate donees listed on Schedule A—count each person only once. ▶		
11a	Have you (the donor) previously filed a Form 709 (or 709-A) for any other year? If the answer is "No," do not complete line 11b .		
11b	If the answer to line 11a is "Yes," has your address changed since you last filed Form 709 (or 709-A)?		
12	Gifts by husband or wife to third parties.—Do you consent to have the gifts (including generation-skipping transfers) made by you and by your spouse to third parties during the calendar year considered as made one-half by each of you? (See instructions.) (If the answer is "Yes," the following information must be furnished and your spouse must sign the consent shown below. **If the answer is "No," skip lines 13–18 and go to Schedule A).**		
13	Name of consenting spouse **14** SSN		
15	Were you married to one another during the entire calendar year? (see instructions)		
16	If the answer to 15 is "No," check whether ☐ married ☐ divorced or ☐ widowed, and give date (see instructions) ▶		
17	Will a gift tax return for this calendar year be filed by your spouse?		
18	**Consent of Spouse**—I consent to have the gifts (and generation-skipping transfers) made by me and by my spouse to third parties during the calendar year considered as made one-half by each of us. We are both aware of the joint and several liability for tax created by the execution of this consent.		

Consenting spouse's signature ▶   Date ▶

Part 2—Tax Computation

1	Enter the amount from Schedule A, Part 3, line 15	
2	Enter the amount from Schedule B, line 3	
3	Total taxable gifts (add lines 1 and 2)	
4	Tax computed on amount on line 3 (see Table for Computing Tax in separate instructions). . .	
5	Tax computed on amount on line 2 (see Table for Computing Tax in separate instructions). . .	
6	Balance (subtract line 5 from line 4)	
7	Maximum unified credit (nonresident aliens, see instructions)	211,300 00
8	Enter the unified credit against tax allowable for all prior periods (from Sch. B, line 1, col. C) . .	
9	Balance (subtract line 8 from line 7)	
10	Enter 20% (.20) of the amount allowed as a specific exemption for gifts made after September 8, 1976, and before January 1, 1977 (see instructions)	
11	Balance (subtract line 10 from line 9)	
12	Unified credit (enter the smaller of line 6 or line 11)	
13	Credit for foreign gift taxes (see instructions)	
14	Total credits (add lines 12 and 13)	
15	Balance (subtract line 14 from line 6) (do not enter less than zero)	
16	Generation-skipping transfer taxes (from Schedule C, Part 3, col. H, Total)	
17	Total tax (add lines 15 and 16)	
18	Gift and generation-skipping transfer taxes prepaid with extension of time to file	
19	If line 18 is less than line 17, enter BALANCE DUE (see instructions)	
20	If line 18 is greater than line 17, enter AMOUNT TO BE REFUNDED	

Under penalties of perjury, I declare that I have examined this return, including any accompanying schedules and statements, and to the best of my knowledge and belief it is true, correct, and complete. Declaration of preparer (other than donor) is based on all information of which preparer has any knowledge.

Donor's signature ▶   Date ▶

Preparer's signature (other than donor) ▶   Date ▶

Preparer's address (other than donor) ▶

Attach check or money order here.

For Paperwork Reduction Act Notice, see page 8 of the separate instructions for this form.   Cat. No. 16783M   Form **709** (1999)

Figure F-2

Form 709, page 1

Form 709 (1999)   Page **2**

SCHEDULE A   Computation of Taxable Gifts (Including Transfers in Trust)

A   Does the value of any item listed on Schedule A reflect any valuation discount? If the answer is "Yes," see instructions . . Yes ☐ No ☐

B   ☐ ◄ Check here if you elect under section 529(c)(2)(B) to treat any transfers made this year to a qualified state tuition program as made ratably over a 5-year period beginning this year. See instructions. Attach explanation.

Part 1—Gifts Subject Only to Gift Tax. *Gifts less political organization, medical, and educational exclusions—see instructions*

A Item number	B • Donee's name and address • Relationship to donor (if any) • Description of gift • If the gift was made by means of a trust, enter trust's identifying number and attach a copy of the trust instrument • If the gift was of securities, give CUSIP number	C Donor's adjusted basis of gift	D Date of gift	E Value at date of gift
1				

Total of Part 1 (add amounts from Part 1, column E) . . . . ▶

Part 2—Gifts That are Direct Skips and are Subject to Both Gift Tax and Generation-Skipping Transfer Tax. You must list the gifts in chronological order. *Gifts less political organization, medical, and educational exclusions—see instructions. (Also list here direct skips that are subject only to the GST tax at this time as the result of the termination of an "estate tax inclusion period." See instructions.)*

A Item number	B • Donee's name and address • Relationship to donor (if any) • Description of gift • If the gift was made by means of a trust, enter trust's identifying number and attach a copy of the trust instrument • If the gift was of securities, give CUSIP number	C Donor's adjusted basis of gift	D Date of gift	E Value at date of gift
1				

Total of Part 2 (add amounts from Part 2, column E) . . . . ▶

Part 3—Taxable Gift Reconciliation

1	Total value of gifts of donor (add totals from column E of Parts 1 and 2)	**1**
2	One-half of items ------------------------------attributable to spouse (see instructions)	**2**
3	Balance (subtract line 2 from line 1)	**3**
4	Gifts of spouse to be included (from Schedule A, Part 3, line 2 of spouse's return—see instructions) . .	**4**
	If any of the gifts included on this line are also subject to the generation-skipping transfer tax, check here ▶ ☐ and enter those gifts also on Schedule C, Part 1.	
5	Total gifts (add lines 3 and 4)	**5**
6	Total annual exclusions for gifts listed on Schedule A (including line 4, above) (see instructions) . . .	**6**
7	Total included amount of gifts (subtract line 6 from line 5)	**7**

Deductions (see instructions)

8	Gifts of interests to spouse for which a marital deduction will be claimed, based on items ---------------------- of Schedule A	8	
9	Exclusions attributable to gifts on line 8	9	
10	Marital deduction—subtract line 9 from line 8	10	
11	Charitable deduction, based on items ----------------less exclusions . .	11	
12	Total deductions—add lines 10 and 11		**12**
13	Subtract line 12 from line 7		**13**
14	Generation-skipping transfer taxes payable with this Form 709 (from Schedule C, Part 3, col. H, Total) .		**14**
15	Taxable gifts (add lines 13 and 14). Enter here and on line 1 of the Tax Computation on page 1 . . .		**15**

(If more space is needed, attach additional sheets of same size.)   Form **709** (1999)

Figure F-2

Form 709, page 2

Form 709 (1999)

SCHEDULE A   Computation of Taxable Gifts *(continued)*

16 Terminable Interest (QTIP) Marital Deduction. (See instructions for line 8 of Schedule A.)

If a trust (or other property) meets the requirements of qualified terminable interest property under section 2523(f), and

   a. The trust (or other property) is listed on Schedule A, and

   b. The value of the trust (or other property) is entered in whole or in part as a deduction on line 8, Part 3 of Schedule A,

then the donor shall be deemed to have made an election to have such trust (or other property) treated as qualified terminable interest property under section 2523(f).

   If less than the entire value of the trust (or other property) that the donor has included in Part 1 of Schedule A is entered as a deduction on line 8, the donor shall be considered to have made an election only as to a fraction of the trust (or other property). The numerator of this fraction is equal to the amount of the trust (or other property) deducted on line 10 of Part 3, Schedule A. The denominator is equal to the total value of the trust (or other property) listed in Part 1 of Schedule A.

   If you make the QTIP election (see instructions for line 8 of Schedule A), the terminable interest property involved will be included in your spouse's gross estate upon his or her death (section 2044). If your spouse disposes (by gift or otherwise) of all or part of the qualifying life income interest, he or she will be considered to have made a transfer of the entire property that is subject to the gift tax (see Transfer of Certain Life Estates on page 3 of the instructions).

17 Election Out of QTIP Treatment of Annuities

☐ ◄ Check here if you elect under section 2523(f)(6) **NOT** to treat as qualified terminable interest property any joint and survivor annuities that are reported on Schedule A and would otherwise be treated as qualified terminable interest property under section 2523(f). (See instructions.) Enter the item numbers (from Schedule A) for the annuities for which you are making this election ►

SCHEDULE B   Gifts From Prior Periods

If you answered "Yes" on line 11a of page 1, Part 1, see the instructions for completing Schedule B. If you answered "No," skip to the Tax Computation on page 1 (or Schedule C, if applicable).

A Calendar year or calendar quarter (see instructions)	B Internal Revenue office where prior return was filed	C Amount of unified credit against gift tax for periods after December 31, 1976	D Amount of specific exemption for prior periods ending before January 1, 1977	E Amount of taxable gifts

1 Totals for prior periods (without adjustment for reduced specific exemption)	**1**		
2 Amount, if any, by which total specific exemption, line 1, column D, is more than $30,000	**2**		
3 Total amount of taxable gifts for prior periods (add amount, column E, line 1, and amount, if any, on line 2). (Enter here and on line 2 of the Tax Computation on page 1.)	**3**		

(If more space is needed, attach additional sheets of same size.)

Form **709** (1999)

Figure F-2

Form 709,
page 3

Form 709 (1999)   Page **4**

SCHEDULE C   Computation of Generation-Skipping Transfer Tax

Note: Inter vivos direct skips that are completely excluded by the GST exemption must still be fully reported (including value and exemptions claimed) on Schedule C.

Part 1—Generation-Skipping Transfers

A Item No. (from Schedule A, Part 2, col. A)	B Value (from Schedule A, Part 2, col. E)	C Split Gifts (enter ½ of col. B) (see instructions)	D Subtract col. C from col. B	E Nontaxable portion of transfer	F Net Transfer (subtract col. E from col. D)
1					
2					
3					
4					
5					
6					

If you elected gift splitting and your spouse was required to file a separate Form 709 (see the instructions for "Split Gifts"), you must enter all of the gifts shown on Schedule A, Part 2, of your spouse's Form 709 here. In column C, enter the item number of each gift in the order it appears in column A of your spouse's Schedule A, Part 2. We have preprinted the prefix "S-" to distinguish your spouse's item numbers from your own when you complete column A of Schedule C, Part 3. In column D, for each gift, enter the amount reported in column C, Schedule C, Part 1, of your spouse's Form 709.	Split gifts from spouse's Form 709 (enter item number)	Value included from spouse's Form 709	Nontaxable portion of transfer	Net transfer (subtract col. E from col. D)
	S-			
	S-			
	S-			
	S-			
	S-			
	S-			
	S-			
	S-			

Part 2—GST Exemption Reconciliation (Section 2631) and Section 2652(a)(3) Election

Check box ▶ ☐   if you are making a section 2652(a)(3) (special QTIP) election (see instructions)

Enter the item numbers (from Schedule A) of the gifts for which you are making this election ▶ ....

1	Maximum allowable exemption (see instructions)	1
2	Total exemption used for periods before filing this return	2
3	Exemption available for this return (subtract line 2 from line 1)	3
4	Exemption claimed on this return (from Part 3, col. C total, below)	4
5	Exemption allocated to transfers not shown on Part 3, below. **You must attach a Notice of Allocation.** (See instructions.)	5
6	Add lines 4 and 5	6
7	Exemption available for future transfers (subtract line 6 from line 3)	7

Part 3—Tax Computation

A Item No. (from Schedule C, Part 1)	B Net transfer (from Schedule C, Part 1, col. F)	C GST Exemption Allocated	D Divide col. C by col. B	E Inclusion Ratio (subtract col. D from 1.000)	F Maximum Estate Tax Rate	G Applicable Rate (multiply col. E by col. F)	H Generation-Skipping Transfer Tax (multiply col. B by col. G)
1					55% (.55)		
2					55% (.55)		
3					55% (.55)		
4					55% (.55)		
5					55% (.55)		
6					55% (.55)		
					55% (.55)		
					55% (.55)		
					55% (.55)		
					55% (.55)		

Total exemption claimed. Enter here and on line 4, Part 2, above. May not exceed line 3, Part 2, above	Total generation-skipping transfer tax. Enter here, on line 14 of Schedule A, Part 3, and on line 16 of the Tax Computation on page 1 . . . .

(If more space is needed, attach additional sheets of same size.)   ✪ Printed on recycled paper   Form **709** (1999)

*U.S. Government Printing Office: 1999 — 461-004/10090

Figure F-2

Form 709, page 4

Form 709-A
(Rev. December 1996)

Department of the Treasury
Internal Revenue Service

United States Short Form Gift Tax Return
(For "Privacy Act" notice, see the Form 1040 instructions)

OMB No. 1545-0021

Calendar year 19.........

1 Donor's first name and middle initial	2 Donor's last name	3 Donor's social security number
4 Address (number, street, and apartment number)		5 Legal residence (domicile)
6 City, state, and ZIP code		7 Citizenship

8 Did you file any gift tax returns for prior periods? . . . . □ Yes □ No

If "Yes," state when and where earlier returns were filed ▶

9 Name of consenting spouse	10 Consenting spouse's social security number

Note: Do not use this form to report gifts of closely held stock, partnership interests, fractional interests in real estate, or gifts for which the value has been reduced to reflect a valuation discount. Instead, use Form 709.

List of Gifts

(a) Donee's name and address and description of gift	(b) Donor's adjusted basis of gift	(c) Date of gift	(d) Value at date of gift

Consent — I consent to have the gifts made by my spouse to third parties during the calendar year considered as made one-half by each of us.

Consenting spouse's signature ▶ _____   Date ▶ _____

Under penalties of perjury, I declare that I have examined this return, and to the best of my knowledge and belief it is true, correct, and complete. Declaration of preparer (other than donor) is based on all information of which preparer has any knowledge.

Donor's signature ▶ ....   Date ▶ ....

Preparer's signature
(other than donor's) ▶ ....   Date ▶ ....

Preparer's address
(other than donor's) ▶ ....

For Paperwork Reduction Act Notice, see the instructions on the reverse side of this form.   Cat. No. 10171G   Form **709-A** (Rev. 12-96)

Figure F-3

Form 709-A,
page 1

Form 709-A (Rev. 12-96)

Page **2**

General Instructions

For Privacy Act notice, see the Form 1040 instructions.

Paperwork Reduction Act Notice.—We ask for the information on this form to carry out the Internal Revenue laws of the United States. You are required to give us the information. We need it to ensure that you are complying with these laws and to allow us to figure and collect the right amount of tax.

You are not required to provide the information requested on a form that is subject to the Paperwork Reduction Act unless the form displays a valid OMB control number. Books or records relating to a form or its instructions must be retained as long as their contents may become material in the administration of any Internal Revenue law. Generally, tax returns and return information are confidential, as required by Code section 6103.

The time needed to complete and file this form will vary depending on individual circumstances. The estimated average time is:

Recordkeeping	13 min.
Learning about the law or the form	11 min.
Preparing the form	14 min.
Copying, assembling, and sending the form to the IRS	20 min.

If you have comments concerning the accuracy of these time estimates or suggestions for making this form simpler, we would be happy to hear from you. You can write to the Tax Forms Committee, Western Area Distribution Center, Rancho Cordova, CA 95743-0001. DO NOT send the tax form to this office. Instead, see **Where To File** below.

General Instructions

Form 709-A is an annual short form gift tax return that certain married couples may use instead of **Form 709**, United States Gift (and Generation-Skipping Transfer) Tax Return, to report nontaxable gifts that they consent to split.

Who May File

Gifts to your spouse.—For gifts to your spouse who is a U.S. citizen, you must only file a gift tax return to report certain gifts of terminable interests. For details on this and for filing rules for gifts to a spouse who is not a U.S. citizen, see the Instructions for Form 709.

Gifts to donee other than your spouse.—You must file a gift tax return if you gave either of the following gifts to someone other than your spouse:

1. Gifts of future interests of any amount; or

2. Gifts of present interests of more than $10,000 to any one donee.

Exceptions.—You do not have to file a gift tax return for any year in which the only gifts you made were for either of the following:

1. Gifts that were paid on behalf of an individual as tuition to an educational organization; or

2. Gifts that were paid on behalf of an individual as payment for medical care to a provider of medical care.

You may use Form 709-A if all of the following requirements are met:

1. You are a citizen or resident of the United States, and were married during the entire calendar year to one individual who is also a citizen or resident of the United States. Both you and your spouse must have been alive at the end of the calendar year.

2. Your only gifts (other than gifts for tuition or medical care) to a third party consisted entirely of present interests in tangible personal property, cash, U.S. Savings Bonds, or stocks and bonds listed on a stock exchange. A "third-party donee" is any donee other than your spouse.

3. Your gifts to any one third-party donee (other than gifts for tuition or medical care) during the calendar year did not total more than $20,000. If the donee is a charity, no part of that gift may be given to a noncharitable donee.

4. During the calendar year, you did not make any gifts of terminable interests to your spouse.

5. During the calendar year, your spouse did not make any gifts to any of the donees listed on this form, did not make gifts of terminable interests to you, did not make gifts (other than gifts for tuition or medical care) of over $10,000 to any other donee, and did not make any gifts of future interests to any other donee.

6. You and your spouse agree to split all of the gifts either of you made during the calendar year.

7. You did not file a Form 709 for this calendar year.

If all seven requirements above are met, you may also use Form 709-A to report gifts made under the Uniform Gifts to Minors Act. **Note:** *Gifts include transfers of property when no money changes hands and also transfers when some payment was made, but the payment was less than the value of the item transferred.*

When To File

Form 709-A is a calendar-year return to be filed on or after January 1 but not later than April 15 of the year following the year when the nontaxable split gifts were made.

Any extension of time granted to file your calendar year income tax return will also extend the time to file Form 709-A. Income tax extensions are made using Forms 4868, 2688, or 2350. If you received an extension, attach a copy of it to Form 709-A.

You may not file Form 709-A later than April 15 (or the extension due date). Instead, you must file Form 709.

Where To File

File Form 709-A with the Internal Revenue Service Center where you would file your Federal income tax return. See the Form 1040 instructions for a list of filing locations.

Additional Help

The Instructions for Form 709 contain further information on the gift tax, including information about the following matters:

1. Annual exclusion.

2. Present and future interest.

3. Fair market value.

4. Adjusted basis. Get Pub. 551, Basis of Assets, and the instructions for Schedule D (Form 1040).

5. Extension of time to file.

6. Terminable interest.

7. Gifts for tuition or medical care.

Specific Instructions

Column (a)

List the names and addresses of all third party donees to whom you made gifts (other than gifts for tuition or medical care) totaling more than $10,000 during the calendar year. Do not list the names of donees to whom you gave only gifts for tuition or medical care or to whom you gave gifts (other than tuition or medical care) of present interests of $10,000 or less.

Describe the gifts in enough detail so they may be easily identified.

If you list **bonds**, include in your description:

- The number of bonds transferred;
- The principal amount of the bonds;
- The name of the obligor;
- The date of maturity of the bonds;
- The rate of interest;
- The date or dates on which interest is payable;
- The series number (if there is more than one issue);
- The exchange where the bond is listed; and
- The CUSIP number. The CUSIP number is a nine-digit number assigned by the American Banking Association to traded securities.

If you list **stocks**, you should include:

- The number of shares transferred;
- Whether the stocks are common or preferred. (If the stocks are preferred, list the issue and par value.);
- Exact name of corporation;
- Principal exchange where the stocks are sold; and
- The CUSIP number (see "bonds" above).

If you list **tangible personal property** (such as a car), describe the property in enough detail so that its fair market value can be accurately figured.

Column (b)

Show the basis you would use for income tax purposes if you sold or exchanged the property.

Column (d)

If you make the gift in property other than money, determine the fair market value as of the date the gift was made.

Consent

Your spouse must consent to split all gifts made by either of you. Your spouse gives this consent by signing in the space provided. You give your consent by signing in the space for the donor's signature. The guardian of a legally incompetent spouse may sign the consent. The executor for a deceased spouse may sign the consent if the spouse died after the close of the calendar year. Although a properly filed Form 709-A will not result in any gift tax liability, you should know that if you and your spouse consent to split gifts, either or both of you will be liable in the event any gift tax is later determined to be due.

Signature

You, as a donor, must sign the return. If you pay another person, firm, or corporation to prepare your return, that person must also sign the return as preparer unless he or she is your regular, full-time employee.

Printed on recycled paper

*U.S. Government Printing Office: 1997 — 417-577/80032

Figure F-3

Form 709-A, page 2

Form 1041

Department of the Treasury—Internal Revenue Service

U.S. Income Tax Return for Estates and Trusts

1999

For calendar year 1999 or fiscal year beginning , 1999, and ending ,

OMB No. 1545-0092

A Type of entity:	Name of estate or trust (If a grantor type trust, see page 8 of the instructions.)	C Employer identification number
☐ Decedent's estate		
☐ Simple trust		D Date entity created
☐ Complex trust		
☐ Grantor type trust	Name and title of fiduciary	E Nonexempt charitable and split-interest trusts, check applicable boxes (see page 10 of the instructions):
☐ Bankruptcy estate–Ch. 7		
☐ Bankruptcy estate–Ch. 11	Number, street, and room or suite no. (If a P.O. box, see page 8 of the instructions.)	
☐ Pooled income fund		☐ Described in section 4947(a)(1)
B Number of Schedules K-1 attached (see instructions) ▶	City or town, state, and ZIP code	☐ Not a private foundation
		☐ Described in section 4947(a)(2)

F Check applicable boxes:	☐ Initial return ☐ Final return ☐ Amended return ☐ Change in fiduciary's name ☐ Change in fiduciary's address	G Pooled mortgage account (see page 10 of the instructions): ☐ Bought ☐ Sold Date:

Income

1	Interest income	1
2	Ordinary dividends	2
3	Business income or (loss) (attach Schedule C or C-EZ (Form 1040))	3
4	Capital gain or (loss) (attach Schedule D (Form 1041))	4
5	Rents, royalties, partnerships, other estates and trusts, etc. (attach Schedule E (Form 1040))	5
6	Farm income or (loss) (attach Schedule F (Form 1040))	6
7	Ordinary gain or (loss) (attach Form 4797)	7
8	Other income. List type and amount	8
9	**Total income.** Combine lines 1 through 8 ▶	9

Deductions

10	Interest. Check if Form 4952 is attached ▶ ☐	10
11	Taxes	11
12	Fiduciary fees	12
13	Charitable deduction (from Schedule A, line 7)	13
14	Attorney, accountant, and return preparer fees	14
15a	Other deductions NOT subject to the 2% floor (attach schedule)	15a
b	Allowable miscellaneous itemized deductions subject to the 2% floor	15b
16	**Total.** Add lines 10 through 15b	16
17	Adjusted total income or (loss). Subtract line 16 from line 9. Enter here and on Schedule B, line 1 ▶	17
18	Income distribution deduction (from Schedule B, line 15) (attach Schedules K-1 (Form 1041))	18
19	Estate tax deduction (including certain generation-skipping taxes) (attach computation)	19
20	Exemption	20
21	**Total deductions.** Add lines 18 through 20 ▶	21

Tax and Payments

22	Taxable income. Subtract line 21 from line 17. If a loss, see page 14 of the instructions	22
23	**Total tax** (from Schedule G, line 8)	23
24	**Payments: a** 1999 estimated tax payments and amount applied from 1998 return	24a
b	Estimated tax payments allocated to beneficiaries (from Form 1041-T)	24b
c	Subtract line 24b from line 24a	24c
d	Tax paid with extension of time to file: ☐ Form 2758 ☐ Form 8736 ☐ Form 8800	24d
e	Federal income tax withheld. If any is from Form(s) 1099, check ▶ ☐	24e
	Other payments: **f** Form 2439 ; **g** Form 4136 ; Total ▶	24h
25	**Total payments.** Add lines 24c through 24e, and 24h ▶	25
26	Estimated tax penalty (see page 15 of the instructions)	26
27	**Tax due.** If line 25 is smaller than the total of lines 23 and 26, enter amount owed	27
28	**Overpayment.** If line 25 is larger than the total of lines 23 and 26, enter amount overpaid	28
29	Amount of line 28 to be: **a** Credited to 2000 estimated tax ▶ ; **b** Refunded ▶	29

Please Sign Here

Under penalties of perjury, I declare that I have examined this return, including accompanying schedules and statements, and to the best of my knowledge and belief, it is true, correct, and complete. Declaration of preparer (other than fiduciary) is based on all information of which preparer has any knowledge.

▶ Signature of fiduciary or officer representing fiduciary / Date

▶ EIN of fiduciary if a financial institution (see page 5 of the instructions)

Paid Preparer's Use Only

Preparer's signature ▶	Date	Check if self-employed ▶ ☐	Preparer's SSN or PTIN
Firm's name (or yours if self-employed) and address ▶		EIN ▶	
		ZIP code ▶	

For Paperwork Reduction Act Notice, see the separate instructions.

Cat. No. 11370H

Form **1041** (1999)

Figure F-4

Form 1041, page 1

Form 1041 (1999)   Page **2**

Schedule A	Charitable Deduction. Do not complete for a simple trust or a pooled income fund.	
1	Amounts paid or permanently set aside for charitable purposes from gross income (see page 15)	**1**
2	Tax-exempt income allocable to charitable contributions (see page 16 of the instructions)	**2**
3	Subtract line 2 from line 1	**3**
4	Capital gains for the tax year allocated to corpus and paid or permanently set aside for charitable purposes	**4**
5	Add lines 3 and 4	**5**
6	Section 1202 exclusion allocable to capital gains paid or permanently set aside for charitable purposes (see page 16 of the instructions)	**6**
7	**Charitable deduction.** Subtract line 6 from 5. Enter here and on page 1, line 13	**7**

Schedule B	Income Distribution Deduction	
1	Adjusted total income (from page 1, line 17) (see page 16 of the instructions)	**1**
2	Adjusted tax-exempt interest	**2**
3	Total net gain from Schedule D (Form 1041), line 16, column (1) (see page 16 of the instructions)	**3**
4	Enter amount from Schedule A, line 4 (reduced by any allocable section 1202 exclusion).	**4**
5	Capital gains for the tax year included on Schedule A, line 1 (see page 16 of the instructions)	**5**
6	Enter any gain from page 1, line 4, as a negative number. If page 1, line 4, is a loss, enter the loss as a positive number	**6**
7	**Distributable net income (DNI).** Combine lines 1 through 6. If zero or less, enter -0-.	**7**
8	If a complex trust, enter accounting income for the tax year as determined under the governing instrument and applicable local law	**8**
9	Income required to be distributed currently	**9**
10	Other amounts paid, credited, or otherwise required to be distributed	**10**
11	Total distributions. Add lines 9 and 10. If greater than line 8, see page 17 of the instructions	**11**
12	Enter the amount of tax-exempt income included on line 11	**12**
13	Tentative income distribution deduction. Subtract line 12 from line 11	**13**
14	Tentative income distribution deduction. Subtract line 2 from line 7. If zero or less, enter -0-	**14**
15	**Income distribution deduction.** Enter the smaller of line 13 or line 14 here and on page 1, line 18	**15**

Schedule G	Tax Computation (see page 17 of the instructions)	
1	**Tax: a** ☐ Tax rate schedule or ☐ Schedule D (Form 1041)	**1a**
	b Tax on lump-sum distributions (attach Form 4972)	**1b**
	c Total. Add lines 1a and 1b	**1c**
2a	Foreign tax credit (attach Form 1116)	**2a**
b	Check: ☐ Nonconventional source fuel credit ☐ Form 8834	**2b**
c	General business credit. Enter here and check which forms are attached: ☐ Form 3800 or ☐ Forms (specify) ▶	**2c**
d	Credit for prior year minimum tax (attach Form 8801)	**2d**
3	**Total credits.** Add lines 2a through 2d	**3**
4	Subtract line 3 from line 1c	**4**
5	Recapture taxes. Check if from: ☐ Form 4255 ☐ Form 8611	**5**
6	Alternative minimum tax (from Schedule I, line 39)	**6**
7	Household employment taxes. Attach Schedule H (Form 1040)	**7**
8	**Total tax.** Add lines 4 through 7. Enter here and on page 1, line 23	**8**

Other Information

		Yes	No
1	Did the estate or trust receive tax-exempt income? If "Yes," attach a computation of the allocation of expenses. Enter the amount of tax-exempt interest income and exempt-interest dividends ▶ $		
2	Did the estate or trust receive all or any part of the earnings (salary, wages, and other compensation) of any individual by reason of a contract assignment or similar arrangement?		
3	At any time during calendar year 1999, did the estate or trust have an interest in or a signature or other authority over a bank, securities, or other financial account in a foreign country? See page 18 of the instructions for exceptions and filing requirements for Form TD F 90-22.1. If "Yes," enter the name of the foreign country ▶		
4	During the tax year, did the estate or trust receive a distribution from, or was it the grantor of, or transferor to, a foreign trust? If "Yes," the estate or trust may have to file Form 3520. See page 19 of the instructions		
5	Did the estate or trust receive, or pay, any qualified residence interest on seller-provided financing? If "Yes," see page 19 for required attachment		
6	If this is an estate or a complex trust making the section 663(b) election, check here (see page 19) ▶ ☐		
7	To make a section 643(e)(3) election, attach Schedule D (Form 1041), and check here (see page 19). ▶ ☐		
8	If the decedent's estate has been open for more than 2 years, attach an explanation for the delay in closing the estate, and check here ▶ ☐		
9	Are any present or future trust beneficiaries skip persons? See page 19 of the instructions		

Form **1041** (1999)

Figure F-4

Form 1041, page 2

Schedule I	**Alternative Minimum Tax** (see pages 19 through 24 of the instructions)

Part I—Estate's or Trust's Share of Alternative Minimum Taxable Income

1	Adjusted total income or (loss) (from page 1, line 17)	**1**	
2	Net operating loss deduction. Enter as a positive amount	**2**	
3	Add lines 1 and 2	**3**	
4	**Adjustments and tax preference items:**		
a	Interest	**4a**	
b	Taxes	**4b**	
c	Miscellaneous itemized deductions (from page 1, line 15b) . . .	**4c**	
d	Refund of taxes	**4d** ( )	
e	Depreciation of property placed in service after 1986	**4e**	
f	Circulation and research and experimental expenditures	**4f**	
g	Mining exploration and development costs	**4g**	
h	Long-term contracts entered into after February 28, 1986	**4h**	
i	Amortization of pollution control facilities	**4i**	
j	Installment sales of certain property	**4j**	
k	Adjusted gain or loss (including incentive stock options)	**4k**	
l	Certain loss limitations	**4l**	
m	Tax shelter farm activities	**4m**	
n	Passive activities	**4n**	
o	Beneficiaries of other trusts or decedent's estates	**4o**	
p	Tax-exempt interest from specified private activity bonds	**4p**	
q	Depletion	**4q**	
r	Accelerated depreciation of real property placed in service before 1987	**4r**	
s	Accelerated depreciation of leased personal property placed in service before 1987	**4s**	
t	Intangible drilling costs	**4t**	
u	Other adjustments	**4u**	
5	Combine lines 4a through 4u	**5**	
6	Add lines 3 and 5	**6**	
7	Alternative tax net operating loss deduction (see page 22 of the instructions for limitations) . .	**7**	
8	Adjusted alternative minimum taxable income. Subtract line 7 from line 6. Enter here and on line 13	**8**	

Note: *Complete Part II below before going to line 9.*

9	Income distribution deduction from line 27 below	**9**	
10	Estate tax deduction (from page 1, line 19)	**10**	
11	Add lines 9 and 10	**11**	
12	Estate's or trust's share of alternative minimum taxable income. Subtract line 11 from line 8 .	**12**	

If line 12 is:
- $22,500 or less, stop here and enter -0- on Schedule G, line 6. The estate or trust is not liable for the alternative minimum tax.
- Over $22,500, but less than $165,000, go to line 28.
- $165,000 or more, enter the amount from line 12 on line 34 and go to line 35.

Part II—Income Distribution Deduction on a Minimum Tax Basis

13	Adjusted alternative minimum taxable income (from line 8)	**13**	
14	Adjusted tax-exempt interest (other than amounts included on line 4p)	**14**	
15	Total net gain from Schedule D (Form 1041), line 16, column (1). If a loss, enter -0-	**15**	
16	Capital gains for the tax year allocated to corpus and paid or permanently set aside for charitable purposes (from Schedule A, line 4) .	**16**	
17	Capital gains paid or permanently set aside for charitable purposes from gross income (see page 23 of the instructions) .	**17**	
18	Capital gains computed on a minimum tax basis included on line 8	**18** ( )	
19	Capital losses computed on a minimum tax basis included on line 8. Enter as a positive amount	**19**	
20	Distributable net alternative minimum taxable income (DNAMTI). Combine lines 13 through 19. If zero or less, enter -0- .	**20**	
21	Income required to be distributed currently (from Schedule B, line 9)	**21**	
22	Other amounts paid, credited, or otherwise required to be distributed (from Schedule B, line 10) .	**22**	
23	Total distributions. Add lines 21 and 22	**23**	
24	Tax-exempt income included on line 23 (other than amounts included on line 4p)	**24**	
25	Tentative income distribution deduction on a minimum tax basis. Subtract line 24 from line 23 .	**25**	
26	Tentative income distribution deduction on a minimum tax basis. Subtract line 14 from line 20. If zero or less, enter -0- .	**26**	
27	**Income distribution deduction on a minimum tax basis.** Enter the smaller of line 25 or line 26. Enter here and on line 9	**27**	

Form **1041** (1999)

Figure F-4

Form 1041,
page 3

Form 1041 (1999)   Page **4**

Part III—Alternative Minimum Tax

28	Exemption amount		**28**	$22,500 00
29	Enter the amount from line 12	**29**		
30	Phase-out of exemption amount	**30** $75,000 00		
31	Subtract line 30 from line 29. If zero or less, enter -0-	**31**		
32	Multiply line 31 by 25% (.25).		**32**	
33	Subtract line 32 from line 28. If zero or less, enter -0-		**33**	
34	Subtract line 33 from line 29		**34**	

35   If the estate or trust completed Schedule D (Form 1041) and has an amount on line 24 or 26
     (or would have had an amount on either line if Part V had been completed) (as refigured for the
     AMT, if necessary), go to Part IV below to figure line 35. **All others:** If line 34 is—
     • $175,000 or less, multiply line 34 by 26% (.26).
     • Over $175,000, multiply line 34 by 28% (.28) and subtract $3,500 from the result **35**

36	Alternative minimum foreign tax credit (see page 23 of instructions).	**36**	
37	Tentative minimum tax. Subtract line 36 from line 35	**37**	
38	Enter the tax from Schedule G, line 1a (minus any foreign tax credit from Schedule G, line 2a).	**38**	
39	**Alternative minimum tax.** Subtract line 38 from line 37. If zero or less, enter -0-. Enter here and on Schedule G, line 6	**39**	

Part IV—Line 35 Computation Using Maximum Capital Gains Rates

Caution: *If the estate or trust did not complete Part V of Schedule D (Form 1041), complete lines 19 through 26 of Schedule D (as refigured for the AMT, if necessary) before completing this part.*

40	Enter the amount from line 34		**40**
41	Enter the amount from Schedule D (Form 1041), line 26 (as refigured for AMT, if necessary)	**41**	
42	Enter the amount from Schedule D (Form 1041), line 24 (as refigured for AMT, if necessary)	**42**	
43	Add lines 41 and 42. If zero or less, enter -0-	**43**	
44	Enter the amount from Schedule D (Form 1041), line 21 (as refigured for AMT, if necessary)	**44**	
45	Enter the **smaller** of line 43 or line 44		**45**
46	Subtract line 45 from line 40. If zero or less, enter -0-		**46**
47	If line 46 is $175,000 or less, multiply line 46 by 26% (.26). Otherwise, multiply line 46 by 28% (.28) and subtract $3,500 from the result . . . . ▶		**47**
48	Enter the amount from Schedule D (Form 1041), line 35 (as figured for the regular tax) . . .		**48**
49	Enter the **smallest** of line 40, line 41, or line 48		**49**
50	Multiply line 49 by 10% (.10) . . . . ▶		**50**
51	Enter the **smaller** of line 40 or line 41		**51**
52	Enter the amount from line 49		**52**
53	Subtract line 52 from line 51. If zero or less, enter -0-		**53**
54	Multiply line 53 by 20% (.20) . . . . ▶		**54**
55	Enter the amount from line 40		**55**
56	Add lines 46, 49, and 53		**56**
57	Subtract line 56 from line 55		**57**
58	Multiply line 57 by 25% (.25) . . . . ▶		**58**
59	Add lines 47, 50, 54, and 58		**59**
60	If line 40 is $175,000 or less, multiply line 40 by 26% (.26). Otherwise, multiply line 40 by 28% (.28) and subtract $3,500 from the result		**60**
61	Enter the **smaller** of line 59 or line 60 here and on line 35 . . . . ▶		**61**

*U.S.GPO:1999-456-252   ⊛ Printed on recycled paper   Form **1041** (1999)

Figure F-4

Form 1041,
page 4

APPENDIX G

What's on the CD-ROM?

Τhe CD-ROM that accompanies this book contains the following:

- A functional version of WillWriter, provided by Business Logic Corporation
- Example wills prepared by the author
- A beneficiary worksheet
- An estate inventory worksheet
- A guardian checklist

 NOTE   Two versions of the WillWriter software are on the CD and will be installed on your hard drive. The "full" version contains all the functionality of the program. This is the version that you should use. The demo version is much more limited, so there is no reason to use it.

Running the CD-ROM

To make the companion CD-ROM more user-friendly and to take up less space on your hard drive, we've designed the CD-ROM so that you can install only those files that you desire.

Before you attempt to install any software, however, please be sure that your computer meets the following minimum system requirements:

- 486 or faster processor
- Microsoft Windows 95/98 or Windows NT
- 4MB of RAM
- CD-ROM drive

Windows 95/98/NT4

To begin using the companion CD-ROM, simply insert it into your CD-ROM drive, close the tray, and wait for the CD-ROM to load.

If the CD-ROM interface does not load automatically (which means that Autorun is disabled), follow these steps:

1. Click on the Start menu, and select Run from the menu.
2. Type **D:\CDInstaller.exe** (where *D* is the letter of your CD-ROM drive).
3. Click on OK.

The Prima License

Take a moment to read the license agreement. If you accept the agreement, click on the I Agree button and proceed to the user interface. If you do not accept the agreement license, click on the I Decline button to close the user interface and return to Windows.

The Prima User Interface

Prima's user interface is designed to make viewing and using the CD-ROM contents quick and easy. The opening screen contains a two-panel window with three buttons across the bottom. The left panel contains entries that point to information about Prima Tech and the files available on the disc. The right panel displays a description page for the selected entry in the left panel. The three buttons across the bottom of the user interface make it possible to install programs to your hard drive, view the contents of the disc using Windows Explorer, and view the contents of a Help file for the selected entry. If a button is "grayed out," that button is currently unavailable. For example, if the Help button is grayed out, it means that no Help file is available.

 NOTE Each time you click on the Explore button, a new Explorer window opens, so be sure to close Explorer when you are finished by selecting File and then Close or by clicking on the Close button (the *x*) in the upper-right corner of the window.

Resizing and Closing the User Interface

As with any window, you can resize the user interface. To do so, position the mouse over any edge or corner, hold down the left mouse button, and drag the edge or corner to a new position.

To close and exit the user interface, either double-click on the small icon in the upper-left corner of the window, or click on the Close button (marked with a small *x*) in the upper-right corner of the window.

Using the Left Panel

The left panel of the Prima user interface works very much like Windows Explorer. To view the description of an entry in the left panel, simply click on the entry. General information about Prima Publishing is shown by default, but if, for example, you want to view information about the example wills, click on the entry called Example Wills.

Some items have subitems that are nested below them. Such parent items have a small plus (+) sign next to them. To view the nested subitems, simply click on the plus sign. When you do, the list expands, and the subitems are listed below the parent item. In addition, the plus (+) sign becomes a minus (-) sign. To hide the subitems, click on the minus sign to collapse the listing.

● ●

NOTE You can control the positon of the line between the left and right panels. To change the position of the dividing line, move the mouse over the line, hold down the left mouse button (the mouse becomes a two-headed arrow) and drag the line to a new position.

● ●

Using the Right Panel

The right panel displays a page that describes the entry you choose in the left panel. (For example, if you click on Example Wills, the right panel displays a page that describes the wills provided on the CD-ROM.) Use the information provided in the right panel for details about your selection—such as what functionality an installable program provides. In addition to a general description, the page may provide the following information:

✪ **World Wide Web site.** Many program providers have a Web site. If one is available, the description page provides the Web address. To navigate to the Web site using your browser, simply click on the

Web address (you must be connected to the Internet). Alternatively, you can copy the Web address to the Clipboard, and paste it into the URL line at the top of your browser window.

○ **E-mail address.** Many program providers are available via e-mail. If available, the description page provides the e-mail address. To use the e-mail address, click on it to open your e-mail program (to send e-mail, you must be connected to the Internet). Alternatively, copy the address to the Clipboard, and paste it into the address line of your e-mail program.

○ **Readme, License, and other text files.** Many programs have additional information available in files with such names as Readme, License, Order, and so on. If such a file exists, you can view the contents of the file in the right panel by clicking on the indicated hyperlink (such as the word *here* displayed in blue). When you are done viewing the text file, you can return to the description page by reclicking on the entry in the left panel.

Command Buttons

○ **Install.** Use this button to install the program corresponding to your selection onto your hard drive. Note that when you click on the Install button, a window appears that enables you to unzip the file that you selected. For example, if you select Example Wills in the left panel and click the Install button, a window pops up that enables you to install the files to a directory named WriteYourWill on your hard drive. (If you want to install the files to a different location, you must enter the new pathname in the Unzip to folder window.)

When you are ready to install, click on the Unzip button, and the files will be copied to your hard drive.

For specific instructions on how to install and run the WillWriter software, please refer to the Saturday Evening session.

When you install any of the sample files, the program creates a new program group and copies the files into a folder named C:\WriteYourWill. To access these files, open Windows Explorer (go to Start, select <u>P</u>rogram, and then select Windows Explorer). Scroll down the left panel until you see the WriteYour Will folder. Click on the folder to select it, and the sample files will appear in the right panel. To open and view any one of them, double-ckick on the file.

- ✪ **Explore**. Use this button to view the contents of the CD-ROM using Windows Explorer.
- ✪ **Help**. Click on this button to display the contents of the Help file provided with the program.

Pop-Up Menu Options

- ✪ **Install.** If the selected title contains an install routine, choosing this option begins the installation process.
- ✪ **Explore**. Selecting this option allows you to view the folder containing the program files using Windows Explorer.
- ✪ **View Help**. Use this menu item to display the contents of the Help file provided with the program.

The Software

This section gives you a brief description of the version of WillWriter that is on the CD-ROM.

WillWriter is a complete legal will-writing program available for residents of North America. The program offers a fast, easy method of protecting yourself, your family, and your property without hiring the costly services of a lawyer. WillWriter is provided by Business Logic Corporation.

This version of WillWriter enables you to do the following:

○ Answer simple, straightforward questions that help you write your will.

○ Create your will at the press of a button.

○ Review the document before printing.

○ Print wills that look professional.

○ Get extensive on-line help.

Files Supplied by the Author

○ **Beneficiary Worksheet for Specific Requests (Benefic.doc).** This worksheet is designed to help you determine to whom you want to leave specific gifts at your death.

○ **Estate Inventory Worksheet (Estate.doc).** Use this worksheet to calculate your estate's worth by determining what you own and what you owe.

○ **Guardian Checklist (Guardian.doc).** Use this checklist to choose the appropriate person to raise minor children that you might leave at your death.

○ **Example wills.** You will find five example wills. The first one (living.doc) is an example of a living will, which allows a person to state his wishes about certain medical treatments if he is unable to communicate them at a later time. The next four wills represent specific situations—that is, married (married.doc), married with children (married-child.doc), single (single.doc), and single with children (single-children.doc).

For More Information

FIND IT ON ▶
THE WEB

For more information about WillWriter, you can visit the Business Logic Corporation Web site at **www.blcorp.com**. For more information about Prima Tech books, visit **www.prima-tech.com**.

GLOSSARY

AB trust: A trust created by a married couple to minimize estate tax, where the surviving spouse inherits a life estate in the deceased spouse's property at his or her death.

abatement: The reduction of a general or specific bequest under a will because of the insufficiency of the estate to pay debts and liabilities owed.

ademption by extinction: The failure of a bequest under a will because the property left in the will no longer exists at the time of the testator's death.

ademption by satisfaction: The failure of a bequest under a will because the property left in the will was given to the named beneficiary during the testator's life.

administrator: Individual appointed by a court to handle an estate without a will.

(Also referred to as a *personal representative.*)

affidavit: A voluntary, written declaration sworn to by the declarant in front of a notary public.

beneficiary: An individual designated to receive an interest in another's property or assets under a will, trust, or other legal instrument such as a life insurance policy.

bequest: A gift left under a will.

claims: The debts and other obligations of a decedent that survive the decedent's death, including funeral and administration expenses, as well as all estate and inheritance taxes.

codicil: A written document that supplements, amends, or changes a will without revoking the entire will document.

community property: The property acquired during a marriage that is considered to be owned equally between a husband and wife—excluding property acquired as a result of an inheritance or gift, which is not considered community property. (Community property is recognized in nine states: Arizona, California, Idaho, Louisiana, Nevada, New Mexico, Texas, Washington, and Wisconsin.)

contingent bequest: A gift left in a will, the receipt of which is contingent on an event or condition. (Also referred to as a *conditional gift*.)

custodian: An individual named to handle property for a minor under a state's Uniform Gift or Transfer to Minors Act.

death tax: An estate or inheritance tax imposed by a decedent's state of domicile.

decedent: One who dies testate (with a will) or intestate (without a will).

directive to physicians: A legal document wherein an individual states his or her intentions to refuse certain medical treatments (for example, artificial life support) should he become incapacitated. (Also referred to as a *living will*.)

disinterested witness: One who has no financial interest in the will that he or she witnesses; not receiving an interest.

dispositive provisions: In a will, the provisions of conveyance by which the testator directs how to dispose of his or her property at death.

domicile: An individual's permanent and legal residence.

domiciliary state: An individual's state of legal and permanent residence.

durable power of attorney: A written document that grants an individual full legal authority to act on behalf of another when that person becomes incapacitated or disabled.

encumbrances: Claims or liabilities of a decedent's estate.

escheat: The passing of property to the state upon the death of an individual who had no will and no legal heirs.

estate: The real and personal property of a decedent.

estate planning: The preparation for the orderly transfer of an individual's property at death, by instruments such as a will, trust, life insurance policy, and so on.

estate tax: The federal and state taxes levied upon the transfer of property and the value of assets remaining at death.

executor: An individual named by a testator in his or her will to carry out the testator's directives and to handle the testator's estate at death. (Also referred to as a *personal representative*.)

fiduciary: An individual entrusted with representing another or another's affairs in good faith and with fair dealing. Examples of fiduciaries include a guardian, a trustee, and an executor.

forced heirship: A testator's inability to disinherit an individual because the law reserves a part of the testator's estate for that individual.

formal will: A computer-generated or typewritten, witnessed will.

guardian: One who is legally responsible for caring for a minor or incompetent person.

healthcare power of attorney: A written document that grants an individual full legal authority to act on behalf of another individual concerning certain medical and health care decisions.

heir: An individual who is legally entitled to receive the property of another through inheritance; those persons, including a surviving spouse, entitled under state statute to the real and personal property of a decedent who died without a will.

holographic will: A handwritten, unwitnessed will.

***in terrorem* clause**: Latin term for "in order to frighten." A provision or clause in a will that acts to disinherit anyone who unsuccessfully contests the will. (Also referred to as a *no-contest clause*.)

Individual Retirement Account (IRA): An account established by an individual to prepare for his or her continuing financial support at retirement. (Contributions may be tax deductible.)

inheritance tax: A tax levied by some states on the value of inherited property.

intangible personal property: Property that lacks physical existence. For example, stocks, bonds, mutual funds, bank accounts, and intellectual property rights.

inter vivos: Latin term for "between the living." An *inter vivos* gift is given during the giver's lifetime; it's not left to a beneficiary in a will.

intestate (noun): One who dies without a valid will.

intestate (verb): Dying without a valid will to dispose of property.

intestate succession: A state-determined order in which property owned at a person's death is distributed to his or her heirs.

joint tenancy: The property owned jointly between two individuals, usually with a right of survivorship (ROS), where the surviving party becomes the sole owner of the property at the other person's death. Property owned in this manner is not subject to probate.

legally competent: The minimal ability required to perform an act. In the case of drafting a will, the testator must also be an adult—that is, at least 18 years old (19 in Wyoming).

life estate: An interest in the property or assets of another that lasts only for a specific duration (the lifetime of the recipient beneficiary).

living will: A legal document wherein an individual states his or her intentions to refuse certain medical treatments (for example, artificial life support) should he or she become incapacitated. (Also referred to as *directive to physicians*.)

marital deduction: A federal estate tax deduction for property transferred by a decedent to his or her surviving spouse.

minor: Individual who has not reached full legal age—typically a person under the age of 18 (except in Wyoming, where, in regard to drafting a will, minors are considered to be those under the age of 19).

movable property: An individual's personal property (all property—excluding real estate—owned by an individual).

no-contest clause: A provision or clause in a will that acts to disinherit anyone who unsuccessfully contests the will.

nonprobate property: The property of an estate that is effectively transferred to a beneficiary or heir without being subject to the probate process.

nuncupative will: An oral will made in contemplation of death or by an active member of the armed forces in time of war.

pay-on-death account: An account, typically a bank account, in which one person deposits money in his or her own name as a trustee for another person. These funds are automatically paid to a previously designated beneficiary upon the death of the trustee.

per stirpes: Latin term for "by roots or stocks." The division of interest among beneficiaries, according to their deceased ancestor's share. (The beneficiaries stand in the shoes of their ancestor and are entitled to what the ancestor would have received had he not predeceased the testator.)

performance bond: A type of bond required of a fiduciary in a will to ensure that the fiduciary's good faith and fair dealing in administering the estate or performing his or her role. (More commonly referred to as a *surety bond*.)

personal estate tax exemption: An amount allowed as a deduction from estate tax. More specifically, beginning in the year 2000, a decedent is allowed to leave an estate worth as much as $675,000 without it being subject to federal estate tax. This allowable exemption amount will increase steadily until it reaches $1 million in 2006. (Also referred to as the *unified estate and gift tax credit*.)

personal property: The tangible (movable) and intangible property owned by an individual (includes interests in goods, money, evidences of debt, and life estates in real property).

personal representative: An individual appointed by a court to handle an estate with or without a will. (Also referred to as an *administrator* or *executor*.)

personality: All property owned by an individual, excluding real estate.

pick-up tax: A tax that is levied by some states on the value of a decedent's estate but that is paid out of the estate's federal tax liability. Hence, the estate pays no additional state tax.

prenuptial agreement: A legal agreement made between a soon-to-be husband and wife that outlines how property is to be owned upon the divorce of the couple or the death of a spouse.

pretermission: The accidental act of omitting an heir from a will.

probate: A judicial procedure to prove the validity of a will and to administer an estate.

probate estate: The property owned by an individual at his death that is subject to probate administration.

Qualified Domestic Trust (QDOT): A trust established by a husband and wife in which one spouse is not a U.S. citizen and wherein the deceased spouse's property is transferred to the surviving spouse tax-free.

Qualified Terminable Interest Property (QTIP) trust: A trust established by a husband and wife wherein the deceased spouse's property is transferred to the surviving spouse tax-free.

real property: The real estate (lands) owned by an individual.

remainder interest: A future interest belonging to a person who is entitled to the property upon the death of the life estate beneficiary.

residuary beneficiary: An individual named in a will who will receive the decedent's residuary estate.

residuary estate: The residue (or the remainder) of a decedent's estate after all bequests are distributed and all encumbrances are paid.

right of survivorship (ROS): A joint tenant's right to receive the entire property upon the death of the other joint tenant.

separate property: The property owned solely by an individual regardless of whether he or she is married or lives in a community property state.

sound mind: The mental capacity required of a testator for drafting a valid will.

surety bond: A type of bond required of a fiduciary in a will to ensure the fiduciary's good faith and fair dealing in administering the estate or performing his or her role. (Also referred to as a *performance bond*.)

surviving spouse: A widow or widower of the decedent.

take against the will: A surviving spouse's right in a common law state to choose his or her intestate share of the decedent spouse's estate instead of what was left to him or her in the will.

tangible personal property: The movable, personal property of an individual that can be seen and touched (jewelry, automobiles, clothes, household furnishings, art, antiques, sports equipment, and so on).

taxable estate: A decedent's gross estate minus allowable deductions, such as charitable and marital deductions.

tenancy by the entirety: The property owned jointly between a husband and wife. (This type of ownership exists in only a few states.)

tenancy in common: The property owned by two or more persons, in equal or unequal shares, in which all persons have the right to use or enjoy the property or asset. (No right of survivorship exists with a tenancy in common.)

testate (noun): One who dies with a valid will.

testate (verb): Dying with a valid will.

testator: The drafter of a will. (A female drafter is called a *testratrix*.)

totten trust: A revocable trust created when one deposits money into an account in his or her own name as the trustee for another. (Also called a *pay-on-death account*.)

unified estate and gift tax credit: A tax credit that allows an individual to pass a certain amount of money free from federal estate or gift tax. Beginning in the year 2000, an individual is allowed to leave an estate worth as much as $675,000 without it being subject to federal tax. The credit increases gradually until it reaches $1 million in 2006.

Uniform Transfer to Minors Act: A state statute that allows an individual to name an adult custodian to manage or handle property left to a minor. (Not all states have enacted the Uniform Transfer to Minors Act.)

will: A document in which a person outlines his or her wishes about how his or her estate should be distributed upon death.

will contest: A legal challenge to the validity of a will.

INDEX

Your Will May Not Provide Enough Protection!

...sonal will executes your wishes after you pass away. However, you may often need a document ...xpresses your wishes when you are still alive, but be unable to make your wishes known in person. ...er of attorney is used for situations where an individual cannot be present, but that individual has ...ted someone to do the job in their place. When someone holds "a power of attorney," they are able ...er into contracts, negotiate, and settle matters as if they were that person. An ordinary power of ...ey expires when a grantor becomes incompetent or passes away. The theory is that if the principal ...n't do so on his own, then the agent shouldn't be able to do so either. This makes sense in many ...ial and commercial situations, but makes little sense when dealing with elderly issues. For such ..., there are other forms of the Power of Attorney document that you can write for added protection.

...le Power of Attorney

...le Power of Attorney can act on a person's behalf even ...at person is still alive. For example, people suffering from ...a, or senility, need to continue to make financial and med-...sactions long after they have the capacity to do so. A ...Power of Attorney allows them to do that.

...g Up a Durable Power of Attorney

...asy as signing a single legal document, naming who you ...ke to appoint as your agent. There are no hearings or court ...ings to go through.

...happens If You Don't Have One?

...ave not named an agent to act on your behalf, you can only ...at someone will become a conservator for you.

...s a Conservator?

...appointed person, who volunteers to look after ...airs is called a conservator. To give a conserva-...s a lengthy and expensive legal procedure. ...a volunteer, to suddenly appear and want to be ...aservator is rare.

...urable Power of Attorney Safe?

...e that an elderly man is declared incompetent, ...given his adult child a Durable Power of Attorney. ...cannot turn around and put his father's house ...me or sell off his father's assets for his own ...e law maintains that agents have a fiduciary ...he grantor and cannot take advantage of his or ...tion.

...o You Need a Durable Power Of ...ey?

...ou become unable to look after your own ...he Durable Power of Attorney will:
- that the person of your choice will be ...ted to make decisions for you.
- your assets are looked after.
- t expensive court costs.
- t disputes between family members.
- piece of mind.

Medical Power of Attorney (or a Living Will)

A Medical Power of Attorney (also known as a Durable Power of Attorney for Health Care or Living Will) is so critical, because it allows a trusted agent to make healthcare decisions on your behalf. Few hospitals wish to take on the responsibility of determining your healthcare decisions for you, especially in this litigious society.

How Will a Medical Power of Attorney Help You?

The Medical Power of Attorney helps your doctor determine when life-supporting measures should be stopped. If your wish is to not use life-sustaining measures, you can convey this wish to the person you've named, and that person will be able to fulfill your wishes on your behalf.

How Does a Medical Power of Attorney Differ from a Durable Power Of Attorney?

A Medical Power of Attorney applies only to your healthcare decisions and cannot empower the agent to make financial or other decisions on your behalf (unless, of course, you've granted both Powers of Attorney to the same person).

Why Do You Need A Medical Power Of Attorney?

- ensures medical treatment is carried out according to your wishes.
- ensures piece of mind and saves unnecessary, and painful decision making for family members.

How Do I Write My Own Power of Attorney Document?

Writing your own power of attorney is as easy as writing the personal will that you just created. If you feel that you need the added protection of these types of documents, we encourage you to visit our Web site and inquire about **WillWriter Deluxe**. A free trial version is available for your convenience.

www.blcorp.com

License Agreement/Notice of Limited Warranty

By opening the sealed disk container in this book, you agree to the following terms and conditions. If, upon reading the following license agreement and notice of limited warranty, you cannot agree to the terms and conditions set forth, return the unused book with unopened disk to the place where you purchased it for a refund.

License:
The enclosed software is copyrighted by the copyright holder(s) indicated on the software disk. You are licensed to copy the software onto a single computer for use by a single concurrent user and to a backup disk. You may not reproduce, make copies, or distribute copies or rent or lease the software in whole or in part, except with written permission of the copyright holder(s). You may transfer the enclosed disk only together with this license, and only if you destroy all other copies of the software and the transferee agrees to the terms of the license. You may not decompile, reverse assemble, or reverse engineer the software.

Notice of Limited Warranty:
The enclosed disk is warranted by Prima Publishing to be free of physical defects in materials and workmanship for a period of sixty (60) days from end user's purchase of the book/disk combination. During the sixty-day term of the limited warranty, Prima will provide a replacement disk upon the return of a defective disk.

Limited Liability:
THE SOLE REMEDY FOR BREACH OF THIS LIMITED WARRANTY SHALL CONSIST ENTIRELY OF REPLACEMENT OF THE DEFECTIVE DISK. IN NO EVENT SHALL PRIMA OR THE AUTHORS BE LIABLE FOR ANY OTHER DAMAGES, INCLUDING LOSS OR CORRUPTION OF DATA, CHANGES IN THE FUNCTIONAL CHARACTERISTICS OF THE HARDWARE OR OPERATING SYS-TEM, DELETERIOUS INTERACTION WITH OTHER SOFTWARE, OR ANY OTHER SPECIAL, INCI-DENTAL, OR CONSEQUENTIAL DAMAGES THAT MAY ARISE, EVEN IF PRIMA AND/OR THE AUTHOR HAVE PREVIOUSLY BEEN NOTIFIED THAT THE POSSIBILITY OF SUCH DAMAGES EXISTS.

Disclaimer of Warranties:
PRIMA AND THE AUTHORS SPECIFICALLY DISCLAIM ANY AND ALL OTHER WARRANTIES, EITHER EXPRESS OR IMPLIED, INCLUDING WARRANTIES OF MERCHANTABILITY, SUITABILITY TO A PARTICULAR TASK OR PURPOSE, OR FREEDOM FROM ERRORS. SOME STATES DO NOT ALLOW FOR EXCLUSION OF IMPLIED WARRANTIES OR LIMITATION OF INCIDENTAL OR CON-SEQUENTIAL DAMAGES, SO THESE LIMITATIONS MAY NOT APPLY TO YOU.

Other:
This Agreement is governed by the laws of the State of California without regard to choice of law prin-ciples. The United Convention of Contracts for the International Sale of Goods is specifically dis-claimed. This Agreement constitutes the entire agreement between you and Prima Publishing regard-ing use of the software.